Taxing Freedom in Thessalian Manumission Inscriptions

Mnemosyne

Supplements

History and Archaeology
of Classical Antiquity

VOLUME 361

The titles published in this series are listed at brill.com/mns

Taxing Freedom in Thessalian Manumission Inscriptions

By

Rachel Zelnick-Abramovitz

TUTA SUB AEGIDE PALLAS · 1683 ·

BRILL

LEIDEN · BOSTON
2013

Cover illustration: Silver stater of the Thessalian League (late second–mid-first century BC). Obverse: head of Zeus, wearing a laurel wreath. Reverse: Athena Itonia flinging a spear in her right hand, holding a shield in her left; ΘΕΣΣΑ/ΛΩΝ to her right and left; [Σ]ΩΣΙΠ-ΑΤΡΟΣ above the spear, [Γ]ΟΡΓΩΠΑΣ in exergue. The Classical Numismatic Group, Inc. (www.cngcoins.com).

Library of Congress Cataloging-in-Publication Data

Zelnick-Abramovitz, Rachel, author.
Taxing freedom in Thessalian manumission inscriptions / by Rachel Zelnick-Abramovitz.
pages cm – (Mnemosyne. Supplements ; volume 361)
Includes bibliographical references and index.
ISBN 978-90-04-25389-6 (hardback : alk. paper) – ISBN 978-90-04-25662-0 (e-book)
1. Taxation–Greece–Thessaly. 2. Slaves–Emancipation–Greece–Thessaly. 3. Inscriptions, Greek–Greece–Thessaly. I. Title. II. Series: Mnemosyne, bibliotheca classica Batava. Supplementum ; v. 361.

HJ217.Z45 2013
336.2'7–dc23

2013024126

This publication has been typeset in the multilingual "Brill" typeface. With over 5,100 characters covering Latin, IPA, Greek, and Cyrillic, this typeface is especially suitable for use in the humanities. For more information, please see www.brill.com/brill-typeface.

ISSN 0169-8958
ISBN 978-90-04-25389-6 (hardback)
ISBN 978-90-04-25662-0 (e-book)

This book is printed on acid-free paper.

In Memoriam
Zeev Rubin

CONTENTS

PREFACE AND ACKNOWLEDGMENTS

The question posed at the core of this book, namely the purpose of payments made "to the polis" by manumitted slaves in Thessaly, has occupied my mind for a long time. Our knowledge of the process by which slaves in the Greek world became free and of their lives after manumission is still full of 'black holes', especially in respect of Thessaly. One of these riddles is the numerous records of such payments, which adds to the notion (which I argued in my book *Not Wholly Free: The Concept of Manumission and the Status of Manumitted Slaves in the Ancient Greek World,* Brill 2005) that there were many obstacles to full freedom, and that as a non-citizen, the freed slave's status had to be clearly and publicly advertised—for his or her sake as well as in the interest of the polis.

Research for this book was partly carried out during my stay as a visiting fellow (March to August 2011) at the Institute of Classical Studies, School of Advanced Study at the University of London. I am deeply indebted to the former Director of the Institute, Professor Michael Edwards, and to the Deputy Director and Administrator, Dr Olga Krzyszkowska, for their warm welcome and support, and to the staff in the library for their useful help.

Richard Bouchon, who is planning a new edition of all the Thessalian manumission inscriptions, kindly sent me his articles on Thessaly in the age of Augustus (2008) and on the fee paid by manumitted slaves in Thessaly (2009). I am most grateful to the anonymous readers for Brill for their wise comments and suggestions. Caroline van Erp of Brill and Laurie Meijers of TAT Zetwerk were most helpful, efficient, and supportive. Special thanks are due to Murray Rosovsky for polishing my English and saving me, as always, from embarrassing pitfalls. Needless to say, any errors still left are my responsibility.

This book is dedicated to the memory of Zeev Rubin, a great scholar, teacher, and friend, who passed away before his time in the early summer of 2009. He never failed to avail me of his enormous knowledge and to contribute his sage advice. His unfailing guidance and support are greatly missed.

LIST OF ABBREVIATIONS

Abbreviations of ancient sources cited in this book are those found in *Oxford Classical Dictionary*[3]; abbreviations of Journals follow *L'Année Philologique*. The following list includes abbreviations of literary editions, and of epigraphic and papyrological collections and journals.

AAA	*Archaiologika Analekta ex Athenon*, Athens, 1968–
AD	*Archaiologikon Deltion*, Athens.
AE	*Archaiologike Ephemeris*, Athens.
Agora XXVIII	The Athenian Agora 28: *The lawcourts at Athens: Sites, Buildings, Equipment, Procedure, and Testimonia*, by A.L. Boegehold, Princeton, N.J., 1995.
ASAtene	*Annuario della Scuola archeologica di Atene e delle Missioni italiane in Oriente*, Rome.
BCH	*Bulletin de Correspondance Hellénique*, Paris.
BGU XIII	W.M. Brashear (ed.), *Aegyptische Urkunden aus den Staatlichen Museen zu Berlin, Griechische Urkunden*, Berlin, 1976.
BL	*British Library Papyri.*
Chr. Mitt.	L. Mitteis and U. Wilcken (eds.), *Grundzüge und Chrestomathie der Papyruskunde*, II Bd. *Juristischer Teil*, II Hälfte *Chrestomathie*. Leipzig-Berlin 1912.
CID	*Corpus des inscriptions de Delphes*, Paris, 1977–1992.
CIL	*Corpus Inscriptionum Latinarum*, Berlin, 1928–
Clara Rhodos	*Studi e materiali pubblicati a cura dell' Istituto storico-archeologico di Rodi*, Rhodes, 1928–1941.
EAM	T. Rizakis and G. Touratsoglou (eds.), *ΕΠΙΓΡΑΦΕΣ ΑΝΩ ΜΑΚΕΔΟΝΙΑΣ ('Ελίμεια, 'Εορδαία, Νότια Λυγκηστίς, 'Ορεστίς); Τόμος Α'. ΚΑΤΑΛΟΓΟΣ ΕΠΙΓΡΑΦΩΝ*, Athens, 1985.
EKM 1. *Beroia*	L. Gounaropoulos, and M.B. Hatzopoulos (eds.), *ΕΠΙΓΡΑΦΕΣ ΚΑΤΩ ΜΑΚΕΔΟΝΙΑΣ. ΤΕΥΧΟΣ Α'. ΕΠΙΓΡΑΦΕΣ ΒΕΡΟΙΑΣ*, Athens, 1998.
FD III	G. Daux et al. (eds.), *Fouilles de Delphes*, Vol. 3, Paris, 1909–1954.
FGrH	F. Jacoby (ed.), *Die Fragmente der griechischen Historiker*, Berlin, 1923–1999.
FIRA III	V. Arangio-Ruiz (ed.), *Fontes Iuris Romani Antejustiniani*, pars tertia, *Negotia*, 2nd ed., Florence 1943.
Gonnoi II	B. Helly (ed.), *Gonnoi*, Vol. II: *Les Inscriptions*, Amsterdam, 1973.
IBouthrotos	P. Cabanes and F. Drini, *Corpus des inscriptions grecques d'Ilyrie méridionale et d'Épire* 2, Athènes: Ecole Française d'Athènes, 1997.

IC	M. Guaeducci (ed.), *Inscriptiones Creticae*, Rome, 1935.
IDidyma	A. Rehm (ed.), *Didyma*, II. *Die Inschriften*, Berlin, 1958.
IEphesos	H. Wankel et al. (eds.), *Die Inschriften von Ephesos*, Bonn, 1979–1984.
IG	*Inscriptiones Graecae*, Berlin, 1873–
IJG	R. Dareste, B. Haussoulier, T. Reinach (eds.), *Recueil des inscriptions juridiques grecques*, 2 Vols., Paris, 1898–1904.
IK	T.B. Mitford (ed.), *The Inscriptions of Kourion*, Filadelfia 1971.
IK Estremo Oriente	F. Cannali de Rossi (ed.), *Icrizioni delle Estremo Oriente Greco*, Inschriften griechischer Städte aus Kleinasien 65, Bonn, 2004.
ILS	H. Dessau (ed.), *Inscriptiones Latinae Selectae*^{3}, Berlin, 1962.
IMagnesia	O. Kern, *Die Inschriften von Magnesia am Maeander*, Berlin, 1900.
IMylasa	W. Blümel, *Die Inschriften von Mylasa*, Bonn 1987–1988.
IosPE I^2	V.V. Latyshev (ed.), *Inscriptiones Antiquae Orae Septentrionalis Ponti Euxeni Graecae et Latinae*, St. Petersburg, 1885–1901.
I.Perg.	M. Fraenkel, *Die Inschriften von Pergamon*, I–II, Berlin, 1890–1895.
I.Priene	F. Hiller von Gaertringen (ed.), *Inschriften von Priene*, Berlin, 1906.
Iscr. di Cos ED	M. Segré (ed.), *Iscrizioni di Cos*, Roma, 1994.
ISE II	L. Moretti (ed.), *Iscrizioni storiche ellenistiche*, I–II, Florence, 1967–1975.
ISmyrna	G. Petzl, *Die Inschriften von Smyrna*, Bonn 1982–1990.
I Thess. I	J.-C. Decourt, *Inscriptions de Thessalie. Les cités de la vallée de l'Énipeus*, Paris, 1995.
I.Thrace.Aeg.	L.D. Loukopoulou et alii, *Ἐπιγραφὲς τῆς Θράκης τοῦ Αἰγαίου μεταξὺ τῶν ποταμῶν Νέστου καὶ Ἕβρου (Νομοὶ Ξάνθης, Ροδόπης καὶ Ἕβρου)*, Athens, 2005.
Jur. Pap.	P.M. Meyer (ed.), *Juristische Papyri*, Berlin, 1920.
Kassel-Austin	R. Kassel and C. Austin (eds.), Poetae Comici Graeci, Berlin and New-York, 1983–1995.
Lindos II	Ch. Blinkenberg and K.F. Kinch (eds.), *Lindos, fouilles et recherches 1902–1914*, II, *Inscriptions*, Copenhagen, 1941.
LSAG	L.H. Jeffery, 1961. *The Local Scripts of Archaic Greece: A Study of the Origin of the Greek Alphabet and its Development from the Eighth to the Fifth Centuries B.C.*, Oxford, 1961.
LSAM	F. Sokolowski (ed.), *Lois sacrés de l'Asie Mineure*, Paris: E. de Boccard, 1955.
LSCG	F. Sokolowski (ed.), *Lois sacrés des cités grecques*, Paris: E. de Boccard, 1969.
MDAI(A)	*Mitteilungen des deutschen archäologischen Instituts* (*Athenische Abteilung*), Athens.
MDAI(I)	*Mitteilungen des deutschen archäologischen Instituts* (*Abteilung Istanbul*), Tübingen.
Mélanges Daux	*Mélanges helléniques offerts à Georges Daux*, Paris: E. de Boccard, 1974.

Milet I(2)	C. Fredrich, 'Die Inschriften', en *Milet. Ergebnisse der Ausgrabungen und Untersuchungen seit dem Jahre 1899*, Heft II, *Das Rathaus von Milet*, Berlin, 1908.
Milet I(3)	A. Rehm, 'Die Inschriften', en *Milet. Ergebnisse der Ausgrabungen und Untersuchungen seit dem Jahre 1899*, Heft III, *Das Delphinion in Milet*, Berlin, 1914.
ML	R. Meiggs and D. Lewis (eds.), *A Selection of Greek Historical Inscriptions to the End of the Fifth Century B.C.*², Oxford, 1989.
Nomima	H. van Effenterre and F. Ruze (eds.), *Nomima: Recueil d'inscription politiques et juridiques de l'archaïsme grec*, Rome: Ecole française de Rome, 1994–1995.
Nouveau Choix	*Nouveau Choix d'inscriptions grecques*, ed. Institut F. Courby, Paris, 1971.
OGIS	W. Dittenberger (ed.), *Orientis Graeci Inscriptiones Selectae*, Leipzig, 1903–1905.
P. Freib. II	J. Partsch (ed.), *Mitteilungen aus der Freiburger Papyrussammlung*, Heidelberg 1916.
P. Hib.	B.P. Grenfell and A.S. Hunt (eds.) *The Hibeh Papyri* I, London, 1906.
P. Mich.	*Michigan Papyri*. Ann Arbor, 1931–1999.
P. Oslo III	B.P. Grenfell and A.S. Hunt (eds.), *Papyri Osloenses*, Oslo, 1903.
P. Oxy. I	B.P. Grenfell and A.S. Hunt (eds.), *The Oxyrhynchus Papyri*, London, 1898.
P. Oxy. XVII	A.S. Hunt (ed.), *The Oxyrhynchus Papyri*, London, 1927.
P. Oxy. XX	E. Lobel, E.P. Wegener and C.H. Roberts (eds.), *The Oxyrhynchus Papyri*, London, 1952.
P. Oxy. XXXVIII	G.M. Browne, J.D. Thomas, E.G. Turner, M.E. Weinstein et al. (eds.), *The Oxyrhynchus Papyri*, London, 1971.
P. Oxy. XLV	A.K. Bowman, M.W. Haslam, S.A. Stephens, M.L. West et al., *The Oxyrhynchus Papyri*, London, 1977.
P. Strasb. II	F. Preisigke (ed.), *Griechische Papyrus der Kaiserlichen Universitäts- und Landes-bibliothek zu Strassburg*, Leipzig, 1920.
P. Strasb. III	P. Collomp et ses élèves (eds.), *Griechische Papyrus der Kaiserlichen Universitäts- und Landes-bibliothek zu Strassburg* Paris, 1948.
P. Strasb. IV	J. Schwartz et ses élèves (eds.), *Griechische Papyrus der Kaiserlichen Universitäts- und Landes-bibliothek zu Strassburg*, Leipzig, 1963.
P. Tebt. II	B.P. Grenfell and A.S. Hunt (eds.), *The Tebtunis Papyri*, London, 1907.
P. Tebt. III 1	A.S. Hunt and J.G. Smyly (eds.), *The Tebtunis Papyri*, London, 1933.
P. Turner	P.J. Parsons, J.R. Rea et al. (eds.), *Papyri Greek and Egyptian Edited by Various Hands in Honour of Eric Gardner Turner on the Occasion of his Seventieth Birthday*, London, 1981.
P. UB Trier	*Papyrus Collection Trier*, 1982–

PH	W.R. Paton and E.L. Hicks (eds.), *The Inscriptions of Cos*, Oxford, 1981.
RPh	*Revue de philologie, de littérature et d'histoire anciennes*, Paris.
SB	*Sammelbuch griechischer Urkunden aus Aegypten*, Strassburg and Berlin 1913–1915.
SDHI	*Studia et Documenta Historiae et Iuris*, Roma.
SEG	*Supplementum Epigraphicum Graecum*, 1923– Electronic resource, ed. by A. Chaniotis et al., Leiden: Brill.
Sel. Pap. I	A.S. Hunt and C.C. Edgar (eds.), *Select Papyri*, London and Cambridge, Mass., 1932.
SGDI	H. Collitz et al. (eds.), *Sammlung der griechischen Dialekt-Inschriften*, Göttingen, 1884–1915.
SIA VI	M.C.J. Miller (ed.), *Supplementum Inscriptionum Atticarum*, Ares, 1992.
*Syll.*³	W. Dittenberger (ed.), *Sylloge Inscriptionum Graecarum*, 3rd ed., Leipzig, 1915–1924.
TC	M. Segré (ed.), *Tituli Calymni*, Bergamo 1952.
ZPE	*Zeitschrift für Papyrologie und Epigraphik*, Bonn.

MAP

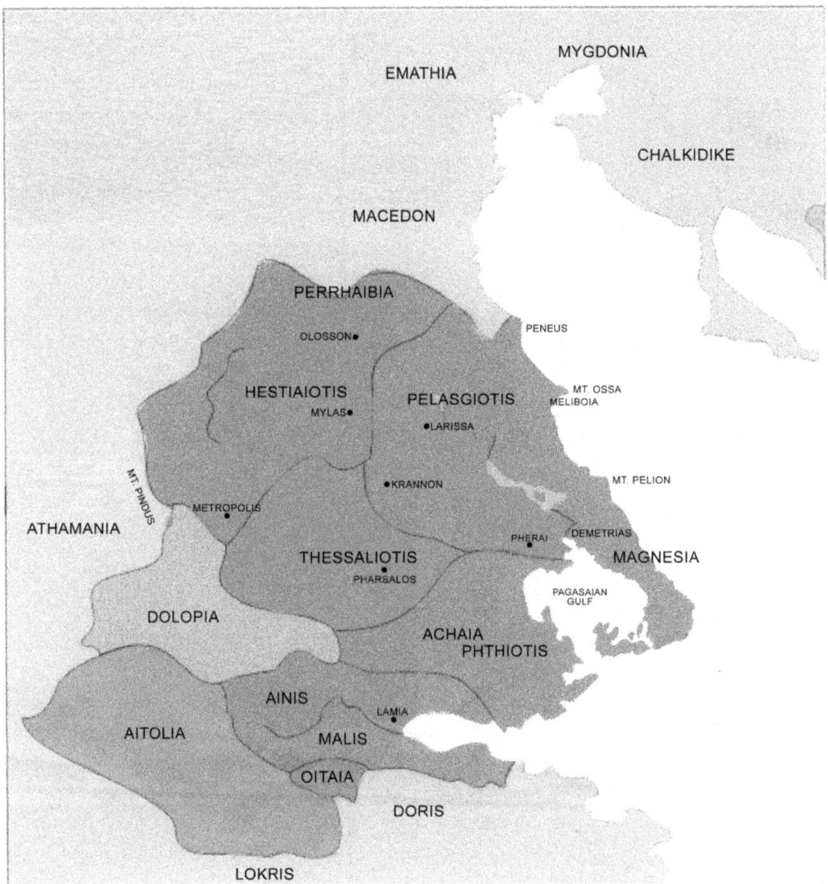

Map of Thessaly.

INTRODUCTION

> *Chremylos*: You're talking nonsense. All these crafts which you've just listed—our slaves will toil over them.
> *Poverty*: But where will you get slaves from?
> *Chremylos*: We'll buy them for money, of course!
> *Poverty*: But first, who'll be the seller, when that one too will have money?
> *Chremylos*: Some profit-seeking dealer from Thessaly, where the most slave-traders are.[1]

Chremylos, a character in the early fourth-century BC comedy *Ploutos* by Aristophanes, refers offhandedly to Thessaly as a source of slave trade. This passage is one of the very few literary texts that mention chattel slavery in classical Thessaly.[2] Conversely, for the late Hellenistic and Roman periods we have abundant epigraphic evidence, on which this study focuses. The book examines the nature and purpose of, and the motivation behind, payments apparently exacted by Thessalian poleis from slaves upon or immediately after their manumission, as attested by the numerous inscribed manumission documents found in this region, starting in the early second century BC. Though still debated on some points, literary sources and archaeological excavations give us a more or less fair picture of the history of Thessaly and its political and social organization, from the classical period down into the Roman era. However, our knowledge of the economic administration and the social structure in Thessaly, on the local level of the polis-member and on the higher level of the federal government in the Hellenistic and Roman periods, remains inadequate. The evidence supplied by the manumission inscriptions is therefore important as a means to augment our understanding of the economic and social life of the Thessalian League at this time.

Thessaly was a "land apart" or "une autre Grèce" owing to the geographical conditions obtaining there,[3] but it grew in economic and political

[1] Ar. *Pl.* 517–521: **Χρεμύλος**: λῆρον ληρεῖς. ταῦτα γὰρ ἡμῖν πάνθ' ὅσα νῦν δὴ κατέλεξας οἱ θεράποντες μοχθήσουσιν. **Πενία**: πόθεν οὖν ἕξεις θεράποντας; **Χρεμύλος**: ὠνησόμεθ' ἀργυρίου δήπου. **Πενία**: τίς δ' ἔσται πρῶτον ὁ πωλῶν, ὅταν ἀργύριον κἀκεῖνος ἔχῃ; **Χρεμύλος**: κερδαίνειν βουλόμενός τις ἔμπορος ἥκων ἐκ Θετταλίας παρὰ πλείστων ἀνδραποδιστῶν.

[2] As against the Penestai. See also below.

[3] I borrow the expression "land apart" from Larsen 1968, 292; "une autre Grèce" is the

importance from ancient times. Its large and fertile plains were a source of grain imports for other parts of Greece from antiquity, and later for Rome, but were also the theatre of battles between other forces. The federal organization of Thessaly in the period under discussion had its predecessor in the fifth century BC (according to some scholars even earlier). Already then, and traditionally from the reign of Aleuas of Larisa (second half of the sixth century BC), the land was divided for administrative purposes into four regions, *tetrades* (see map):[4] Pelasgiotis in the east, with its chief polis Larisa (which in the second century BC became the chief city of the Thessalian League); Phthiotis in south-east; Hestiaiotis in the west; and Thessaliotis in south-west. These *tetrades* were surrounded by the neighbouring, *perioikoi*, regions: Perrhaibia in the north, Magnesia in the east, and Achaia Phthiotis in the south. These regions were subject in one way or another to the Thessalians.[5] Some such relationship may also have been created between the Thessalians and the ἔθνη (*ethne*) of Malis, Ainis, Oitaia, and Dolopia in the Spercheios valley.

In the mid-fourth century BC, probably during the Third Sacred War (354–346 BC), Thessaly and its perioecic regions fell under Macedonian control. Despite some setbacks, such as the revolt of most of Thessaly in the Lamian War (323–322 BC), Macedonian rule remained firm. But in the 270s BC the Aitolians began extending their control to the perioecic regions to the south of Thessaly: Oitaia, Dolopia, Ainis, and Malis. In 229 BC, when the Macedonian king Demetrios II died, a large part of Thessaly seems to have rebelled, and the Aitolians took advantage of the situation to invade these parts and incorporate many Thessalian cities into their κοινόν (*koinon*).[6] Antigonos III Doson crushed the revolt (probably in 228 BC) and regained control of the Thessalian regions, except for most of Achaia Phthiotis.[7] During the First Macedonian War (214–205 BC) the Aitolians used the polis of

---

expression used by Pouilloux 1979, vii, who describes the special geographical conditions which kept Thessaly isolated and unique. See also Westlake 1935, 1–20.

4 On the topography of Thessaly and its history from archaic times to the fourth century BC, see Westlake 1935; Sordi 1958; Helly 1995; Beck 1997, 119–134; Morgan 2003, 22–24, 85–86; Hatzopoulos 2003; Graninger 2011, 7–23. On Thessaly in the third century BC, and after its reorganization by the Romans in 196 BC, see Bowersock 1965; Larsen 1968, 281–294, 378–406; Bouchon 2008; Bouchon 2009; Graninger 2011, 23–42.

5 Morgan 2003, 23, points out that the separate representation of the perioecic regions in the Delphic Amphictionic League suggests that their dependence on the Thessalians was more economic than political. See also Graninger 2011, 13–19.

6 See Scholten 2000, 165–166, with the ancient evidence.

7 Just. 28.3.14–15; cf. Scholten 2000, 167–173.

Phthiotic Thebes as their chief base for raids against Demetrias, Pharsalos, and Larisa—which were still under Macedonian control—acts which prompted Philip V to attack in retaliation.[8]

Following the Roman victory in the Second Macedonian War (200–197 BC), the Roman consul Titus Quinctius Flamininus declared in 196 BC at the Isthmian Games that the Thessalians, the Magnesians, the Perrhaibians, and the Phthiotic Achaians (together with other Greeks) were to be free.[9] Other changes were soon made: Achaia Phthiotis, except for Thebes and Pharsalos, which were to remain under Aitolian rule, was given over to the Thessalians, and Dolopia too was declared free.[10] Initially it seems that the Leagues of the Thessalians (including part of Achaia Phthiotis), the Magnesians, and the Perrhaibians managed their own affairs independently. But in 194 BC a commission of ten men, headed by Flamininus, reorganized the Thessalian League.[11] Flamininus also seems to have given it a new constitution, as is suggested by an inscription from Narthakion in Achaia Phthiotis (*IG* IX(2) 89b), recording a decision about a border dispute, dated to ca. 140 BC. Lines 15–18 of the inscription state that the polis of Narthakion won the case,

> κατὰ νόμους τοὺς Θεσσαλῶν, οἷς ν̣[ό]-
> μοις ἕ̣ως τα̣[ν]ῦν χρῶνται, ο[ὓ]ς νόμους Τίτος
> Κοΐγκτιος ὕπατος ἀπὸ τῆς τῶν δέκα πρεσ-
> βευτῶν γνώμης ἔδωκεν

> according to the laws of the Thessalians, which laws they use even now, that the consul Titus Quinctius (Flamininus) gave them by the decision of the ten commissioners.

What these "laws" were, and whether they were based on a Greek or a Roman model is not known. Judging by the Thessalian League's organization (described below), Larsen suggests that Flamininus' model was a mixture of elements taken from other Greek federations, especially the Achaian League.[12] As will be shown below, the payments exacted from manumitted slaves have been interpreted by some scholars as a manumission tax resembling the Roman *vicesima libertatum*, so the question of Flamininus' model for the reorganization of the Thessalian League, whether Greek or Roman,

[8] Philip captured Phthiotic Thebes in 217 BC, sold its inhabitants into slavery, repopulated the city with Macedonians, and changed its name to Philippopolis: see Polyb. 5.99–100.8; Larsen 1968, 354–355; Grainger 1999, 292–294; Scholten 2000, 217.

[9] Polyb. 18.46.5; Liv. 33.32.5.

[10] Polyb. 18.47.6–9; Liv. 33.34.6–7.

[11] Liv. 34.51.4–6.

[12] Larsen 1968, 284.

and whether he dictated to the Thessalians their financial policy, is of great significance.

In 194 BC the Thessalian League after its reorganization by Flamininus comprised the original Thessalian *tetrades* (Thessaliotis, Pelasgiotis, Hestiaiotis, and Phthiotis), while for some time Perrhaibia remained an independent League. Some manumission inscriptions from Pythion in Perrhaibia, the earliest of which is probably from ca. 146–137 BC, are dated by Thessalian *strategoi*, the annually elected chief magistrates of the League, which suggests that by this time Pythion, and most likely Perrhaibia as a whole, was Thessalian.[13]

Although the Magnesians were declared free in 196 BC, Philip V of Macedonia captured Demetrias in 191 BC and was allowed by the Romans to hold Magnesia in reward for his military service in the war against Antiochos III (191–188 BC).[14] Probably after the Third Macedonian War, Magnesia became free and remained an independent League at least until the third century AD.[15] Dolopia too seems to have remained under Macedonian control until the Third Macedonian War, after which (at an unknown date) it was incorporated into the Thessalian League.[16] Quite early Malis too joined the Thessalian League: this can be inferred from the fact that in 186/5 BC Lamia, its head city,[17] was dating its decrees by the eponymous Thessalian στρατηγοί (*strategoi*).[18]

In 167 BC, after the Third Macedonian War, Oitaia was taken away from the Aitolians and formed a separate federation, but by the middle of the second century, possibly in 146 BC, it seems to have joined the Thessalian League (perhaps after first being incorporated into the Achaian League).[19] Ainis too was under Aitolian control possibly until the end of the Third Macedonian War, when it seems to have become an independent League, with Hypata at its head. The last extant independent decree of the Ainian *koinon* is dated to ca. 88–80 BC (*IG* IX(2) 38).[20] A manumission inscrip-

---

13 See e.g. *AE* (1924), 155, no. 400; Graninger 2011, 37. Kramolisch 1979, suggests that Perrhaibia joined the Thessalian League in 146 BC, following the Achaian War.

14 Liv. 39.23.11.

15 See Larsen 1968, 295; Graninger 2011, 33.

16 Graninger 2011, 34.

17 The city was captured from the Aitolians by the Roman consul Manius Acilius Glabrio in 190 BC; see Liv. 37.4.8–37.5.4.

18 See *IG* IX(2) 67, dated by the Thessalian *strategos* of 186/5 BC, Leontomenos of Pherai, and by the city's chief magistrates.

19 Graninger 2011, 34–35.

20 Larsen 1968, 282; Kramolisch 1978, 32.

tion from Hypata, dated to the 30s AD (*IG* IX(2) 15), has the στρατηγός (*strategos*) of the Thessalian League as the eponymous magistrate, so that decade may serve as a *terminus ante quem* for the incorporation of Ainis into the Thessalian League.[21] In 148 or 146 BC, following the suppression of Andriskos' revolt, Thessaly was joined to the newly organized province of Macedonia,[22] and in 27 BC it was probably incorporated into the province of Achaia.[23]

The reorganized Thessalian League was headed by an annually elected *strategos*, who was the eponymous magistrate of the League as well as its chief military leader. The League also had a council, the συνέδριον (*synedrion*), whose members were the representatives of the cities belonging to the League, their number apparently in proportion to the size of each city's population. The *synedrion* seems to have met regularly at Larisa, the League's chief city; among the issues handled by this institution judicial matters (such as border disputes among members) seem to have loomed large.[24] The League started minting its own coins in the second century BC in two standards: the Attic standard, which was used for foreign trade and dealings, and a local one—which became legal tender in all the cities of the League; the Thessalian drachma weighed three-fourths of the Attic drachma, so that a Thessalian stater (a two-drachma coin) was worth one Attic drachma and a half or one Roman denarius and a half.[25] In 27 BC, following a διόρθωμα (*diorthoma*), a revision, by Augustus, the formal rate of exchange was established between the Thessalian stater and the Roman denarius,[26] but the epigraphic evidence shows that Thessalian cities continued to use staters and obols (the Roman denarius being considered worth eight obols).[27]

So although given its constitution by Rome, the Thessalian League apparently enjoyed considerable freedom and used Greek laws, currency (at least until 27 BC), and institutions. It also seems to have had its own system of

---

21 Graninger 2011, 38–39; but see Sekunda 1997, 208–214, who argues for an earlier date, possibly after the battle of Pharsalos in 48, or even before it.

22 See Vanderspoel 2010, 259.

23 Graninger 2011, 40.

24 Larsen 1968, 286–287, 290.

25 Graninger 2011, 32 and n. 103.

26 Helly 1997.

27 Larsen 1968, 291. See Helly 1997, 79–81, who argues that despite this fact the only legal currency after the publication of the *diorthoma* was the Roman denarius; cf. Bouchon 2008, 434–436. On the *diorthoma* and the currency indicated by the Thessalian manumission inscriptions see also Chapter 2 below.

customs duties.[28] But so little is known about Flamininus' reorganization and the actual political dealings of the League that we cannot rule out some Roman influence, as might be the case of the payments imposed on manumitted slaves discussed in this book (as some scholars postulate). Note that in border disputes, members of the Thessalian League often preferred Rome's arbitration.[29]

Another question is how centralized the federal government was. On the one hand, as we saw, the League had a uniform currency and perhaps even a common calendar,[30] and decisions concerning foreign and internal matters were made by a representative institution, the *synedrion*.[31] The League also had a federal army, to which each member contributed a contingent, probably in proportion to its size.[32] On the other hand, the cities belonging to the League seem to have been considerably independent in their relations with each other and with the central government. Citizens in any given city did not enjoy citizenship and other privileges in any other member of the League unless granted by the sovereign body of that city.[33] Each city seems to have had its own army; and although federal imposts might have existed, each city had its own tax system.[34] Border disputes were usually referred to the federal *synedrion*, or later to the Roman Senate, but many cities applied to poleis outside the League. Also, the ἱερομνήμονες (*hieromnemones*) sent to the Delphic Amphictyony are recorded separately, according to their city or region and not as delegates of the Thessalians as a League.[35]

---

28 Larsen 1968, 291.

29 As shown by *IG* IX(2) 89, mentioned above (a decision in a dispute between Melitaia and Narthakion in ca. 140 BC). Cf. Th.D. Axenides, *Hellenika* 11 (1939), 263–271 (Larisa, second century BC); and perhaps IG IX(2) 261 (= *SEG* 45.610) dated to AD 15–35.

30 On the common Thessalian calendar after 196 BC, see Graninger 2011, 95–106.

31 The federal decrees were published in two federal sanctuaries: that of Zeus Eleutherios at Larisa and that of Athena Itonia at Philia (Itonos). On the identification of Itonos with Philia see B. Helly and J.-C. Decourt, *Bulletin épigraphique* 2004, no. 211; B.C. Intzesiloglou, "Η Ἰτωνία Ἀθηνᾶ καὶ τὸ Θεσσαλικὸ ὁμοσπονδιακὸ ἱερό της στὴ Φίλια Καρδίτσας', in A. Mazarakis Ainian (ed.), *Ἀρχαιολογικὸ Ἔργο Θεσσαλίας καὶ Στερεᾶς Ἑλλάδας. Πρακτικὰ Ἐπιστημονικῆς Συνάντησης, Βόλος 27.2–2.3.2003 I* (Volos 2006), 227–237. I owe these references to Angelos Chaniotis. On the Thessalian sanctuaries, see Graninger 2011, 43–86.

32 On the Thessalian cavalry in the Hellenistic period, see Helly 1995, 264–277.

33 See Larsen 1968, 287–288, who also points out that even if the League, for instance, granted foreign judges from Miletos citizenship and other privileges in all the cities of the League (*IG* IX(2) 508; 49/8 BC), it meant that if these honorands chose to implement the grant in some city they had to obtain the city's consent to register them as citizens, even though it could not refuse them.

34 See Baker 2001. See also in Chapters 1 and 2 below.

35 See e.g. *CID* 4.108, of 178/7 BC, where lines 8–10, for instance, record the *hieromnemones* sent from Achaia Phthiotis.

Like other Greek communities, the Thessalians too made use of labour provided by people of servile status. Until the fourth or the third century BC, the main servile population in Thessaly was the group called the Penestai, an indigenous people, collectively reduced to servitude but privately owned by landlords, whose status has often been compared (erroneously) to that of the Spartan Helots.[36] In contrast to the Helots, the Penestai belonged to private owners. Thessalian aristocrats possessed numerous Penestai who cultivated their lands and could also be drafted to military service.[37] There is no direct evidence of collective or private manumission of Penestai. Jean Ducat argues that the existence of private armies of landlords may suggest that these nobles granted freedom to Penestai working their land in return for military service.[38] There is also the evidence from Theopompos of Chios (*FGrH* 115 F 81 = Ath. 6, 259f–260a) that Agathokles, who enjoyed great power with Philip II, had been a slave and one of the Penestai; this detail makes it plausible that Agathokles had been manumitted. An inscription from Pharsalos, *IG* IX(2) 234, dated to the last third of the third century BC,[39] is a decree which grants citizenship and land to two categories of people in reward for military service, no doubt because of a decrease in the number of the citizens in Pharsalos. These people have been unanimously seen as Penestai. According to Ducat's interpretation the first group consisted of those manumitted some time before the decree was issued but were not yet citizens; the second of those manumitted on the occasion of the grant of citizenship, thus receiving both freedom and citizenship in one step.[40] This decree is sometimes taken as indication that the system of Penestai was declining at this time.[41] The origin, the exact status, and the decline of the Penestai system are still matters of debate, but their existence as a servile population in Thessaly is firmly attested.

---

36 The most recent and full discussion on the Penestai and their status as conceived by the Greeks is Ducat 1994, who argues that the Penestai still existed as a servile category in the first half of the third century BC. See also Westlake 1935, 28, 32–37; Sordi 1958, 325–327; Lotze 1959, 48–53, 74–77; Morgan 2003, 190–192.

37 Ducat 1994, 71–89.

38 Ducat 1994, 73.

39 The inscription has been re-edited and studied by Decourt 1990.

40 See Ducat 1994, 107–113 (with a discussion of earlier interpretations), esp. 111–112. As Ducat comments (107), the same period saw other grants of citizenship by Thessalian cities (*IG* IX(2) 517 by Larisa, and *IG* IX(2) 1228 by Phalanna), but the beneficiaries in these cases were foreigners of free, not servile, status.

41 See, however, the cautious remarks of Ducat 1994, 112–113.

Less certain is whether chattel slavery was practised extensively in Thessaly before the second century BC, that is, before it is attested in the manumission inscriptions. Two passages from Attic Comedy refer to Thessaly as an important centre of the slave trade in the second half of the fifth century BC: Hermippos in his *Phormophoroi* (Kassel-Austin V, 591–594, line 19 = Ath. 1, 27e–28a), performed in the 420s, includes "slaves and branded men" (δούλους καὶ στιγματίας) from Pagasai in a list of merchandise imported to Athens from various countries. Chremylos in Aristophanes' *Ploutos* (lines 520–521)—in a passage cited at the beginning of this Introduction—presents Thessalians as predominantly engaged in the slave trade out of greed (κερδαίνειν βουλόμενός τις ἔμπορος ἥκων ἐκ Θετταλίας παρὰ πλείστων ἀνδραποδιστῶν). Yet as Ducat observes, these passages may simply imply that Thessalian ports, such as Pagasai, were centres of this traffic but cannot attest to the extent of chattel slavery inland.[42] Ducat comments that it is possible that this form of slavery was introduced into Thessaly in the second half of the fourth century BC, but as in Sparta, such slaves were not the primary productive labour force. The fact that Greek authors often use the terminology of chattel slavery (especially δοῦλος, and δουλεία) to describe the Penestai impedes attempts to verify the existence of chattel slavery in Thessaly prior to the second century BC.[43]

According to an aetiological story, preserved in a fragment of the historical work of the third-century BC historian Baton of Sinope, the Thessalians celebrate the festival called Peloria, "even to this day", in imitation of an ancient celebration in honour of Peloros. He brought the king Pelasgos the good news that, following a great earthquake, the mountain Tempe had broken apart, and water cascaded through the cleft into the stream of the Peneios. After the water dried up there appeared large and beautiful plains. In this festival, says Baton, they welcome all the foreigners (ξένοι) to the feast, set free the prisoners, and feast the house slaves (οἰκέται).[44] If Baton's terminology is reliable, this story can be used to indicate that chattel slavery existed in Thessaly in the third century BC; however, in this case too we cannot be sure that Baton's (or Athenaeus') use of the term οἰκέται refers to chattel slaves and not to Penestai. Yet some epigraphic evidence from the third century BC, again meagre, may attest to the existence of chattel

---

42 Ducat 1994, 87. Pagasai, who later took part in the *synoikismos* of Demetrias, was an important port in the fifth and fourth centuries BC, serving military and commercial needs; see e.g. Hdt. 7.193; Plut. *Them.* 20.1; Xen. *Hell.* 5.4.56.

43 See Ducat 1994, 79–80.

44 Ath. 14, 639d–640a (= *FGrH* 268 F 5). See Zelnick-Abramovitz 2012, 103–104, 108.

slavery and manumission in this period.[45] Moreover, the possibility should be considered that the decree from Pharsalos mentioned above recorded the grant of citizenship to chattel slaves; although the military service for which the beneficiaries in this inscription were rewarded is usually associated with Penestai, chattel slaves in other places were often recruited in times of emergency and granted freedom.[46] The Pharsalos decree, together with Philip V's letters to Larisa and that city's grant of citizenship to metics in 217/16 BC (*IG* IX(2) 514), as well as a similar measure adopted by Phalanna (*IG* IX(2) 1228), may also indicate the introduction, or intensification, of chattel slavery which, being perhaps more suited to the changing economic and social conditions, gradually rendered the Penestai system obsolete. This would explain the few inscriptions that record manumission in the third century BC.

The principal evidence on chattel slavery in Thessaly appears in the second century BC, in the form of numerous manumission inscriptions, which also record the payments discussed in the present study. These inscriptions, mostly long lists enumerating manumission acts in chronological order, are the largest body of epigraphic evidence of manumission we have next to the Delphic inscriptions, if not larger.[47] They also constitute the main source of information we have on chattel slavery and manumission in Hellenistic and Roman Thessaly. Moreover, because not much is known about the economic activity in Thessaly or the conditions of chattel slaves there, the abundant epigraphic evidence of payments apparently made to the state treasurers in many Thessalian poleis in the late Hellenistic and Roman periods is of great value. These payments feature in inscriptions recording manumission, so they most probably relate to that very act. The sum paid—fifteen staters or, after 27 BC, twenty-two and a half denarii—was the same in all the poleis where these payments are recorded, making it plausible to consider this a federal charge.[48] An example of the more frequently encountered forms is this (*IG* IX(2) 463, lines 1–10; Krannon, 49/8 BC):

---

45 Inscriptions recording slavery and manumission in third-century BC Thessaly are discussed in Chapter 5.

46 See e.g. Ar. *Ran.* 693–694 on the manumission in Athens of slaves who fought at Arginousai in 406 BC; D.S. 20.100.1–4, on the manumission in Rhodes of slaves who helped the city during the siege of Demetrios Poliorketes in 305/4 BC; cf. Ephesos' decision in 86 BC to grant freedom (but not citizenship) to public slaves who rendered military help in the war against Mithradates VI Eupator (*OGIS* 253).

47 On the manumission inscriptions from Delphi see Hopkins 1978, 133–171; Mulliez 1992. On the estimated number of the manumissions recorded in Thessaly see in Chapter 2 below.

48 On Thessalian federal coinages see Head 1911, 291–312; Helly 1987; and below.

στρατηγοῦντος Φιλοκρά-
τους τοῦ Ἀρχελάδου Λαρι-
σαίου, ταμιεύοντος τὴν δε[υ]-
τέραν ἑξάμηνον Θέωνος
τοῦ Παρμενίσκου οἱ φάμενο[ι]
[γ]εγονέναι ἀπελεύθεροι καὶ δε-
δωκότες τῇ πόλει τοὺς δε-
καπέντε στατῆρας· Εὐφροσύ-
νη ἡ ἀπελευθερωθεῖσα ἀπὸ Ἀ-
γλαοφῶντος τοῦ Αἰσχρίωνος ...

When Philocrates, son of Archelades, of Larisa was the *strategos*, when Theon, son of Parmeniscos, was the treasurer in the second half of the year, those declared to be manumitted and who paid to the polis the fifteen staters (were): Euphrosyne, the manumitted slave by Aglaophon, son of Aischrion ... (more names in the same form follow).

Since our knowledge of Thessalian poleis is still limited, understanding the purpose of these payments might contribute to our knowledge of Thessaly's economic activity and how its poleis and their federation tried to secure revenues. A grasp of the function of these payments might also help us see the extent to which the poleis intervened in their citizens' economic lives.[49] It may likewise shed light on the status of the Thessalian League and its individual members under the Roman rule.

But the purpose of these payments is not easy to determine. Many inscriptions which mention payments are damaged and fragmentary, so the information extracted from them is often based on conjectured restorations of the lost text. When the inscriptions are legible they are laconic, and for the most part offer no details beyond the mere record of the payments. Some scholars who studied these inscriptions interpret the payments as a manumission tax, similar to the Roman *vicesima manumissionum* (or *libertatis*); the Roman tax, five percent of the market value of every slave manumitted, which presumably was paid by the master, was introduced already in 357 BC by the consul Gnaeus Manlius.[50] Other scholars regard these payments as

49 One aspect of such intervention can be seen in decrees of Thessalian cities encouraging their citizens to contribute to various public projects; see *SEG* 33.460 from Larisa (= *SEG* 13.390+13.393; Habicht, 1983; Migeotte 1992, 90–93, no. 33); Helly 1973, 133–134, no. 113, from Gonnoi (= A.S. Arvanitopoulos, *AE*, 1913, 48, no. 177; Migeotte 1992, 96–97, no. 35); Y. Béquignon *BCH* 59 (1935), 37, face 2, from Krannon (= *SEG* 15.371; cf. McDevitt 1970, 310; Migeotte 1992, 93–96, no. 34). And see below.

50 Interpreting the payments as manumission tax: Calderini 1965, 141–142; Rensch 1908, 92–95; Busolt 1920, 290; Reilly 1971; Helly 1976, 143–158, at 154; Habicht 1987, 287; Bielman 1989, 25–41, at 30. On the *vicesima manumissionum*/*libertatis*, which was first paid to the

fees exacted for registering freed slaves or for publishing the manumission acts, and indeed some considerations seem to support this conclusion.[51] It should be stressed that whether this impost was a manumission tax or a publication fee, in either case the polis exploited manumission to raise money. Moreover, in either case these inscriptions provide important evidence on the economic and social life of these Thessalian poleis and on steps taken by them or by the Thessalian League to increase their revenues. Yet the answer to the question whether this was a tax or a publication fee may enhance our understanding of the fiscal and political administration of Thessaly in the late Hellenistic and the Roman periods: was this impost a sign of Roman influence or even dictate? If it was, it might throw more light on the extent of the Thessalian League's dependence on Rome; or were these payments yet more evidence of a Greek practice attested elsewhere (as we shall see in Chapter 4)? Furthermore, these inscriptions are the only testimony we have of federal taxation in Thessaly besides the partial evidence of customs duties collected by or for the federal treasury in earlier

---

aerarium Saturnini and later (under the Antonines) to the *fiscus* (but see Bradley 1984b, 178), see Liv. 7.16.7; Epict. *Disc.* 2.1.26, where the manumittor pays the tax to the magistrate before whom the act of manumission is being done, and the payment is presented as a condition for the freedom of the slave. But in 4.1.33 it is the manumitted slave who pays it to the εἰκοστῶναι (*eikostonai*), namely the farmers of the εἰκοστή (*eikoste*), that is, one twentieth of the slave's value (see in Chapter 3 below). See also Vigié 1881 (who on p. 7 argues that usually the tax was paid by the manumitted slaves from their *peculium*); Treggiari 1969, 17; Luzzato 1984, 708 (who suggests that the master or his heir paid the tax when the initiative for the manumission came from the master, but the slave did so if he bought his freedom with his own money; cf. for a similar view Bradley 1984a, 150, and 1984b, 177, who nonetheless remarks that it is not clear "when such a convention developed, and whether it was ever legally ratified"); Eck 1999, 120–130; Mouritsen 2011, 88 n. 95 (who argues that in the case of Latin freedmen it was the manumittor who paid the tax; on p. 180 n. 280 he states that the payment fell to the slaves, "unless the master was particularly generous"; and on p. 187 it is again the master who paid the tax in cases of slave children, manumitted because they faced death).

[51] Interpreting the payments as registration/publication fees: *IJG* II, 312; Parker and Obbink 2000, 442; Rädle 1969, 119, 158–161, who, however, follows Calderini in arguing that the sum was too high for a publication fee. Accepting the reasoning of Busolt (1920, 290) and Rensch (1908, 95) that this was an important source of income for the states, Rädle suggests that under the label of publication fee a manumission tax was collected (see below). See also Beauchet 1969, 474–475, who suggests that in return for this payment the polis recognized and guaranteed the manumission. This suggestion presupposes that manumission in Thessaly had to be practised in accordance with a procedure established by law, for which there is indeed some evidence: see Helly 1976; Zelnick-Abramovitz 2005a, 303–305. See also te Riele 1982, 161. It is not clear what Larsen 1958, 126–127, and 1968, 291–292, means by calling this payment "a manumission fee". On similar payments in other places, see below.

times.[52] Here, however, the question also arises as to whether the payment was set by the federal government, and perhaps also collected centrally, or if it was a local concern—the uniformity deriving merely from some sense of federal or ethnic identity. In addition to the financial aspect, these payments might indicate a federal interest in controlling the non-citizen population in all the poleis members of the League. Such a concern might imply a much stricter federal structure in Thessaly than hitherto assumed, and attest to intervention by the state—whether the Thessalian *koinon* or each individual Thessalian polis—in its members' economic life: since manumission was a private transaction, taxing it or exacting fees for its registration meant that the state interfered in the private sphere.

The aim of this study is to elucidate the questions arising in our subject as best we can, and to arrive at some plausible answers. In Chapter 1, I briefly survey the place of taxation in the Greek poleis' economy and the evidence for taxes imposed in various places in Greece in the context of slavery. Slave ownership, slave sale, and slave trade were taxed in many places from early times. Since manumission was a in a way a transfer of property, it seems reasonable that poleis would deem it taxable like any other transaction.[53] Chapter 2 reviews and analyses the Thessalian evidence on manumission and the payments made upon this act. It discusses the mode of manumission prevalent in Thessaly; questions concerning the formulae used for registering the payments; the currency and amount of money paid; the recipient(s) of the money; whether it was the manumittor or the manumitted slave who paid; and variations in these documents and their significance. Chapter 3 discusses the evidence and the arguments for and against each of the two possible interpretations of the payments in Thessaly. As I hope to show, the evidence seems to support interpreting the payments as

[52] In the fourth century BC customs duties and market levies were collected, perhaps by each member-city, for the federal government, as can be inferred from Demosthenes' comment (1.22) that the Thessalians decided to cease handing over to Philip II their proceeds from the harbours and the markets, claiming that these monies belonged to the Thessalian federation. It is not known whether and how such taxes were collected after 196 BC. Larsen 1968, 292, suggests that since Thessaly continued to exist under Roman rule as "a land apart", it is likely that the League also had its own system of customs duties, perhaps administered by elected officials; he also notes that there is no evidence of any Roman magistrate levying *portoria* in Thessaly. But proof for his thesis is lacking. On taxation in the Thessalian and other leagues see Chapter 1 below.

[53] In some places manumission took the form of a sale to a deity, as e.g. in Delphi; but even in most of the so called 'civil' or 'secular' manumissions slaves paid for their freedom, therefore negotiated with their former masters. See Zelnick-Abramovitz 2005a, 86–99, 208–222.

registration and publication fees. In Chapter 4 I adduce evidence from other places on fees levied in the context of manumission which might help us situate the Thessalian manumission inscriptions in a wider historical context. Finally, Chapter 5 returns to some of the questions posed in this Introduction and offers some answers as to the historical and economic background of this levy, and the motives for it. In the Conclusions I recapitulate the subjects raised in the previous chapters and restate my arguments.

All translations from the Greek and Latin sources in this book are mine, unless otherwise indicated. Transliteration of Greek words and names adheres as closely as possible to the Greek spelling, but familiar names keep their Latinized forms.

CHAPTER ONE

TAXATION AND SLAVERY

Until the Hellenistic period government intervention in the Greek cities' economic activity was usually limited. The Greek states' intervention in their citizens' private economic activity chiefly manifested itself in laws that regulated prices and market activity[1] and in obtaining revenues (πρόσοδοι), through taxes, to pay for public expenses. For the latter purpose the poleis often imposed regular taxes or charged *ad hoc* levies. Taxes were the Greek cities' main source of revenue,[2] but except in emergencies, when εἰσφορά (*eisphora*, war tax on property)[3] was levied or ἐπίδοσις (*epidosis*, voluntary contribution) was collected, direct taxes on the citizen's person were generally avoided, perhaps because they were deemed tyrannical.[4] Instead, in some poleis, notably Athens, public works and institutions were financed through liturgies.[5] By contrast, indirect taxes were often resorted to, normally as customs or levies on trade and on market activity, but also on produce.[6] In fifth- and fourth-century Athens, for instance, only metics paid a poll tax, the μετοίκιον, at an annual rate of twelve drachmae for a man and six for an unmarried woman. Indirect taxes were imposed *ad valorem* on goods

---

1 See e.g. Dem. 20.9; Hyper. 3.14; Arist. *Pol.* 6, 1321b12–17; Theophr. *Nomoi*, fg. 20 Szegedy-Maszak; *IG* II² 1013; *SEG* 46.678G; *SEG* 47.1026.

2 Andreades 1979, 125–185; Littman 1988, 797; Gabrielsen 2008, 124–125; Migeotte 2009, 49. On taxes as an important principle of modern states, involving redistribution and conflict, see Newton and Confalonieri 1995.

3 On the *eisphora* in Athens and elsewhere in Greece see Thomsen 1964.

4 See Zimmern 1961, 288–289; Austin and Vidal-Naquet 1977, 121–123; Lyttkens 1994, 69–70; Möller 2007, 375–378. In the fourth-century work on economics ascribed to Aristotle it is tyrants and kings who usually impose direct taxes (Ps.-Arist. *Oec.* 2, 1346a31–1353b29; on this work see below), and the *Ath. Pol.* 15.5, and Thuc. 6.54.5 ascribe to Peisistratos the imposition of a five-percent tax on agricultural produce. The ancient Greek poleis' aversion to direct taxation did not derive, of course, from any systematic 'liberal' thinking on the role of the government in the nation's economy. For different views of the nature of ancient Greek economy see Finley 1973, against Burke 1992; and Mattingly and Salmon 2001.

5 Two of the liturgies in Athens are discussed in recent studies: Gabrielsen 1994 on the trierarchy, and Wilson 2000 on the *choregia*. See also Christ 2006, especially 143–204, on the Athenians' attitude to liturgies and on strategies of tax evasion. For examples of direct taxation in Greece see Migeotte 2003.

6 See Finley 1973, 95–96, 164–165; Austin and Vidal-Naquet 1977, 121–123; Migeotte 2003.

imported or exported through the Piraeus, on goods sold in the Athenian *agora*, on foreigners who did business there, on sales of lands and confiscated goods, and so on.[7] The polis farmed out collection to companies of private tax farmers (τελῶναι) who were obliged to provide sureties and who paid a lump sum.

Evidence of taxation in the classical period is found for other poleis as well, but it is often too meagre and obscure for any safe inference on state revenues and state intervention outside Athens. Thus a decree of the polis Teos from the second half of the fourth century BC grants the citizens of another city, or perhaps new citizens, privileges and exemption from several liturgies and taxes.[8] One of Olynthos' major sources of revenue was the tax on ports and trading posts (Xen. *Hell.* 5.2.16). The author of the late fourth-century work on economics ascribed to Aristotle registers in the second book measures (some of which are hard to believe) taken by various poleis, politicians (including Athenians), and rulers in times of need (Ps.-Arist. *Oec.* 2, 1346a31–1353b29). Before recounting these anecdotes, the author analyses the sources of revenues unique to each kind of government (1345b19–1346a10):

> πρῶτον μὲν τοίνυν τὴν βασιλικὴν ἴδωμεν. ἔστι δὲ αὕτη δυναμένη μὲν τὸ καθόλου, εἴδη δὲ ἔχουσα τέσσαρα: περὶ νόμισμα, περὶ τὰ ἐξαγώγιμα, περὶ τὰ εἰσαγώγιμα, περὶ τὰ ἀναλώματα. τούτων δὲ ἕκαστον μὲν περὶ ... τὸ νόμισμα λέγω ποῖον καὶ πότε τίμιον ἢ εὔωνον ποιητέον, περὶ δὲ τὰ ἐξαγώγιμα καὶ εἰσαγώγιμα πότε καὶ τίνα παρὰ τῶν σατραπῶν ἐν τῇ ταγῇ ἐκλαβόντι αὐτῷ λυσιτελήσει διατίθεσθαι, περὶ δὲ τὰ ἀναλώματα τίνα περιαιρετέον καὶ πότε, καὶ πότερον δοτέον νόμισμα

---

[7] On taxes and other revenues in Athens see Finley 1973, pp. 163–164; Littman 1988, 799–802; Cohen 1992, 194–195; Burke 1992; Kyrtatas 2002, 147; Amemiya 2007, 92–99; Engen 2010, *passim*. See also Lyttkens 1994, who argues that the implicit bargaining between Athenian politicians and the poor majority generated predatory rule (defined as the tendency to maximize state revenue). According to [Xen.] *Ath. Pol.* 1.17, a tax of 1% (ἑκατοστή) was levied in the Piraeus, probably on all goods imported or exported. In Ar. *Vesp.* 658, performed in 422 BC, Bdelykleon mentions the "many 1% taxes" among other levies (on court proceedings, on leases of mines, on transactions in the *agora*, and on using the harbours). By 400/399 BC the harbour tax had risen to 2% (the πεντεκοστή; see Andoc. 1.133; Dem. 35.29). Sales taxes, ἐπώνια (*eponia*), of 1% to 2% were paid on confiscated property sold by the πωληταί (*poletai*; see references in Lambert, 1997, 270 and n. 209). See also Stroud 1998 on the tax law of 374/3 BC, establishing the procedures for farming the tax of 8 1/3% (the 1/12 part, δωδεκάτη) on the grain harvest collected in kind from the Athenian cleruchies on the islands of Lemnos, Imbros, and Skyros, and another tax of 1/50 (see especially pp. 119–120 on the historical setting of the law); and Lambert 1997, 270–273, on the ἑκατοστή (*hekatoste*), the 1% tax on sales of land by Attic corporate groups in the second half of the fourth century BC. For a recent overview of Athenian taxation see Möller 2007, 375–383.

[8] *SEG* 26.1305 = J. & L. Robert, *JS* 1976, 175–188. See Kyrtatas 2002, 147–148.

εἰς τὰς δαπάνας ἢ ἃ τῷ νομίσματι ὤνια. δεύτερον δὲ τὴν σατραπικήν. ἔστι δὲ ταύτης εἴδη ἓξ τῶν προσόδων ἀπὸ γῆς, ἀπὸ τῶν ἐν τῇ χώρᾳ ἰδίων γινομένων, ἀπὸ ἐμπορίων, ἀπὸ τελῶν, ἀπὸ βοσκημάτων, ἀπὸ τῶν ἄλλων. αὐτῶν δὲ τούτων πρώτη μὲν καὶ κρατίστη ἡ ἀπὸ τῆς γῆς, αὕτη δέ ἐστιν ἣν οἱ μὲν ἐκφόριον, οἱ δὲ δεκάτην προσαγορεύουσιν, δευτέρα δὲ ἡ ἀπὸ τῶν ἰδίων γινομένη, οὗ μὲν χρυσίον, οὗ δὲ ἀργύριον, οὗ δὲ χαλκός, οὗ δὲ ὁπόσα δύναται γίνεσθαι, τρίτη δὲ καὶ ἡ ἀπὸ τῶν ἐμπορίων, [1346α] τετάρτη δὲ καὶ ἡ ἀπὸ τῶν κατὰ γῆν τε καὶ ἀγοραίων τελῶν γινομένη, πέμπτη δὲ ἡ ἀπὸ τῶν βοσκημάτων, ἐπικαρπία τε καὶ δεκάτη καλουμένη, ἕκτη δὲ ἡ ἀπὸ τῶν ἄλλων, ἐπικεφάλαιόν τε καὶ χειρωνάξιον προσαγορευομένη. τρίτον δὲ τὴν πολιτικήν. ταύτης δὲ κρατίστη μὲν πρόσοδος ἡ ἀπὸ τῶν ἰδίων ἐν τῇ χώρᾳ γινομένων, εἶτα ἡ ἀπὸ τῶν ἐμπορίων καὶ διαγωγῶν, εἶτα ἡ ἀπὸ τῶν ἐγκυκλίων.

Taking first the royal administration, we see that while theoretically its power is unlimited, it is in practice concerned with four departments, namely currency, exports, imports, and expenditure. Taking these severally, I assign to that of currency the seasonable regulation of prices; to imports and exports, the profitable disposition, at any given time, of the dues received from provincial governors; and to expenditure, the reduction of outgoings as occasion may serve, and the question of meeting expenses by currency or by commodities. The second kind of administration, that of the governor, is concerned with six different classes of revenue: namely, those arising from agriculture, from the special products of the country, from markets, from taxes, from cattle, and from other sources. Taking these in turn, the first and most important of them is revenue from agriculture, which some call tithe and some produce tax. The second is that from special products; in one place gold, in another silver, in another copper, and so on. Third in importance is revenue from markets, [1346a] and fourth that which arises from taxes on land and on sales. In the fifth place we have revenue from cattle, called tithe or first-fruits; and in the sixth, revenue from other sources, which we term poll tax, or tax on industry. Of our third kind of administration, that of a free state, the most important revenue is that arising from the special products of the country. Next follows revenue from markets and occupations; and finally that from everyday transactions.[9]

It is noteworthy that the anonymous author places great emphasis on revenues, including taxes of various sorts.[10] Significantly, one of the anecdotes he gives to illustrate the above account tells how the people of Mende used for the administration of their polis the taxes (τέλη) imposed on the harbour and taxes of other kinds, but refrained from collecting the imposts on land

9 The English translation is by G.C. Armstrong for the Loeb Classical Library (1935), with minor adaptations.

10 Finley 1973, 20–21, comments "what is noteworthy about these half a dozen paragraphs is not only their crashing banality but also their isolation in the whole of surviving ancient writing".

and on houses (τὰ δὲ ἀπὸ τῆς γῆς καὶ οἰκιῶν τέλη); however, they kept a register of the owners and collected arrears only when the city needed funds (1350a7–12).[11]

Evidence of taxation in Greek cities increases in volume in the Hellenistic and Roman periods. The Hellenistic kingdoms and Roman rule introduced a change: to meet military and economic demands the Hellenistic kings, and later the Romans, imposed new levies, even taxes on land and person.[12] In Ptolemaic Egypt a variety of taxes were imposed: on agricultural produce (in kind and in money), a capitation tax on salt, on transfers of property (later known as the ἐγκύκλιον), and on professional occupation.[13] However, a passage from a work by the third-century BC historian Phylarchos, preserved by Athenaeus (3, 73b–d = *FGrH* 81 F 65), whatever its historical value, may illustrate the Greeks' attitude to taxation. Phylarchos offers three examples of Hellenistic kings who imposed taxes on the use of natural resources, or prohibited their use, only to find out that these resources miraculously disappeared:

> Φύλαρχος δέ φησιν· οὐδέποτε πρότερον ἐν οὐδενὶ τόπῳ κυάμων Αἰγυπτίων οὔτε σπαρέντων οὔτ' εἰ σπείρειέ τις τικτομένων εἰ μὴ κατὰ Αἴγυπτον, ἐπὶ τοῦ βασιλέως Ἀλεξάνδρου τοῦ Πύρρου παρὰ τὸν Θύαμιν ποταμὸν τῆς ἐν Ἠπείρῳ Θεσπρωτίας ἐν ἕλει τινὶ συνέβη φυῆναι. δύο μὲν οὖν ἤνεγκέ πως ἔτη καρπὸν ἐκτενῶς καὶ ηὔξησε· τοῦ δ' Ἀλεξάνδρου φυλακὴν ἐπιστήσαντος καὶ κωλύοντος οὐχ ὅτι λαμβάνειν τὸν βουλόμενον, (73c) ἀλλὰ μηδὲ προσέρχεσθαι πρὸς τὸν τόπον, ἀνεξηράνθη τὸ ἕλος καὶ τὸ λοιπὸν οὐχ ὅτι τὸν προειρημένον ἤνεγκε καρπόν, ἀλλ' οὐδὲ ὕδωρ εἴ ποτε ἔσχε φαίνεται. τὸ παραπλήσιον ἐγένετο καὶ ἐν Αἰδηψῷ. χωρὶς γὰρ τῶν ἄλλων ὑδάτων ναμάτιόν τι ἐφάνη ψυχρὸν ὕδωρ προιέμενον οὐ πόρρω τῆς θαλάσσης. τούτου πίνοντες οἱ ἀρρωστοῦντες τὰ μέγιστα ὠφελοῦντο· διὸ πολλοὶ παρεγίνοντο καὶ μακρόθεν τῷ ὕδατι χρησόμενοι. οἱ οὖν τοῦ βασιλέως Ἀντιγόνου (73d) στρατηγοὶ βουλόμενοι οἰκονομικώτεροι εἶναι διάφορόν τι ἔταξαν διδόναι τοῖς πίνουσι, καὶ ἐκ τούτου ἀπεξηράνθη τὸ νᾶμα. καὶ ἐν Τρῳάδι δὲ ἐξουσίαν εἶχον οἱ βουλόμενοι τὸν πρὸ τοῦ χρόνον τὸν Τραγασαῖον ἅλα λαμβάνειν. Λυσιμάχου δὲ τέλος ἐπιβαλόντος ἠφανίσθη. θαυμάσαντος δὲ καὶ ἀφέντος τὸν τόπον ἀτελῆ πάλιν ηὐξήθη.
>
> Phylarchos says: "Never before, in any region, had Egyptian beans been sown; or if they had, nowhere did they grow except in Egypt. But in the reign of Alexander, son of Pyrrhos, they chanced to spring up in a swamp near the Thyamis river in Thesprotia, a region of Epeiros. For perhaps two years, then, they bore fruit luxuriantly and spread; but when Alexander stationed a guard

---

[11] Thomsen 1964, 39, interprets the tax on lands and houses as *eisphora*. For this incident see Migeotte 1984, no. 37.

[12] Rostovtzeff 1964, 316–346, 471, 954, 966, 994. See also Finley 1973, 95–96, 175.

[13] See Manning 2007, 446–458. Taxes in Egypt varied regionally. For the taxation system in Roman Egypt see Rathbone 2007, 716–718.

over them to see that no one should even approach the spot, to say nothing of gathering them at will, the swamp dried up, and not only did not produce the aforesaid fruit again, but whatever water it had contained never reappeared. The same also occurred in Aidepsos. For, not to mention other waters, a spring came to light which sent forth cold water not far from the sea. The sick who drank of it received the greatest benefit, so that many came even from great distances to use the water. Accordingly the generals of King Antigonos, desiring to be more efficient in collecting revenue, imposed a special tax on all who drank, and as a result the stream dried up. In the Troad, also, all who desired were at liberty in old times to collect salt at Tragasai. But when Lysimachos levied a tax on it, it disappeared. Surprised at this, he exempted the place from taxation, whereupon the salt increased once more".[14]

In Hellenistic Greece and Asia Minor local traditional taxes were often still collected in the poleis and by local tax collectors (the τελῶναι). The poleis themselves imposed taxes on agricultural production, on transfers of landed property, and on goods imported and exported.[15] Thus in the late second or early first century BC, the city of Kos issued a decree (*Syll.*[3] 1000 = *LSCG* 168) presenting a list (probably not complete) of obligatory sacrifices imposed, among others, on farmers of taxes exacted in Kos at the time of the inscription, but perhaps even earlier. The taxes in the list are on trading materials, cult requisites, prostitutes, workers (slaves?) in vineyards, female house-slaves, medical treatment, house rentals, etc.[16]

However, the poleis increasingly relied on contributions and loans made by generous and ambitious citizens.[17] For instance, in the third century BC the polis Akraiphia in Boiotia twice acknowledged a debt to private citizens (*SEG* 3.356 and 359).[18] In the early years of the second century BC Larisa raised funds for the renovation of the gymnasium; among the contributors were King Philip V and his son, the later King Perseus (*SEG* 33.460 = Ch. Habicht, *Chiron* 13, 1983, 21–32; 197–186 BC).[19] The citizens of the Xanthos agreed in 206/5 BC to contribute 500 drachmae to the polis Kytenion for the restoration of its walls, justifying their inability to make a more generous

---

14 The English translation is by Charles Burton Gulick for Loeb Classical Library (1927–1941), with minor changes. See also Davies 2001; Aperghis 2001; Paterson 2001.

15 See Reger 2007, 464–465.

16 Wiemer 2003a argues that the extant text of the inscription is a fragment of a law concerning the cult of Poseidon and the Nymphs of Kos and Rhodos, to whom the sacrifices were made.

17 See Migeotte 1984; Gabrielsen 2008, 125–126. The practice of relying on wealthy citizens' generosity is already noticeable in fourth-century Athens: see Aeschin. 3.27–31; Dem. 18.114.

18 Cf. Migeotte 1984, 74, nos. 16A and 16B.

19 On this inscriptions and other fundraisings in Thessaly see also Chapter 5 below.

contribution by referring to the economic troubles of Xanthos, to a previous decree which forbade any further impost for the next nine years, and to the fact that their wealthy citizens had already made generous donations to their city (*SEG* 38.1476, lines 52–58).[20]

Numerous clay seals (βοῦλλαι) found in the archives of second-century Seleucid Babylonia attest to the existence of various taxes that the depositors of the documents to which these seals were attached paid or were exempted from. The most common tax recorded in these seals is the ἁλική (*halike*), a tax levied on salt, which was a major source of revenue in the ancient world.[21]

Thessalian cities too imposed taxes on their citizens, but this is only indirectly attested by honorary decrees granting exemption, ἀτέλεια (*ateleia*), from taxes. Thus an inscription, dated to ca. 250–215 BC, records a decree by the city of Krannon to grant citizenship and other privileges, including an "exemption from imposts and from everything else" (ἀτέλειαν τᾶν φοράουν καὶ τοῦν ἄλλουν πάντουν, lines 4–6), to a man from Pharsalos (*SEG* 23.437 = *REA* 66, 1964, 312–315).[22] The existence of taxes is also indicated by grants of ἰσοτέλεια (*isoteleia*), equality of taxes, also accorded to foreign benefactors of the cities, as in *IG* IX(2) 61 from Lamia, then in the Aitolian League (216–212 BC).[23] Although direct evidence on taxation in Thessalian cities is practically absent,[24] these privileges could have been granted only where taxes were usually exacted.

This practice continued after Flamininus' declaration in 196 BC that the Thessalians were free, and after his reorganization of the Thessalian League. Decrees issued by individual Thessalian cities granting exemption from or equality of taxes therefore show that the federal government notwithstanding, each polis exercised its own fiscal administration and tax system.[25] Thus a decree of the polis Krannon (*IG* IX(2) 461b; ca. 168 BC) is dated by the

---

20 See also Ps.-Arist, *Oec.* 2, 1347b–1348a, on fourth-century BC Chios, and *IG* XII(7) 67 B on fourth-century BC Arkesine.

21 On the clay seals of Seleukia and Uruk see McDowell 1935; Lindström 2003; Invernizzi 2003. See also Rostovtzeff 1932, and below.

22 For another such grant from Krannon see *SEG* 31.572, ca. 200 BC (to Philip V and his *strategos*). See also *SEG* 16.373 (= *AE*, 1955, 81–84) from Lamia, ca. 300–250 BC; *IG* IX(2) 513 from Larisa, third century BC; *IG* IX(2) 260a from Kierion, third century BC.

23 Cf., from Lamia, *SEG* 53.540 (mid-third century BC). See also *SEG* 33.448 from Atrax (230–200 BC).

24 See, however, *SEG* 37.450 and 37.451 from second- or third-century AD Demetrias, discussed in detail in Chapter 4, where taxes and tax collectors are mentioned in the context of manumission of slaves.

25 See Baker 2001, 191–192.

Thessalian federal *strategos*, but it grants a citizen of Metropolis προξενία (*proxenia*) and other privileges, including "an exemption from all things" (ἀτ⟨έ⟩[λειαν πάντουν], line 31).[26] A decree issued by Lamia in 125/4? BC (*IG* IX(2) 66b) grants *proxenia* and *isoteleia* (equality of imposts) to a man from Kierion.[27]

In contrast to the taxation systems of the individual members of the Thessalian League, no extant text indicates that the Thessalian federal government collected directly taxes of any kind.[28] It may be significant that no evidence survives of federal taxation for other federations either, except the contributions by the poleis belonging to the various leagues, which were probably proportional to the number of their representatives on the federal councils.[29] The only evidence of a federal levy is found in an inscription concerning the Akarnanian League, dated to 216 BC. According to this decree, the people of Anaktorion customarily imposed taxes on various commercial transactions which took place during the festival in honour of Apollo in Aktion. The inscription records the Anaktorians' agreement to share with the Akarnanian Federation, to which they belonged, the revenues accruing from these taxes (*IG* IX(1) 2^2 583, lines 31–34):[30]

> 31 τᾶς δὲ πεντηκοστᾶς καὶ τῶν λοιπῶν τελέων ἁπάντων
> [τ]ῶγ γινομένων ἐν τᾶι παναγύρει καὶ τῶν ἄλλων τῶμ
> πιπτόντων ἐκ τᾶς
> [τ]ῶν σωμάτων πωλήσιος τὰ μὲν ἥμισα τῶν Ἀκαρνάνων εἶμεν,
> τὰ δὲ ἥμισα
> [τᾶ]ṣ πόλιος τῶν Ἀνακτοριέων·
>
> Of the two percent tax, and of all the other taxes which are (collected) during the festival, and of other revenues that derive from the sale of slaves, half shall go to the Akarnanians and half to the polis of the Anaktorians.

---

26 See also Habicht 1970, 139, lines 7–8, from Metropolis, dated to the first years of the second century BC (though it is not certain that the decree was issued after the reorganization of the League); *IG* IX(2) 65 from Lamia (184/3 BC); *AE* (1910), 344, no. 3 from Larisa (ca. 186 BC); *IG* IX(2) 1230 from Phalanna (second century BC), which grants a man named Glaukos, son of Apollonios, citizenship and exemption from taxes on all goods imported or exported by him; *SEG* 36.552 from Pythion (180–170 BC).

27 Cf. *IG* IX(2) 67 (186/5 BC) and 69 (ca. 130 BC), both from Lamia; *IG* IX(2) 519 from Larisa (late second century BC).

28 As mentioned in the Introduction above, according to Dem. 1.22 the Thessalians collected proceeds from the harbours, but nothing is known about later times.

29 See Larsen 1968, 36 on the Boiotians, 212–213 on the Aitolians, 232–233 on the Achaians, and 253 on the Lykians.

30 Cf. Habicht 1957, 86–122; Larsen 1968 271–272.

However, as Larsen notes, this was a special arrangement for the duration of the festival alone—indicating that the Akarnanian federal government normally did not collect taxes in the cities of the League.[31] The absence of any evidence of central collection of taxes by the Greek federations may imply that the payments also recorded in the Thessalian manumissions, though most probably imposed by a federal decision, were collected locally by the individual cities (see Chapter 5 below).

In addition to the aforementioned taxes, slaveholding and slave sales were often subject to taxation.[32] This category of taxation reveals the ambiguous conception of slavery. On the one hand, the slave was considered a piece of property which could be bought, sold, and transferred, hence slaveholding and slave sales were taxed like other items of property. On the other hand, the ancient Greeks also treated slaves as human beings, albeit of inferior status, as the capitation taxes in Ptolemaic and Roman Egypt attest.[33] This apparent contradiction is already detectable in Aristotle's definition of the slave:

> τίς μὲν οὖν ἡ φύσις τοῦ δούλου καὶ τίς ἡ δύναμις, ἐκ τούτων δῆλον: ὁ γὰρ μὴ αὑτοῦ φύσει ἀλλ' ἄλλου ἄνθρωπος ὤν, οὗτος φύσει δοῦλός ἐστιν, ἄλλου δ' ἐστὶν ἄνθρωπος ὃς ἂν κτῆμα ᾖ ἄνθρωπος ὤν. (*Pol.* 1, 1254a13–16)
>
> Therefore, the slave's nature and capacity are clear from these considerations: a human being who by nature belongs not to himself but to another is by nature a slave, and a human being belonging to another is anyone who, although being a man, is an item of property.

Discussing relationships of φιλία (*philia*) in *Nicomachean Ethics*, Aristotle claims that *philia* does not exist in relation to inanimate things (τὰ ἄψυχα), and so there can be no *philia* in relation to a slave in his capacity as a slave (ᾗ δοῦλος); but in respect of the slave's being a human being (ᾗ ἄνθρωπος) *philia* can exist (*EN* 1161b1–5). This ambiguous conception of slavery enabled the Greeks to tax slaves both as property and as persons.[34]

---

31 Larsen 1968, 272. On the taxation of slave sales, mentioned in this inscription, see below.

32 See Migeotte 2003.

33 See Straus 1973b on the property tax and capitation tax relating to slaves in Roman Egypt ("l' esclave ... est frappé de taxes comme les biens, dans le cas de sa vente par exemple. Mais, come être humain, il sera aussi soumis à des impôts et à des corvées", p. 364). For poll taxes levied on slaves in Ptolemaic Egypt see Muhs 2005. See also below.

34 On the conceptions of slavery in modern times and as reflected by the use of slavery terms in the ancient Greek sources see Vlassopoulos 2011a, arguing for relationships of domination, rather than of property, as the basis of understanding Greek slavery. See also Waldstein 2001, 32–36. Such conflicting conceptions are also revealed by the Three-Fifths Clause of the U.S. Constitution, a compromise reached in 1783 for the purpose of taxation

The oldest evidence known of slaves as taxable commodities in Greece is an inscription from Kyzikos from the last quarter of the sixth century BC (*Syll.*^{3} 4 = *Nomima* 32):[35]

A
[τὴν δὲ στ]ήλην τήνδε πόλις Μ-
ανῆ ἔδωκε τῶι Μεδίκ[εω].

B
ἐπὶ Μαιανδρίου·
πόλις ⟨Μανῆ ἔδωκε τῶι⟩ Μηδίκεω καὶ τοῖσιν Αἰσήπου παισὶν
καὶ τοῖσιν ἐκγόνοισιν ἀτε⟨λ⟩είην καὶ πρυ-
τανεῖον· δέδοται παρὲξ ναύτο
καὶ τὸ τάλαντο καὶ ἱππονίης καὶ
τῆς τετάρτης καὶ ἀνδραποδωνίης·
τῶν δὲ ἄλλων πάντων ἀτελές· καὶ ἐπὶ
τούτοισιν δῆμος ὅρκιον ἔταμον· τὴν
δὲ στήλην τήνδε πόλις Μ[α]νῆ ἔδ[ω]κ[ε]
τῶι Μηδίκεω.

Side A: The polis granted this stele to Manes, son of Medikes.

Side B: In the year of Maiandrios. The polis granted to (the son of) Medikes and to the sons of Aisepos and to their descendents exemption and (the right to dine in the) *prytaneion*. It was granted except for the *nautos*, the (tax on the use of) public weights and measures, the (tax on) horses, the (tax of) one-quarter and the (tax on) slaves. From all other (taxes) they shall be exempt. Concerning these (stipulations) the people swore over a sacrifice. The polis granted this stele to Manes, son of Medikes.

The inscription, issued in the sixth century BC, is a decree in honour of two citizens, bestowing on them and their offspring exemption (*ateleia*) from some taxes; it was re-inscribed in the first century BC (probably by descendents of the original beneficiaries). From the original decree (Side A) only the text of last line, repeated in the later decree (Side B), survives. The extant text gives only the list of taxes from which the family was *not* exempted. Line 6 of the inscription mentions the ἀνδραποδωνίη (*andrapodonie*), which probably was a tax on the sale of slaves. Together with the other taxes mentioned (one on the use of weights and measures, one on horses, and two others whose nature is not clear), this tax attests to Kyzikos' financial policy

---

and representation between the northern states' demand to treat slaves as property and the southern states' demand to count them as people, which would win them larger representation in Congress; under this compromise, only three-fifths of the slave population were counted. See Einhorn 2006.

35 The ed. pr. is J.H. Mordtman, *Hermes* 15 (1880), 92–98. See also Jeffery, *LSAG*, 367, no. 51.

of increasing its revenues by taxing the business transactions of its private citizens.[36]

In Athens, the harbour tax imposed on all goods imported through the Piraeus, which, as mentioned above, had risen by the end of the fifth century BC from one to two percent (the πεντηκοστή, *pentekoste*), may also have included the import of slaves, as can be inferred from a lexical entry in *Anecdota Graeca* (Bekker), 297:

> πεντεκοστεύονται καὶ τὸ πεντεκοστευόμενον· τῶν εἰσαγομένων εἰς τὸν Πειραιᾶ φορτίων καὶ ἀνδραπόδων ἐκ τῆς ἀλλοδαπῆς πεντηκοστὴν ἐτέλουν οἱ ἔμποροι. καὶ τοῦτο ἐκαλεῖτο πεντηκοστεύεσθαι. καὶ αὐτοὶ δὲ οἱ τὸ τέλος εἰσπράττοντες πεντηκοστολόγοι καλοῦνται.
>
> "To pay the fiftieth part" and "the payer of the fiftieth part": those merchants who pay the fiftieth-part tax on goods and slaves brought to the Piraeus from another country. And this is called "to pay the fiftieth part". And those who exact the tax are called πεντηκοστολόγοι (*pentekostologoi*).[37]

In his *De Vectigalibus* (ca. 355 BC) Xenophon suggested increasing Athens' revenues by the state's buying slaves and leasing them out to work in the mines; he argued that this plan could bring great profit to the city, noting that before the Dekelean War the tax on slaves (τὸ τέλος ... τῶν ἀνδραπόδων) brought in a great amount of money.[38] Westermann believes that Xenophon meant a tax on slave sales, but also argues that an integral part of that levy was a tax on manumission.[39] Still, Xenophon's argument is unsound because the tax he mentions was imposed by the state on private slave-owners, whereas the slaves he has in mind would belong to the state itself.

As we saw above, discussing the various types of household management (*oikonomia*) and the forms of revenues appropriate to each type, Pseudo-Aristotle provides in the second book of the *Economics* a collection of cases exemplifying the means adopted in the past by certain statesmen to replenish the treasury (*Oec.* 2, 1346a20–30). Some of these measures were

---

36 See the comments of Mordtman, *Hermes* 15 (1880), 97–98; *Nomima* 32, p. 138. Westermann 1955, 4, notes that this inscription indicates that slavery increased in importance in the sixth century BC.

37 For other attestations of this tax in Athens, but without specifying the goods taxed, see Andoc. 1.133; Dem. 24.120; 35.29–30, 59.27 (who describes this tax as being imposed on grain). Andreades 1979, 282, believes that in Athens the tax was imposed on the import and export of slaves.

38 Xen. *Vect.* 4.25 (see sections 18–24 on Xenophon's program). According to Thuc. 7.27.3–5, after the Spartans had occupied Dekelea 20,000 slaves deserted, a great many of them artisans (ἀνδραπόδων πλέον ἢ δύο μυριάδες ηὐτομολήκεσαν, καὶ τούτων τὸ πολὺ μέρος χειροτέχναι).

39 Westermann 1955, 16.

mentioned above. Some other examples given by the author relate to slaves. Thus the people of Mende,

> πολεμοῦντες τὲ πρὸς Ὀλυνθίους καὶ δεόμενοι χρημάτων, ὄντων αὐτοῖς ἀνδραπόδων, ἐψηφίσαντο καταλειπομένων ἑνὶ ἑκάστῳ θήλεος καὶ ἄρρενος τὰ ἄλλα ἀποδόσθαι τῇ πόλει, ὡς ἐκδανεῖσαι τοὺς ἰδιώτας χρήματα.
>
> needing funds because of the war with Olynthos, decreed that all the citizens should sell their slaves, with the exception of one male and one female each, in the name of the polis, as if it was borrowing money from private citizens.[40]

Another example is that of Antimenes of Rhodes, appointed by Alexander the Great to supervise the roads in Babylon:

> πάλιν τε πορίζων τἀνδράποδα τὰ ἐπὶ στρατοπέδῳ ὄντα ἐκέλευσε τὸν βουλόμενον ἀπογράφεσθαι ὁπόσου θέλοι, μέλλειν δὲ τοῦ ἐνιαυτοῦ ὀκτὼ δραχμὰς ἀποτίσαι, ἂν δὲ ἀποδρᾷ τὸ ἀνδράποδον, κομίζεσθαι τὴν τιμὴν ἧς ἀνεγράψατο.
>
> He also raised money by urging the owners of any slaves in the camp to register them at whatever value they wished, but at the same time to agree to pay him eight drachmai a year. If a slave ran away, the owner was to receive the registered value.[41]

The result was that many slaves were registered and a large sum of money was paid, and when a slave ran away Antimenes instructed the satrap to recover the runaway or pay the master the slave's value. We cannot be sure how historically reliable these examples are, but they surely reflect a general perception of slaves as a kind of private property which could be used to increase the state revenues.[42]

A decree of the polis Teos from the second half of the fourth century BC, cited above, grants the citizens of another city privileges and exemption from taxes, one of which is on the sale of slaves (ἀτέλειαν ... [ἀνδραπόδων]).[43] The inscription mentioned above, recording the agreement between the citizens of Anaktorion and the Akarnanian League to share the revenues accruing from taxes imposed on commercial transactions during the festival in honour of Apollo in Aktion (*IG* IX(1) 2^2 583; 216 BC), included the sharing of proceeds from a tax on slave sales (lines 2–3).[44]

---

40 Ps.-Arist. *Oec.* 2, 1350a13–16. For this passage see Migeotte 1984, 120–121, who also discusses the possible circumstances of this subscription.

41 Ps.-Arist. *Oec.* 2, 1352b33–1353a4.

42 For means taken to increase revenues not involving slaves, see the whole list in Ps.-Arist. *Oec.* 2, 1346a31–1353b29. See also in the Introduction above.

43 *SEG* 26.1305, lines 7, 11–13 (= J. and L. Robert, *JS*, 1976, 175–188). See Rostovtzeff 1964, 242.

44 Cf. Habicht 1957, 86–122. Larsen 1968, 271 n. 2, understands the phrase καὶ τῶν ἄλλων

In Seleukia on the Tigris a tax named ἀνδραποδική (*andrapodike*) was imposed, probably on slave sales, as is attested by a number of second-century BC clay seals (*boullai*) recording names of slave-owners who were subject to this tax (e.g. ἀνδραποδικῆς Σελευκείας ἀγορᾶς ἐπιτελῶν, *IK Estremo Oriente* 79c[2]) or exempt from it (e.g. ἀνδραποδικῆς Σελευκείας ἀγορᾶς ἀτελῶν, *IK Estremo Oriente* 79c[1]). Another seal bears the inscription ἀνδραπ[οδικῆς] / Σελευκε[ίας] / βκρ' / εἰσαγωγ[ῆς] (*IK Estremo Oriente* 79g; 190/89 BC), which may indicate the import of slaves.[45] McDowell suggests that the seals bearing the legend ἀνδραποδικῆς with ἐπιτελῶν or ἀτελῶν indicate the assessment of slave's value prior to the payment of the tax due on the slave's sale; in the latter seal he restores εἰσαγω[γικῶν] instead of εἰσαγωγ[ῆς] and explains that it registers the payment of tax on the import of slaves.[46]

Slave sales were also taxed in Ptolemaic Egypt. From at least the reign of Ptolemy II all sales and other transfers of property, including slaves, by Greeks were taxed and registered in the office of the *agoranomos*.[47] However, the evidence is often ambiguous. Thus the tax known as ἐγκύκλιον was imposed on transfers of property, including slaves, and is also mentioned in some papyri in the context of manumission, but other names are also attested for taxes on sales of slaves.[48]

Taxation on selling or trading in slaves continued in the Greek East under Roman rule. In 71/70 BC Lucullus imposed new taxes on slaves and houses (App. *Mith.* 83: τέλη δ' ἐπὶ τοῖς θεράπουσι καὶ ταῖς οἰκίαις ὥριζεν), though these

τῶμ πιπτόντων ἐκ τᾶς [τ]ῶν σωμάτων πωλήσιος as denoting manumissions, and refers to the Delphic manumission inscriptions which attest numerous manumissions in the form of fictive sales to Apollo; see also Cabanes 1998, 443, who suggests that this tax may also have been imposed on manumissions. But as much as this interpretation is attractive and may indicate the existence of manumission tax in third-century BC Akarnania, there is no other evidence for the use of πώλησις in sale-manumissions.

45 See also *IK Estremo Oriente* 126a, 126b (Nippur, 164 BC); 132a, 132b (Uruk); and see above for another tax recorded by the Babylonian seals. On these clay seals see McDowell 1935, 41–42, 64; Rostovtzeff 1932, 99–105; 1964, vol. 2, 1261; Invernizzi 2003, 317; Lindström 2003; Messina 2005, 140.

46 McDowell 1935, 138–141, 175–179.

47 See Rostovtzeff 1964, 322; Muhs 2005, 21–22. For the Roman period see Straus 1973b, and Straus 2004, 71–78.

48 See Muhs 2005, 71–72, who describes the *enkyklion* as a sale tax, first levied at the rate of eight for each 100 drachmai and later at the rate of 5–10% the sale price. Muhs also notes that although sale taxes at this rate are known earlier, the first attested appearance of the term *enkyklion* is in 210 BC. On the various names used for taxes see Straus 2004, 72, who explains that in slave sales the name of the tax depended on whether it was used in the title of the collector or in the text of the document. In the latter case the variants are much more numerous and more individualized by elements specific to the taxed slaves. On manumission taxes in Egypt see Chapter 4 below.

taxes were probably collected by the cities themselves. Likewise Pompey, Apius Claudius, and Piso imposed in Asia a poll tax on both free persons and slaves, as well as on houses.[49] The Customs Law of Asia, composed over two centuries, contains provisions on the import, export, and sale of slaves, for which actions a tax (*telos*) was to be collected.[50]

This evidence, though scant and not always unequivocal, indicates that transactions involving slaves were taxed in many places. It is therefore plausible that manumission of slaves, often regarded as a transaction—habitually entailing, as it were, the payment of money in exchange for freedom and often including stipulations—would also be subject to imposts.[51] As we shall see in Chapter 4, in many places in the Greek world, as well as in Ptolemaic and Roman Egypt, payments were exacted from slaves upon their manumission. Yet in many cases it is not easy to determine whether money was exacted as a tax on manumission or for registration. Our best evidence is the Roman tax of five percent (*vicesima manumissionum/libertatis*), introduced, as we saw in the Introduction, in 357 BC by the consul Manlius. Livy (7.16.7), who reports this event, gives no motive for Manlius' action, but comments that although the manner of passing the law was without precedent, the Senate ratified it *quia ea lege haud parvum vectigal inopi aerario additum esset* ("since by this law no small income was added to the destitute treasury").[52] It is reasonable to assume that a similar motive drove Greek poleis and Hellenistic kings who imposed a tax on manumission. Where the impost was exacted to cover registration and publication costs, we may assume that besides the financial profit the poleis wished to have a formal record of manumitted slaves.[53]

To determine the nature of the uniform payments made in the context of manumission in Thessaly, the next chapter analyses the relevant documents recording such payments.

---

49 See Rostovtzeff 1964, 954.

50 See Cottier et al. 2008, lines 12, 74–76, 98, 117, 121, and p. 228.

51 The commercial aspect of manumission is perhaps particularly noticeable in the mode of manumission whereby the slave was sold to a third party with the agreed intention of the latter to manumit the slave (sometimes called πρᾶσις ἐπὶ λύσει, sale for the purpose of release). Such was the case described in Hyperides' oration *Against Athenogenes*. But manumission made by selling the slave to a deity can also be seen as belonging to this type; see Zelnick-Abramovitz 2005a, 86–99. On manumission as a taxable transaction see also Stewart 2012, 6.

52 See Bradley 1984a, 149; 1984b, 175.

53 Having a public record of the slaves' new status was also in the interest of the latter and of their former masters, who thus anticipated any future claims from heirs. See Zelnick-Abramovitz 2005a, 184–187, 191–192.

CHAPTER TWO

THE THESSALIAN MANUMISSION INSCRIPTIONS

Most of the inscriptions which mention money paid to the polis in the context of manumission in various Thessalian cities are long lists of names of manumittors and manumitted slaves, arranged in chronological order; some, however, record individual acts of manumission in more elaborate language.[1] The extant inscriptions are dated by eponymous local magistrates and by the annual federal *strategos*,[2] and span more than four hundred years, from the early second century BC to sometime in the third century AD. The manumission acts recorded in these inscriptions are often arranged by years and months.[3] However, the precise number of the manumissions in these inscriptions is difficult to determine. Calculating by the occurrences of manumission verbs, manumission formulae ("X by Y"), names of slaves, and mentions of payment, I count more than 1,700 acts of manumission, grouped in more than 300 inscriptions, to which must be added many entries not preserved on the stones.[4] The extant inscriptions contain hundreds of allusions to this payment, but there must have been many more: since most of the inscriptions mentioning the payment are fragmentary, those that comprise long lists of manumission acts are certain to have included more references.

The inscriptions reveal that chattel slavery was an important institution in Thessaly, at least in the centuries following Flamininus' reorganization of the League; as noted in the Introduction, there is also some evidence that may attest to the existence of chattel slavery in earlier times.[5] It is

---

[1] See e.g. *IG* IX(2) 1296 (= *AE*, 1945–1947, 110, no. 59) from Azoros (20–18 BC), which records five individual elaborate manumission acts; and *SEG* 26.670 from Pythion (150–100 BC), which is a record of a single manumission act.

[2] On the federal *strategoi* and their dates, until the late first century BC, see Arvanitopoulos, *AE* (1917), 146–150; Étienne and Knoepfler1976; Kramolisch 1978.

[3] On the Thessalian calendar see Reilly 1971, 668; Graninger 2011, 95–106.

[4] For a list of the Thessalian manumission inscriptions see Appendix. This list holds 313 inscriptions, recording ca. 1,760 manumitted slaves. The new editions of the Thessalian manumission inscriptions planned by Richard Bouchon for the *Collection Bibliothèque des Ecoles françaises d'Athènes et de Rome*, might change the count.

[5] See also Chapter 5 below.

difficult to assess the number of slaves in any given period and city, since our information comes from inscriptions that record those who were no longer slaves and it is likely that in any given period the latter were fewer than those still in slavery. As noted above, even the exact number of manumitted slaves per annum cannot be safely deduced because not all the Thessalian poleis yielded manumission inscriptions, and the extant inscriptions are often fragmentary.

Since the inscriptions discussed in this book are our sole evidence of manumission in Thessaly, it is worthwhile briefly reviewing its characteristics. According to the extant inscriptions manumission in Thessaly was 'secular' or 'civil', that is, the slave's freedom was not attained by a fictive dedication or sale to a divinity as was the case in Delphi, for instance;[6] slave owners in Thessaly freed their slaves by a simple declaration, most likely in the presence of witnesses, or ordered their manumission in their last will.[7] The most common verb used in the Thessalian inscriptions to refer to the act of manumission is ἀπελευθερόω.[8] Many inscriptions also use the participle ἀπελευθερωθέντες[9] or the adjective ἀπελεύθεροι[10] in headings or to introduce a new year or month. Less frequently used is ἀφίημι—mostly in Perrhaibia, where it appears in the construction ἀφίημι ἐλεύθερος or ἀπελεύθερος ("release as free").[11] Several manumission records note the obligation of the manumitted slave to παραμονή, that is, to stay on (παραμένειν) with the manumittor or the latter's family members. Interestingly, all these cases come from Pythion in Perrhaibia.[12] Given that the only verb used in Pythion

6 *SEG* 49.629 (Proerna, early second century BC), is a single attestation of manumission by dedication. On manumission modes see Zelnick-Abramovitz 2005a, 69–99.

7 E.g. *IG* IX(2) 546, lines 21–24 (Larisa, AD 131/132). Manumissions made according to the owners' "intention" (κατὰ διανόησιν) are recorded in two manumission acts from Kophi in Achaia Phthiotis: *IG* IX(2) 102, face A, line 4 (185–180 BC), and *IG* IX(2) 109b, line 38 (46/5 BC); see Babacos 1966, 63–64.

8 E.g. *IG* IX(2) 359b, lines 4–6 (from Pagasai, Roman period): Νεικίας Νεικείου ἀπη/λευθέρ⟨ω⟩σεν Μεγειστείωνα.

9 E.g. *IG* IX(2) 18, line 2 (from Hypata, undated): [οἵδε ἀπελευ]θερωθέντες καὶ δόντες τὸ γειν⟨ό⟩μενον ("these are the manumitted slaves and those who paid what is due"), or *IG* IX(2) 474, lines 5–7 (from Atrax, 49/8 BC): Ζωσίμη Λύκου ἡ ἀπελευθ[ε]/ρωθεῖσα ὑπὸ Λύκου τοῦ Φειδίου κατὰ τὸν / νόμον ("Zosime of Lykos, the slave manumitted by Lykos son of Pheidias, according to the law").

10 E.g. *IG* IX(2) 274 (from Metropolis, 186/5 BC), lines 3–4: οἱ γεγο/νότες ἀπελεύθεροι.

11 E.g. *AE* (1945–1947) 110, no. 59, 29–30 (= *IG* IX(2) 1296, from Azoros): τὴν ἑαυτῶν οἰκέτιδα / γεγονυῖαν εὐάρεστον ἀφῆκαν ἐλευθέραν. See also below.

12 See e.g. *SEG* 26.670 from Pythion (on which see also below): παραμενέτω] δὲ Ἀλέξανδρο[ς] / [παρὰ Εὔτυχον ποιῶν] τὸ ἐπιτασσόμε/[νον ἕως ἂν ζῇ Εὔτυχ]ος ("and let Alexandros stay with Eutychos, doing what he is ordered to do as long as Eutychos lives", lines 6–8). See also

to denote manumission is ἀφίημι it may be assumed that Pythion had its unique manumission practices. However, not all the manumission acts from Pythion mention the *paramone*.[13]

There is some evidence of manumitted slaves paying money to their former owners as the price of freedom (λύτρον). Where sums are mentioned—in inscriptions from Pythion and Demetrias in the first century BC and later—they vary between 150 and 300 drachmae.[14] Compared with the prices mentioned in the Delphic manumission inscriptions, the sums paid in Thessaly seem modest; according to Keith Hopkins, prices paid by slaves for their freedom rose from the beginning of the second to the end of the first century BC.[15] Hopkins ascribes this rise to the integration of central Greece into the Roman world, the imposition of taxes, the growing demand for slaves in Italy, and the extension of the slave market from Italy to Greece. But if slaves were brought to Italy from central Greece, Thessaly could have been a supplier too, because although declared free by Flamininus it was under Roman control; yet the prices attested there are much lower. Nonetheless, the evidence we find in Thessalian inscriptions is not enough to infer anything conclusive about prices of freedom (or prices of slaves) in Thessaly as a whole.

Against this evidence, some inscriptions state that the freedom is given "for free" (δωρεάν);[16] possibly the slaves in these cases were related to their owners or distinguished themselves in some way.[17] Slaves often seem to

---

AE (1924), 155, no. 400; 166, no. 405; 173, no. 409 (= *IG* IX(2) 1290); 188, no. 418a (= *IG* IX(2) 1282 IV)—all three from Pythion. On the *paramone* as a stipulation attached to manumissions see Samuel 1965; Hopkins 1978, 133–162; Mulliez 1992; Zelnick-Abramovitz 2005a, 222–248.

13 Babacos 1966, 79–88, argues that the laws in Thessalian poleis established the manumitted slaves' obligations to their manumittors, including the *paramone*, and that is why this obligation is not always mentioned. Cf. Helly 1976. See, however, Zelnick-Abramovitz 2005, 305.

14 Pythion: *IG* IX(2) 1282 II (ca. 50 BC), 150 drachmae. Demetrias: *IG* IX(2) 1117c (Roman period), 300 drachmae; *IG* IX(2) 1119 (Roman period), line 8, 200 drachmae; line 15, 250 drachmae (see also Chapter 4). In several inscriptions the term *lytron* is mentioned without the sums paid: *IG* IX(2) 1100b, 1116b, and *SEG* 44.446 from Demetrias; *IG* IX(2) 1268 from Doliche; *AE* (1916), 78, no. 284 from Olosson; *SEG* 23.460 = *AE* (1930), 100–101, no. 2 from Iolkos in Magnesia. In *SEG* 23.462 from Pythion the manumitted slave is exempted from the *lytron*.

15 See Hopkins 1978, 158–163, for prices paid for freedom in Delphi. From 53 to 1 BC adult male slaves paid 827 drachmai for full freedom (as against deferred freedom); adult females paid 485 drachmai. But see Duncan-Jones 1984.

16 E.g. *IG* IX(2) 1299 (from Azoros), lines 10–12: Ἀ⟨ρ⟩καδίων [ὁ ἀπ]ελευθερω[θ]/εἰς κατὰ δωρεὰν [ὑπὸ Δι]καιο[ο][γ]ένους τοῦ Ἀν[– –]ου. See also below.

17 E.g. *IG* IX(2) 1296 (= *AE*, 1945–1947, 110, no. 59) from Azoros: τὴν ἑαυτῶν οἰκέτιδα / γεγονυῖαν εὐάρεστον ἀφῆκαν ἐλευθέραν δωρεὰν (see also below).

have been held in common ownership by family members: in many records husbands and wives, parents and children manumit their slaves together.[18] Moreover, women manumitted their slaves without a κύριος (*kyrios*), as in *IG* IX(2) 1040b (= *Gonnoi* II, 123), lines 11–15 (Gonnoi, first century BC/AD), where a mother acts as a co-manumittor and as guardian (ἐπίτροπος) of her two sons, although her husband's brothers are still alive.[19] Several manumission documents also mention the consent given by family members to the act of manumission (expressed by the verbs συνευδοκέω and συνεῖπον, or by the phrase μετὰ τῆς γνώμης): husbands to their wives and children, wives to their fathers, husbands, and children, and children to their parents. Thus, the sixth manumission act in an inscription from Pythion (*AE*, 1924, 188, no. 418a = *IG* IX(2) 1282; ca. 50 BC) reads (lines 35–42):

> στρατηγοῦντος Καλλιστ{ρατ}άρχου {[26]Καλλιστάρχου}[26] [τοῦ –]ως μ[η]-
> [νὸς] Ἱπποδρομίου ἐννεακαιδεκάτ[η Ὀλυμ]πία Π[ο]-
> λυστράτου καὶ οἱ υἱοὶ αὐτῆς Κλεογένης καὶ Πολύ-
> [σ]τρατος οἱ Ἐπικράτους συνε[υδοκ]ουσῶν Ἐ[– –]
> [–]νοῦς καὶ Δημοφίλας τῶν Ἐπ[ικρ]άτο[υ κ]α[ὶ]
> [τοῦ] ἀνδρὸς Ἀριστομάχου τοῦ Εὐ[έλθο]ντος [καὶ]
> [Ἀσά]νδ[ρ]ου τοῦ Δημοφίλας, Ἀριστ[ο– – – τὴν ἑαυ]
> [των δ]ού[λην ἀφῆκαν] ⟨ἐ⟩λευθ̣[έ]ραν̣ [κατὰ τὸν νόμον].
>
> When Kallistarchos was the *strategos*, on the nineteenth day of the month of Hippodromios, Olympia, daughter of Polystratos, and her sons Kleogenes and Polystratos, sons of Epikrates, also consenting E[--] and Demophila, daughters of Epikrates, and her husband Aristomachos, son of Euelthon, and Asandros, son of Demophila, released as free their slave Aristo[---] according to the law.[20]

And in *IG* IX(2) 288, lines 3–6 (Gomphoi, undated), we read:

> ἀπὸ Καλλιδίκης
> [τῆς] Ἀπολλωνίου συνε⟨ι⟩πόντων καὶ τῶν τέκνων̣
> [Νι]κάρχου ⟨καὶ⟩ Κωτίλας τῶν Δικα⟨ι⟩άρχου Σωσίας Νικ-
> άρχου.

---

[18] See e.g. *IG* IX(2) 109a, lines 21–22, 25–27, 67–69 (Phthiotic Thebes, 47/6 BC?); 109b, lines 63–65 (Phthiotic Thebes, 46/5 BC?). See Babacos 1966.

[19] Babacos 1963 argues that in Thessaly women could be their children's guardians *ex lege*. Yet in *AE* (1917), 18, no. 309 from Chyretiai (first century BC), lines 19–22, a woman manumits "with the consent (μετὰ τ[ῆς] [γν]ώμης) of her husband"; cf. *AE* (1917), 18, no. 311, lines 17–19 (late first century BC).

[20] When this manumission took place, Olympia the manumittor seems to have been married a second time (to Aristomachos, son of Euelthon); she performs the manumission together with her sons from her first husband (Epikrates), and with the consent of her daughters and her second husband.

> (Manumitted) by Kallidike, daughter of Apollonios, with the consent of her children Nikarchos and Kotila, children of Dikaiarchos—(the slave) Sosias of Nikarchos.[21]

Babacos notes that legally the consent clauses meant collective manumissions, but considering the relative rarity of attested collective manumissions he argues that in Thessaly there was no collective ownership of the household's property; by giving their consent to or taking an active part in the manumission relatives simply waived their legal right to *paramone*.[22] But whether or not slaves were the collective property of the household, such consent clauses show that they were an important household property, and manumission affected all family members and potential heirs.

There is also some evidence of non-citizens manumitting in Thessalian poleis. Some of them acted using their *prostates*. Thus Lines 11–14 of *AD* 11 (1927–1928), 58, no. 5 from Larisa (mid-first century BC) record the manumission of the female slave Nike: "Nike (belonging to) Herakleides (was manumitted) by Herakleides son of Aphrodisios, an Athenian, having appointed as his *prostates* Aineas son of Epikrates" (Νίκη Ἡρακλείδου ἀπὸ Ἡρα/κλείδου τοῦ Ἀφροδισίου, Ἀθηναίου, καθεσ/τακότος προστάτην Αἰνέαν Ἐπ[ι]/κράτους). Lines 18–21 of the same inscription read: "Zeuxis (belonging to) Antigonos (was manumitted) by Antigonos son of Demakos, a Macedonian, having appointed as his prostates Hippolochos son of Hippolochos" (Ζεῦξις Ἀντιγόνου / [ἀ]πὸ Ἀντιγόνου τοῦ Δημάκου, Μακε/δόνος Βονθίτου, καθεστακότ[ος] / [π]ροστάτην Ἱππόλοχον Ἱππολό[χου]). But the *prostates* was not always different than the manumittor even when the latter was a foreigner.[23]

We now come to the payments made to the polis, recorded in the Thessalian manumission inscriptions. As mentioned above, the sum paid is uniform in all places and periods (fifteen staters or twenty-two and a half denarii).

---

[21] In this manumission record, as in many others, the name of the slave is followed by another name in the genitive case, sometimes identical to that of the manumittor or of other participants in the manumission, as in the inscription cited here. For the various interpretations that have been offered (the manumitted slave's father—whether the manumittor himself or a third person, the manumitted slave's προστάτης, or both) see Babacos 1962; Zelnick-Abramovitz 2005a, 259–261. See also *AD* 11 (1927–1928), 58, no. 5, line 13 (cited below), where the *prostates* is explicitly mentioned.

[22] Babacos 1966, 79–86. Collective ownership of slaves is postulated for Epiros by Cabanes 1976, 418–423. See also Zelnick-Abramovitz 2005, 135–140.

[23] See Babacos 1962, 499, who cites *IG* IX(2) 568. See also *SEG* 31.579 from Larisa (100–80 BC), line 30; Llewelyn 1992, 79–81, on Thessalian as against Delphic manumission.

Conversely, the formula referring to the payment varies from place to place. For instance, in *IG* IX(2) 543 from Larisa (reign of Augustus), the formula is:

> στρατηγοῦντο[ς Σω]σιπάτρο[υ – – – – – – – μη]-
> ⟨ν⟩ὸς ⟨Ἰτ⟩ωνίου δευτ̣έ[ρα̣], ταμιεύοντος [τῆς πόλ]-
> εος Ἐπικράτου Ἐλπὶς ἡ ⟨ἀ⟩πελευθερωθ[ῖσα ὑ]-
> πὸ Φιλοδεσποτίδος ἔδωκε τὰ γινό[μενα]
> δι(νάρια) κβ<ʹ.

> When Sostratos was the *strategos*, on the second day of the month of Itonios, when Epikrates was the treasurer of the polis, Elpis, having been manumitted by Philodespotis, paid the due twenty-two and a half denarii.

The other entries on the stone follow the same pattern, recording one manumission act per year. An earlier inscription from Larisa has a different formula: after naming the ταγοί (*tagoi*), the treasurers, the transcriber (ἀντιγραφεύς), the gymnasiarchs, and the federal *strategos*, the inscription (*SEG* 31.577, 136/5 BC, lines 10–13) reads:

> οἱ καττεθειούκοντες τοῦν ἀπελευθέρουν τᾶ πόλι
> τὸ γινόμενον ἐς τοῖ νόμοι· Πανάμμοι ὀδδόα ἐφ' ἰκάδι ν Μέ-
> ν[ο]υ̣ν ὁ φάμενος ἀπειλευθερούσθει̣ν ἀπὸ Μενεστράτοι Πορ-
> τ[ι]νείοι τὸ γινόμενον τᾶ πόλι στατε[ί]ρας δεκάπεμπε·]

> Those among the manumitted slaves who paid to the polis what is due according to the law: on the twenty-eighth day of the month of Panemos, Menon, declared to be manumitted by Menestratos son of Portinos, the due fifteen staters to the polis.

The inscription continues with more names of manumitted slaves and manumittors, following the same formula. Note that since the heading contains the phrase "those ... who paid", no verb denoting payment is used in the following entries, unlike the case in the first example given above. But in a second-century AD inscription from Larisa (*IG* IX(2) 547, AD 131/132) we find a very different formulation:

> ἀγαθῆι̣ τύχηι.
> *Vacat*
> παρὰ Λ(ουκίου) Τιτίου Ὀνησίμου τοῦ
> ταμίου τῆς πόλεως τὴν β
> ἑξάμηνον ἐν στρ(ατηγῷ) Ἱπποκρα-
> τίδῃ ἀναγραφὴ ἀπελ(ευθέρων) τῶν
> δεδωκότων τοὺς στατῆ-
> ρας τῇ πόλει μ(ηνὸς) Ἀφρίου
> Τελεσφόρος, Ἀγάθη, Κασ-
> σάνδρα, Ἡρακλέων, Χαρί-
> τα, Στράτων, Ἰουκοῦνδα

> Good Fortune! When Lucius Titus Onesimus was the treasurer of the polis, in the second half of the year of the *strategos* Hippokratides, a register of the manumitted slaves who paid the staters to the polis. In the month of Aphrios: Telesphoros, Agathe, Kassandra, Herakleon, Charita, Straton, Iucunda ...

Here too the verb of payment is used only in the heading. In Phthiotic Thebes inscriptions were dated by the *strategos* and the local treasurer, followed by a similar but more elaborate formula: "a register (*anagrapha*) of manumitted slaves who paid to the polis the due (sum). (Name of month): from (name of slave), the slave manumitted by (name of manumittor), the fifteen staters due according to the law".[24] A similar formula is found in Pherai (*IG* IX(2) 415 + Add. + *SEG* 28.527, e.g. lines 10–15: οἱ / δεδωκότες ἐπ' αὐτῷ ἀπελεύ/θεροι τῇ πόλει τοὺς δεκαπέν/τε στατῆρας κατὰ τὸν νό/μον· Κλήτα ἀπὸ Ἀρχελάου / τοῦ Ἱπποκράτους). Likewise in Gonnoi (*Gonnoi* II 117 = *IG* IX(2) 1042 I, e.g. lines 4–8: οἱ ἀπη/λευθερωμένοι καὶ δεδω/κότες τῇ πόλει τὰ γεινόμ/ενα τῆς ἀπελευθερώσεω/ς αὐτῶν δεινάρια εἴκοσι δύο ἥμυσυ). That the payment was made in accordance with the law is stated in many other inscriptions from Thessaly, a fact that strengthens the impression that this was a federal decision, accepted by the members of the League.[25]

Some inscriptions, although dated by the local treasurer and registering payment by the manumitted slaves to the polis, omit the sum paid; thus in *IG* IX(2) 288 from Gomphoi (undated), lines 1–3, we find the heading: [ταμιεύοντος – – – –]ẹνίδου τοῦ Σίμου οἱ ἐξε-/[λευθερω]θέν[τ]ες καὶ δεδωκότες τὸ γινόμενον / [εἰς τ]ὴν [π]όλιν κατὰ τὸν νόμον ("[when ---] son of Simos was the treasurer, the manumitted slaves who paid what is due to the polis according to the law"), followed only by the names of the manumittors and their manumitted slaves. Other inscriptions are dated by the treasurer but do not mention any payments at all.[26]

As noted above, the payments registered in the Thessalian manumission inscriptions are of the uniform sum of fifteen staters or, after 27 BC, twenty-two and a half denarii. The transition to Roman currency, at a rate of one stater to one denarius and a half, was part of Augustus' reforms of 27 BC. This is manifest in an inscription from Pherai, *IG* IX(2) 415 + Add. (+ *SEG* 28.527), dated to the late first century BC, recording manumissions and payments

---

[24] E.g. *IG* IX(2) 109a (47/6 BC?): ἀναγραφὰ τῶν δεδωκότων τᾶι / πόλει ἀπελευθέρων τὸ γινόμενον τᾶι πό/λει. παρὰ Εἰράνας τᾶς Διοφάντου / [τᾶ]ς ἀπελευθερωθείσας ἀπὸ Κύλλου τοῦ / Ἀριστονίκου τὸ ἐκ τοῦ νόμου στατῆρες δε/καπέντε (lines 4–9).

[25] See e.g. *IG* IX(2) 13 from Hypata (AD 47); *IG* IX(2) 540 from Larisa (48/9 BC); *IG* IX(2) 288 from Gomphoi (undated); *AE* (1924) 173, no. 407 from Pythion, and many others.

[26] E.g. *IG* IX(2) 274 (186/5 BC) and 277 from Metropolis (undated).

to the polis. The first three entries are dated by the treasurer and the federal *strategos*, and the sum is given in staters (lines 1–53). In the next entry, which is badly preserved, we read (face B, lines 54a–61):

54a [δεκαπέν]-
54b [τε στατῆ]-
54c [ρας κατὰ]
[τὸ]ν νόμ[ον],
[ἃ γ]ίνετα[ι]
[κ]ατὰ τὸ διό[ρ]-
θωμα δει-
νάρια εἴκο-
σ[ι] δύο ἥμυ-
συ·

> ... [fifteen staters according] to the law, which, following the revision (*diorthoma*), are twenty-two and a half denarii.

And again, in lines 84–91: τοὺς δεκα/πέντε στα/τῆρας κατὰ / τὸν νόμον, / ἃ γίνεται / δεινάρια / εἴκοσι δύο / ἥμυσυ ("the fifteen staters, according to the law, which are twenty-two and a half denarii").

Next, and after a record of a manumission act in the month of Hermaios, comes an entry dated by the *strategeia* of Augustus.[27]

Lines 1–3 of an inscription from Echinos, *IG* IX(2) 92 (= *SEG* 39.493), dated to AD 133–134 – ca. 150, are restored to read: [ἔδωκεν τῇ πόλει τὰ γεινόμενα τῆς ἀπελευθερώσεως ἀντὶ τῶν στατήρων ἀργυρίου (δηνάρια) εἴκοσι δύο ἥμ]ισον τῷ ταμίᾳ ("[---] paid the polis the due money on the occasion of manumission, *instead of the staters* twenty-two and a half silver (denarii) to the treasurer").[28] It may seem strange that in the second century AD it was still deemed necessary to note the change in currency, but to judge by some inscriptions, payment in staters continued in some places even after 27 BC (e.g. *IG* IX(2) 546 and 547 from Larisa, AD 131/132; *SEG* 53.512 from Aiginion, second/third century AD). That the Thessalians still used Thessalian currency even for official fees is also evident from the few cases where the sum paid is registered as "twenty-two denarii and four obols", four obols being the equivalent of a half denarius (e.g. *IG* IX(2) 1295 and 1296 [= *AE* 1945–1947, 110, no. 59]).[29]

---

27 The *diorthoma* is also mentioned in *BCH* 99 (1975), 120, no. 1, lines 6–7 (16/5 BC). On this currency change see Larsen 1958, 127; Larsen 1968 291–292; Frank 1959, 456 n. 21; Rädle 1969, 158–159; Helly 1976, 154. See also Helly 1997, who dates Augustus' *strategeia* to 27 BC; Bouchon 2008, 433–435.

28 See Zachou-Kontoyanni 1989, 213, and Chapter 5 below on Echinos.

29 See Helly 1997, 79–81, and Bouchon 2008, 434–436, who do not discuss the second-

The amount paid was uniform in cases of multiple manumissions too. Thus in *IG* IX(2) 553 from Larisa (early first century BC), the same owner manumits two slaves; each pays fifteen staters (lines 18, 21). In the same inscription, another manumitted slave pays thirty staters for himself and for his son—presumably manumitted together with him, that is, twice the sum paid for a single manumission (lines 30–32: Νικόλαος Διοσκουρίδαιος καὶ ὑπὲρ Λυσιμάχοι / τοῖ παιδὸς τὸς γινομένος τᾶ πόλι κὰτ τὸν νόμον ἀργυρίοι στατεῖ/ρας τριάκοντα). Lines 4–8 of *IG* IX(2) 561 from Larisa (Roman period) record the manumission by one man of his three slaves, who paid together sixty-seven and a half denarii. An inscription from first-century AD Pythion (*SEG* 35.646, lines 3–7) records the payment of forty-five denarii by two manumitted slaves, that is, twenty-two and a half denarii each: [ἡ δεῖνα] καὶ Ἀντιοχὶς οἱ ἀ[πε/λευθερω]μένοι ἀπὸ Μεγαλ[– – –] / [– – τ]ῆς Ἱπποδρόμου ξε[νι]/[κῇ ἔδω]καν τῇ πόλει δεινάρι[α] / [τεσσαρά]κοντα πέντε ("[So-and-so] and Antiochis, the slaves manumitted by Megal[---], daughter of Hippodromos, *xenikei*,[30] paid the polis forty-five denarii"). This is also how we should perhaps understand *IG* IX(2) 280 from Metropolis (Roman period), where lines 3–4 read: ἀπηλευθερωμέν]οι ὑπὸ Κλεομάχας τῆς Κλεομέ/[νους ἔδωκαν τὸ γινόμενον τῇ π]όλι μ δ(ηνάρια) ε ταμίᾳ Λέοντι Ἀντι[---]. I understand these lines as saying: "being manumitted by Kleomacha, daughter of Kleomenes, paid what is due to the polis, forty-five denarii to the treasurer Leon, son of Anti[---]". If this is correct, the Metropolis inscription records the manumission by a woman of her two slaves, who each paid twenty-two and a half denarii (forty-five denarii altogether).[31]

The payments in the Thessalian inscriptions are also uniform whether the inscription is a long list of manumissions formulated in concise language (the more common type) or a more elaborate record of a single

century AD inscriptions which still mention staters. Also revealing is the use in some inscriptions of the word χαλκοί, bronze coins, used in Roman Thessaly (e.g. *SEG* 15.370 from Skotoussa, face C1, lines 10–11, 18, 26, 34, 56–57; face D1, line 1). On the payments in bronze coins see also below.

30 On the phrase ξενικῇ (*xenikei*), or ξενικῇ λύσει (*xenikei lysei*), frequently recorded in Thessalian manumission inscriptions, see Zelnick-Abramovitz 2005b, where I interpret this phrase as an exemption from taxes imposed on *xenoi*; for a different view see Dimopoulou-Piliouni 2008, 42–45. See also below.

31 The text of the inscription, however, is not easy to understand. According to the present reading no names of manumitted slaves are given in the first act, the text of which is cited here (the participle ἀπηλευθερωμέν]οι and the name of the manumittor are followed immediately by the payment formula). With a different phrasing, the fragmentary following lines give the name of another slave, manumitted by a man, and state that he paid a sum of money (amount not preserved) to the treasurer.

manumission. The following inscription from Larisa is an example of the first type (*IG* IX(2) 554, lines 1–7, undated):

[–]. ⟨Ἀ⟩μφινίκου τοῦ Εὐδήμου ἀ[πε(λεύθερος)]
σ̣τα(τῆρα̣ς) ιε′ μη(νὸς) Πανήμου, μη(νὸς) Θεμιστίο[υ]·
Ἀπολλώνιος Καλ⟨λ⟩ιστράτου ἀπε(λεύθερος) ⟨σ⟩τα(τῆρας) [ιε′],
Εὐγένεα Εὐτυχίδος ἀπε(λευθέρα) στα(τῆρας) ιε′,
μη(νὸς) Ἀγαγυλίου· Ἐπίκτητος Ἀθηνίωνος
Εὐτυχίδος ἀπε(λεύθερος) στα(τῆρας) ιε′, Ἀπολλών[ιος]
Ἀντιγόνου τοῦ Λύκου ἀπε(λεύθερος) στα(τῆρας) ιε′.

[…] of Amphinikos, son of Eudemos, fifteen staters in the month of Panemos. In the month of Themistios: Apollonios, the freedman of Kallistratos, fifteen staters; Eugenea, the freedwoman of Eutychis, fifteen staters. In the month of Agagylios: Epiktetos, the freedman of Athenion son of Eutychis, fifteen staters; Apollonios, the freedman of Antigonos son of Lykos, fifteen staters. (The inscription continues similarly.)

An example of the other type is *SEG* 26.670 from Pythion (150–100 BC):

[στρατηγοῦντος τῶν Θεσσαλῶν]
[Πετραίου τοῦ Φιλ]οξενίδου, μη-
[νὸς – – – – – – – – –]ου εἰκάδι· Εὔτυ-
[χος – – – – – – – – – ὁ πρεσ]βύτερος Ἀλέ-
[ξανδρον τὸν ἑαυτοῦ] δουλεῖον παιδά-
[ριον ἀφῆκεν ἀπελεύθε]ρον δωρεὰν κατὰ
[τὸν νόμον· παραμενέτω] δὲ Ἀλέξανδρο[ς]
[παρὰ Εὔτυχον ποιῶν] τὸ ἐπιτασσόμε-
[νον ἕως ἂν ζῇ Εὔτυχ]ος· ὅταν δὲ [τε]-
[λευτήσῃ Εὔτυχος, ἐξέστω Ἀ]λεξάνδρῳ καὶ
[........... οἰκῆσαι] καὶ κτ[ή]σ[ασθ]αι
[χρήματα .... κ]αὶ μὴ ὄντι
[.................. καὶ] τοῖς κληρονό-
[μοις Εὐτύχου μὴ πί]πτοντι κατὰ
[μηδένα τρόπον ὑπὸ τ]ὸν τῶν ἀπελευ-
[θέρων νόμον· κοινοξεν]οδόκοι ταγὸς Εὐ-
[......................]A, ἰδιοξενοδόκο[ι]
[......................]μάχου, Ἀρναῖο̣ς
[.......................]ήδης Ἀρναίου·
[ἔδωκε δὲ καὶ τῇ πό]λει στα(τῆρας) ιε′.

When Petraios, son of Philoxenides, was the strategos of the Thessalians, on the twentieth day of the month […], Eutychos [… the elder] manumitted for free his slave-boy Alexandros, according to the law. Let Alexandros stay with Eutychos, doing whatever he is told to do, as long as Eutychos lives. When Eutychos passes away, it will be possible for Alexandros to […] live and possess property […] and he will not fall, in any manner whatsoever, under the law of the manumitted slaves to the benefit of Eutychos' heirs. *Koinoi xenodokoi*: the *tagos* Eu[…], *idioi xenodokoi*: […], Arnaios […] son of Arnaios. And he paid to the polis fifteen staters.

This inscription closely resembles the Delphic manumission documents; the text is long enough to contain a *paramone* clause and a specification of the freedman's rights after its end, a warning against any attempt to re-enslave the freedman, names of witnesses or guarantors and the statement of payment to the polis.[32] We do not know why Alexandros was not required to pay his ex-owner for the freedom granted to him; perhaps he was his son.[33]

There were some exceptions to the uniform payments. In one case, and perhaps in one other, the freed slave was apparently given a discount: in Pythion a freed slave-woman paid ten staters instead of fifteen. Another female from the same city paid sixteen denarii instead of twenty-two and a half. In both cases it is stated that this amount was paid "in accordance with what she convinced/persuaded", or "because she so convinced/persuaded (καθ' ὃ διέπεισε)".[34]

AE (1924), 173, no. 407, lines 2–6 (after 44 BC?):

> [τ]αμιευόντων Ἀμύντου τοῦ Ἀντιγένους, [Φ]ιλί[π]που
> τοῦ Δρεβελάου τὸν ἐνιαυτὸν ⟨τὸν⟩ ἐπὶ στ[ρατ]ηγοῦ Λυκείνο[υ]·
> [Ε]ὐβού⟨λα⟩, ἡ ἀπελ[ε]υθερωθε[ῖ]σα ὑπὸ [Θε]οδότου [τ]οῦ
> [Ε]ὐδή[μου],
> [φ]ύσει δὲ Ἀρ[χελ]άου, κ[αὶ Α]ὐτοδ[ί]κης [τ]ῆς Ἀ[γα]θοβούλου
> ἔ[δ]ωκ[εν]
> [τ]ῇ [π]όλει, [κ]α[θ]' ὃ διέπεισεν, στατῆρ[α]ς δέκ[α].
>
> When Amyntas, son of Antigenes, and Philippos, son of Drebelaos, were the treasurers in the year of the *strategos* Lykeianos: Euboula, the slave manumitted by Theodotos, son of Eudemos, the biological son of Archelaos, and by Autodike, daughter of Agathoboulos, paid the polis, because she so persuaded, ten staters.

SEG 23.462, lines 20–23 (= *AE*, 1923, 150, no. 383; first century BC/first century AD):

---

[32] The text given here (*SEG* 26.670) is that of a completely different reading by Helly (1976, 147–149) of *SEG* 23.462 (= *AE*, 1923, 150, no. 383, lines 1–19). For the ξενοδόκοι (*xenodokoi*) see below. Cf. Babacos 1962, 499–500. See also *AE* (1910) 363, no. 8 from Larisa (AD 131/132), a record of a single manumission act, where the sum paid is recorded as both fifteen staters (line 10) and twenty-two and a half denarii (line 18).

[33] As is the case if we accept the reading of *SEG* 23.462.

[34] I use the feminine pronoun "she", assuming that it was the female slave who paid; on the question of who paid, see below. See Arvanitopoulos, *AE* (1923), 150–153, no. 383 (ed. pr.), who suggests (pp. 152–153) that in this manumission the payment was remitted by the polis, following arbitration or because of an act of persuasion. Note that in the second inscription καθ' ὃ διέπεισε is restored.

[ταμιεύοντος τῆς πόλεως – – –]υ τοῦ Μ[ε]νάνδ[ρ]ο[υ],
[στρατηγοῦντος – – –, – – –] ἡ [ἀπ]ε[λ]ευθερω[θ]-
[εῖσα ὑπὸ – – – – – – – – – –]νος ἔδω[κε]ν [τ]ῇ
[πόλει καθ' ὃ διέπεισε δεινάρ]ια δ[ε]κα[έ]ξ.

When [...], son of Menandros, was the treasurer, when [... was the *strategos*], [...], the slave manumitted by [...], paid the polis, because she so persuaded, sixteen denarii.

Concerning the first example, Arvanitopoulos (in *AE*, 1924, 173, no. 407), argues that the verb διαπείθειν stands for διαιτᾶν, "to arbitrate", indicating that by means of witnesses and other means of proof the manumitted slave convinced the archons that she was unable to pay the whole sum, and won a reduction of one third.[35] The second example (*SEG* 23.462) might appear more puzzling, since in the previous manumission on the same stone (lines 1–19) the freed slave paid in staters; but, as we have seen, other examples are found of the use of both staters and denarii in the same city and period.[36]

Another example, from Azoros, is more challenging: lines 3–4 of *AE* (1945–1947) 110, no. 59, dated to 20–18 BC (= *IG* IX(2) 1296 = *AE*, 1913, 173–174; 1923, 126, no. 361) record a manumission act of the slave-woman Aphrodisia, who is said to be manumitted by Dikaios (his patronymic is not preserved), but then, in line 5–6 and presumably still referring to Aphrodisia, it is said:

[– – –] διεπείσθη(?) ὑπὸ Πεταλοῦ [τοῦ Ἀμύντου(?)]
ἔδωκε τῇ πόλει τὰ γεινόμενα [δ(ηνάρια) κβ' ὀ(βολοὺς) {^{8}4}^{8}].

[...] convinced(?) by Petalos, son of Amyntas, paid the polis the due twenty-two and a half denarii.

The use of the passive voice of the verb διαπείθειν, the mention of someone different from the manumittor, and the slave's paying the full amount make it very difficult to understand the meaning of this statement, and several attempts have been made to amend and explain the text.[37]

---

[35] *AE* (1924), 177.

[36] Lines 20–23 of *SEG* 23.462 are not included in Helly's new reading (1976, 147–149 = *SEG* 26.670). On payments noted both in staters and denarii see above.

[37] In *IG*, Kern reads lines 1–2 (= lines 4–5 in *AE* [1945–1947]) as follows: [– – – – – – – – – –]βεισ[– – – – – – – – – – – –] / [– – – – – – – –]ΕΙΣΘΗΚ ἀπὸ Πε[τ]αλο[ῦ τοῦ Ἀμύντου(?)]. Rensch 1908, 116, restored this line (line 2 according to its publication in *IG*, since at least four lines are missing at the beginning of the inscription) as referring to a manumission performed according to a will: [ὁ δεῖνα ἀπελευθερωθ]εὶς θήκῃ. Arvanitopoulos, in *AE* (1913), 173–174, and (1923), 126, no. 361, suggested reading ἀπεκλείσθη, explaining that the manumitted slave

It is futile to try to guess the reason for the discount, and even the manumitted slaves in both cases being female (i.e. the possibility that they were the spouses or daughters of their owners) is of no help since many other women paid the full amount. However, perhaps it was the manumittors who "convinced" the authorities to reduce the sum, possibly because the manumitted slave women could not pay the full amount for reasons of financial incapability, age, or ill health. We also have evidence, albeit unique and disputable, of what seems to be a postponement of the payment, or part of it, to another time by a decision of the polis: the manumission record of a slave-woman from Chyretiai in Perrhaibia (*AE*, 1917, 18–23, no. 310, lines 25–31) of the late first century BC, reads:

Σωτηρίς, [ἡ φα]μ[έν]η ἀπ[η]λευ[θ]ερῶσθα[ι ὑ]πό
τε Πτο[λεμ]α[ίο]υ [τ]ο[ῦ Π]ολυχά[ρ]μου καὶ Πολυχ[άρ]-
μου τοῦ Πτολεμα̣ί̣{δ}ου {^{26}Πτολεμαίου}^{26} [κα]ὶ Νικαρίστας τῆς Π̣ο̣-
θίωνος, ἔδ[ω]κ[ε]ν [τὰ] γεινόμ[εν]α τῆς ἀπ[ε]-
[λ]ε[υ]θερ[ώ]σεως [δ]ινά[ρ]ι[α εἴκ]οσι δύ[ο, χ]ρο[νι]α̣-
[ῖ]ον, κ[αθ'] ἃ ἔ[δο]ξ[ε]ν [τ]ῇ πόλ[ει],
Φυλ[λ]ικοῦ δευτέρα̣.

Soteris, declared as manumitted by Ptolemaios, son of Polymarchos, by Polymarchos, son of Ptolemaios, and by Nikariste, daughter of Pothion, paid what is due on the occasion of her manumission, twenty-two denarii, deferred, according to the decision of the polis, on the second day of the month of Phyllikos.

Arvanitopoulos, who restored the word χ]ρο[νι]α̣[ῖ]ον in lines 29–30, suggested that the payment of the balance—four obols, or half a denarius—was delayed and that the inscription contains a reminder that it should be paid on the date decided by the polis. Bruno Helly, however, after a revision of the squeeze made by Arvanitopoulos, offers a different reading of lines 16–32 (*SEG* 32.599). For χ]ρο[νι]α̣[ῖ]ον he reads τροπα[ϊκ]ὸν, that is, half a denarius, which means that the manumitted slave paid the *full* amount.[38]

---

was also exempted from the obligation to stay in her manumittor's house, that is, from the *paramone*. But already in 1834 Pesaros read διεπείσθη and his reading was followed by Kougeas, in *AE* (1945–1947), 110, no. 59, although Kougeas asks in a critical note whether διεπιστεύθη is not a preferable reading. For the history of the readings and interpretations of this inscription see Babacos 1961, 223–224, who prefers to keep διεπείσθη, and suggests that this is a new form of expressing the εὐδόκησις, the consent given by family members to the manumission act. See also Helly 1976.

38 B. Helly, who dates the inscription to Augustus' reign, published his new readings in *Actes du 9-ème, congrès international de numismatique*, Berne 1979, Louvain-la Neuve, 1982, 169–171. Helly suggests that the equation of 1/2 denarius = 4 obols = 1/3 stater was introduced

Also challenging is the expression ἐφ' εἴσηι (i.e. ἐπ' ἴσῃ, "equally" or "on equal terms") found in an inscription from Pythion (*AE*, 1924, 173–176, no. 408, mid-first century AD). Some of the manumission acts recorded on the stone have the formula "(name of slave), manumitted by (name of manumitted), ἐφ' εἴσηι, ὡς ἡ ἀπελευθέρωσις περιέχει, paid to the polis the twenty-two and a half denarii due according to the law" (lines 10–11, 19, 26–27).[39] The editor, A. Arvanitopoulos, by analogy with the use of the same expression in a grant of citizenship by the polis of Phalanna (*IG* IX(2) 1230, lines 23–24; second century BC), interprets the words ἐφ' εἴσηι as referring to the grant of full political rights to the manumitted slaves, and in the case of women (as here) the grant of the status of *aste*.[40] The words ὡς ἡ ἀπελευθέρωσις περιέχει indicate, in the editor's opinion, the existence of a document, stored in the archive, which formally stated the rights of the manumitted slave.[41] This interpretation is attractive in light of the evidence in manumission documents of the grant of various rights to manumitted slaves,[42] but it also requires us to assume that this expression became a shortened technical term for bestowing citizenship—an assumption for which there is no other evidence; in all other inscriptions where this phrase is used in the context of granting civic rights—including the inscription from Phalanna which Arvanitopoulos cites—the formula is elaborate (in Phalanna it is: εἶναι / [δ]ὲ κ[αὶ πολίτην αὐτὸν καὶ] ἐκγόνους ἐφ' ἴσ/[ῃ] κ̣αὶ ὁ[μοίᾳ, lines 22–24). Moreover, although Phalanna, like Pythion, was a city in Perrhaibia, *IG* IX(2) 1230 is much earlier than the inscriptions from Pythion and there is no other

by Augustus, probably in 27 BC. Accordingly, he also restores τρ]ο̣παϊκόν in line 16 of *IG* IX(2) 549 (= *SEG* 32.599; 603) from Larisa.

39 In lines 10–11 this formula is applied to one of two manumitted female slaves, but each of them paid twenty-two and a half denarii. In lines 26–27 the order of the words is different: ὡ[ς] ἡ ἀπε[λευθέ]/[ρωσις περιέχει, ἐφ' εἴσηι.

40 In fact, the phrase ἐπ' ἴσῃ appears in many other grants of citizenship and in συμπολιτεία (*sympoliteia*) agreements: e.g. in Kos: *Clara Rhodos* 10 (1941), 27–30, no. 1, lines 13–14 (= C.V. Crowther, *Chiron* 29, 1999, 253–257, no. 1; *IG* XII(6) 150); *Iscr. di Cos* ED 71g, and several others; Samos (*MDAI(A)*, 1957, 218–223, no. 57, and many others); Euboia (*IG* XII(9) 4 and 905); in Asia Minor: Smyrna (*ISmyrna* 573II + II 2 p. 376), Miletos (*Milet* I(3) 143B), Teos (*SEG* 29.1149), Ephesos (*IEphesos* 1389, and many others), Kolophon (*AJP* 1935, 381–382, no. VII, and several others), Priene (*I.Priene* 71); Magnesia (*IMagnesia* 12, and several others), Mylasa (*IMylasa* 868, 913, and several others). The phrase ἐπὶ τᾶι ἴσα[ι κ]α/ὶ τᾶι ὁμοίαι in lines 27–28 of the agreement among the settlers in Kyrene (ML 5) has been interpreted as "on equal terms" and linked to the settlers' equal share in citizenship, offices, and land in the new polis: see ML, p. 7; Burford 1993, 16.

41 Arvanitopoulos, *AE* (1924), 179–180.

42 See Zelnick-Abramovitz 2009.

evidence of the use of this phrase in other manumission inscriptions. I tentatively suggest understanding this expression more literally: according to an agreement made by the manumittors upon manumission (ὡς ἡ ἀπελευθέρωσις περιέχει), they and the manumitted slaves divided the sum between them and each paid half (i.e. "equally").[43] The reason for this agreement escapes us, but since all the relevant freed slaves probably were female,[44] they may have been the spouses or daughters of the manumittors, who therefore helped them with the expenses.

The recipient of the payment of fifteen staters or twenty-two and a half denarii was the polis. This is made clear by the many inscriptions where it is stated that the manumitted slave "paid to the polis". For instance, lines 1–7 of an inscription from Gomphoi (*IG* IX(2) 287a) read:

> [– – –]ου[– – – – – – – ἀπελευ]-
> [θερω]θέντες [τῇ πόλ]ει δ(ε)[δω]-
> [κότε]ς τὸ γινόμενον· [δ(ηνάρια) κβ<']
> *Vacat*
> ἀπὸ Εὐρυδάμαντος τοῦ Ἀγαθά-
> νορος καὶ Θω[ρ]α(κ)ίδος τῆς Νικάνο-
> ρος καὶ Φοννίου τοῦ Εὐρυδά-
> μαντος Φίλων Εὐρυδάμαντος·

> [... the manumitted] slaves who paid to the polis the due twenty-two and a half denarii: by Eurydamas, son of Agathanor, and Thorakis, daughter of Nikanor, and Phonnios, son of Eurydamas—Philon (the freed slave of) Eurydamas. (etc.)

In many other cases the treasurer (ταμίας) is explicitly mentioned as the official to whom the freed slaves paid the money. Thus lines 1–13 of *SEG* 35.602 from Larisa (AD 44) read:

> ἔτους δ Σεβαστοῦ Τιβερί-
> ου Κλαυδίου Καίσαρος Σε-
> βαστοῦ Γερμανικοῦ τοῦ
> καὶ λ καὶ δ, στρατηγοῦν-
> τος Λυκόφρονος μη-
> νὸς Ὁμολῴου ιε, Οἰκο-
> νομία ἡ ἀπελευθερω-
> θεῖσα ὑπὸ Φαιναρέτας

[43] Cf. *BCH* 94, 1970, 109–112 (= G. Kleiner, P. Hommel, and W. Müller-Wiener, *Panonion und Melie* [*JDI* 23 Ergänzungsheft, 1967, 45–63]), line 14: a sacred law concerning sacrifices to Zeus, where the same expression most reasonably means that the priest is to receive half of each item sacrificed in addition to all the parts listed in lines 12–13.

[44] As restored and suggested by Arvanitopoulos, *AE* (1924), 175–180.

τῆς Πασιφίλου χήρας ἔ-
δωκεν Αἰνέᾳ Αἰνέου τῷ
ταμίᾳ τὰ γεινόμενα
τῆς ἐλευθερώσεως
δι(νάρια) εἴκοσι δύο ἥμισυ.

In the fourth year of the august Tiberius Claudius Caesar Augustus Germanicus, which is also the thirty-fourth year, when Lykophron was the *strategos*, on the fifteenth of the month of Homoloios, Oikonomia, the manumitted slave of Phainareta, the widow of Pasiphilos, paid Aineas, son of Aineas, the treasurer, the due money for her manumission, twenty-two and a half denarii.[45]

Even where inscriptions do not specify to whom the payments were made, we may assume that it was the treasurer, or some other fiscal magistrate, who received the money. This is more evident when the headings of the inscriptions, or of the various entries in long lists of manumissions, name the incumbent treasurer as part of the dating.[46] In inscriptions formulated in this way we sometimes find the heading: "the manumitted slaves who paid the polis the sum ...", with slight variations. Thus lines 1–8 in an inscription from Krannon (*IG* IX(2) 463), dated to ca. 49/8 BC, read:

στρατηγοῦντος Φιλοκρά-
τους τοῦ Ἀρχελάδου Λαρι-
σαίου, ταμιεύοντος τὴν δε[υ]-
τέραν ἑξάμηνον Θέωνος
τοῦ Παρμενίσκου οἱ φάμενο[ι]
[γ]εγονέναι ἀπελεύθεροι καὶ δε-
δωκότες τῇ πόλει τοὺς δε-
καπέντε στατῆρας·

When Philokrates, son of Archelades, from Larisa was the *strategos*, Theon, son of Parmeniskos, being the treasurer in the first six months of the year, those declared to be manumitted, who paid to the polis the fifteen staters.[47]

---

[45] The text given here is a different reading by Zachou-Kontoyanni (in *Πρακτικά Α' Ιστορικού-Αρχαιολογικού Συμποσίου: Λάρισα Παρελθόν και Μέλλον, 26–28 April 1985*, Larisa 1985, 186–194) of *IG* IX(2) 545. For the dating by both the Roman emperor and the local calendar cf. *IG* IX(2) 206 III.c, lines 10–16; *IG* IX(2) 544, lines 1–6; *Chiron* 5 (1975), 337 A and B. For other cases where the treasurer is explicitly mentioned as receiving the money see e.g. *IG* IX(2) 280, lines 3–5, from Metropolis; *IG* IX(2) 1297, line 30, from Azoros.

[46] Usually together with the federal *strategos*. See e.g. *IG* IX(2) 72, lines 1–2 (Lamia, ca. 50 BC); 415, lines 5–10 (Pherai, ca. 27 BC).

[47] Lines 1–10 of the inscription are cited in the Introduction. Cf. also *IG* IX(2) 289 (Gomphoi, Roman period); *IG* IX(2) 540 (Larisa, 49/8 BC); *Gonnoi* II 117 (Gonnoi, ca. 10 BC?); *ZPE* 27 (1977), 259–262. Lines 23–24 of *SEG* 30.531A (= *IG* IX(2) 74) read: τού[σδε ὁ τα]/μίας Κλέων Θεύρωνος ἀνέγρα[ψε ("the treasurer Cleon, son of Theuron, registered [or inscribed] these").

In such cases too, the treasurer was apparently the recipient of the payments. Some inscriptions do not mention any payment at all, but their headings include the name of the city's treasurer and they are arranged by month. A good example is *IG* IX(2) 277 I from Metropolis (undated):

[ἱππαρχέοντος – – – – – – – – – –]
.θίου, φύσει δὲ Παι[– – – – – – – – –]
ταμιεύοντος Ἀνδραγάθο[υ – – – – – –]
οἱ ἀπηλευθερωμένοι·
μηνὸς Θύ(ου)· Εὔτυχος ἀπὸ Ὑσ[– – – –]
μηνὸς Θύου· Εὔνομο[ς ἀπὸ – – – – – –]
μηνὸς Ἑρμαίου· Πορφυραία [– – – – –]
μηνὸς Ἑρ(μ)αίου· Ἀθηναγό[ρας ἀπὸ – –]
Ἰτωνίου κʹ· Σωτᾶς ἀπὸ Νεικο[– – – – –]
μηνὸς Θεμιστίου ⟨θʹ· Ε⟩ὔτυχο[ς ἀπὸ – –]

[When the *hipparchos* --- was ---] -thiou, by nature son of [----], when Andragathos, [son of ---] was the treasurer, those manumitted:

In the month of Thyos: Eutychos by Hys[---]
In the month of Thyos: Eunomos [by ---]
In the month of Hermaios: Porphyria [---]
In the month of Hermaios: Athenago[ras by ---]
On the 20th day of Itonios: Sotas by Niko[---]
On the 9th day of Themistios: Eytychos [by ---]

This layout of the inscriptions and the mention of the treasurer make it plausible that payments were made by the manumitted slaves, even though this is not stated.

Other magistrates are mentioned in the Thessalian inscriptions as well: some inscriptions from Larisa and Pythion, dated to the second and first centuries BC, state that the payment was made to or before (or in the presence of) the ξενοδόκος. This official is often named in Thessalian inscriptions in connection with non-citizens: in inter-state agreements, in honorary decrees granting privileges to foreigners, and in manumission inscriptions—sometimes as a private witness and guarantor (ἴδιος ξενοδόκος) or as a public one (κοινὸς ξενοδόκος).[48] In Larisa, for instance, manumitted slaves paid the fifteen staters "in front of" (ἐναντίον) the *koinos xenodokos* (*IG* IX(2)

---

[48] For the character and function of the *xenodokoi* see Zelnick-Abramovitz 2000. The inscription from Atrax, published and discussed by Darmezin and Tziaphalias, 2007, which records the verdict of a local court of law to exclude a *genos* from the community, mentions twelve *xenodokoi* acting as 'official witnesses'. As I suggest in the case of the Basaidai of Metropolis, *SEG* 36.548 (Zelnick-Abramovitz 2000, 113–118), the *xenodokoi* in Atrax may well have been used because the members of the excluded *genos* now had the status of foreigners.

558, lines 3, 5, 8; undated).[49] In Pythion, on the other hand, the *xenodokoi*, whether without any qualifying adjective or as *idioi*, are mentioned together with the eponymous *strategos* and *tagos* (*IG* IX(2) 1282, ca. 50 BC), but no payment to the polis is noted.[50] The *koinos xenodokos*'s role seems to have been to witness and guarantee the payment made by the manumitted slaves to the city, whereas the treasurer was responsible for receiving the money and ordering the inscription.

Inscriptions from Hypata show that in the second century AD a special official, the ἐπιμελητὴς τῶν ἀπελευθερικῶν χρημάτων ("the manager of the money pertaining to manumitted slaves"), was in charge of using the money paid by the manumitted slaves and inscribing the manumission acts on steles (*IG* IX(2) 17, 19, 21, 22). Line 4 of *IG* IX(2) 22 (AD 131/132) seems to imply that this *epimeletes* was also the official to whom the manumitted slaves paid the money. If this is correct, we see that the machinery of collecting fees or taxes in Thessalian poleis varied according to time and place; but it is also significant that in second-century AD Hypata the administration of money exacted from manumitted slaves was separated from the general fiscal administration, presumably still controlled by *tamiai*.[51]

In most cases it is clear that the freed slave made the payment,[52] but in others the wording of the inscription does not allow a definite conclusion.[53]

---

49 Cf. *BCH* 95 (1971), 277 (Larisa, 171 BC); in *BCH* 95 (1971), 562, and in *SEG* 29.532 (both from Larisa, undated) the formula is: "(name of slave) of (name of manumittor), declared (ὁ φάμενος / ἡ φαμένη) to be manumitted by (name of manumittor), the fifteen staters due to the polis, which he/she counted (ἠρίθμησεν) in the presence of (ἐνώπιον) the *koinos xenodokos*"; cf. *SEG* 35.593 (Larisa, early second century BC). For the *idios xenodokos* see e.g. *IG* IX(2) 1282 (Pythion, ca. 50 BC), lines 18–19, 26–27, 33; these persons are noted probably as guarantors to the manumission documents whose details have not been preserved.

50 For the *idioi xenodokoi* mentioned in this inscription see the previous note. Cf. *AE* (1924), 155, no. 400, from Pythion (late first century BC), where at the end of a long list of manumissions, concisely formulated, a more elaborate document is recorded to which the names of both the *xenodokos* (apparently *koinos*) and *idioi xenodokoi* are added; no. 404 (ca. 131–129 BC); no. 405 (131/0 BC?); no. 406 (ca. 60 BC); *SEG* 26.670 (= 23.462, first century BC or AD), mentioning the *idioi xenodokoi* again; *SEG* 26.689 (= *IG* IX(2) 1290, 150–100 BC).

51 Bouchon 2009 argues that *IG* IX(2) 16, 21, 22, and 56—inscribed on the same block—belong together and comprise one inscription, which he interprets as the accounts submitted by the *epimeletes* Zoïlos whose function was to allocate the monies received from the manumitted slaves to the gymnasiarchs and the treasurers. These inscriptions from Hypata and the possible function of the *epimeletes* are further discussed in Chapters 3 and 4 below.

52 E.g. *IG* IX(2) 78b, lines 1–3 from Lamia ([Ἀφρο]δεισίου τοῦ Σω/[τάδ]ο⟨υ⟩ς ὁ ἀπελεύθε/[ρος ἔδω]κε τῇ πό(λει) τὰ κβ<' ✳); *IG* IX(2) 288, lines 1–3 from Gomphoi (οἱ ἐξε/[λευθερω]θέν[τ]ες καὶ δεδωκότες τὸ γινόμενον / [εἰς τ]ὴν [π]όλιν).

53 See Calderini 1965, 142, who argues that in Greece the payment was always made by the manumitted slave; cf. Parker and Obbink 2000, 442.

Thus in an inscription from Azoros (*AE*, 1923, 126, no. 362; ca. 30–1 BC) one manumission act seems to imply that the payment was made on behalf of each of the manumittors (lines 19–22):

> [Θυ]μιλώ, ἡ ἀπελευθερω[θ]εῖσα ὑ[πὸ δεῖνος τοῦ Ἀ]-
> [λ]εξά[νδ]ρο⟨υ⟩ ⟨καὶ⟩ Ὑ⟨π⟩α⟨τ⟩ίας τῆς Παυσανίου {καὶ} [μετὰ δεῖνος καὶ Ἀρχ]-
> ẹπό[λ]ε[ω]ς τῶν τέκνων μου· ἔδωκεν [τῆι πόλει ὑπὲρ ἑκα]-
> τέρων {[δ]εινάρια} ⟨στατῆρας⟩ ιε′.

> Thymilo, the slave-woman manumitted by [----, son of A]lexander, and by Hypatia, daughter of Pausanias, {and} [together with ---- and Arch]epolis my children, paid the polis on behalf of each fifteen {[d]enarii} staters.

If the restoration of this sentence is correct, this phrasing is quite exceptional in the Thessalian manumission inscriptions, because we have no other evidence that slaves manumitted by more than one person paid more than fifteen staters (or twenty-two and a half denarii) or that they did so for every member of the family of their owners. But it may well be that the words "[together with ---- and Arch]epolis my children" actually refer to the children of the slave-woman who were manumitted together with her, and that the word "my" (μου) extant on the stone is an error of the cutter who perhaps was copying from a written declaration of the freedwoman Thymilo (see below); in such a case, it makes sense that she paid the due sum for each.[54] Likewise in *IG* IX(2) 553 from Larisa (early first century BC), lines 24–27, it seems that a third person paid on behalf of the manumitted slave-woman. In other manumission acts on the same stone the regular formula appears: "(name of slave) of (name of manumittor), declared (ὁ φάμενος / ἁ φαμένα) to be released by (name of manumittor), (paid) the due fifteen staters to the polis, according to the law"; but lines 24–27 read:

> Νικά-
> τουρ Μνασέαιος ὑπὲρ Ἀφροδισίας Δαϊμαχείας {τ} ὃς ἔφα ⟨ἀ⟩πει-
> λευθερούσθειν ἀπὸ Δαϊμάχοι Θ⟨ε⟩ιριμαχείοι τὸς γινομένος τᾶ
> πόλι κὰτ τὸν νόμον ἀργυρίοι στατεῖρας δεκαπέμπε.

> Nicatour son of Mnaseas, on behalf of Aphrodisia (the slave) of Daïmachos, who said (she) was released by Daïmachos son of Thirimacheios, the due fifteen staters to the polis, according to the law.[55]

---

[54] In fact, another document on the same stone (A, lines 3–6) records the manumission of two slave-women together with their children (μ]ẹ/[τὰ τῶ]ṿ τέκνων αὐτ[ῶν). Although it is not stated that they paid for their children as well, the words ἔδωκαν τῆι πόλει ἑκατέρα τὰ γι]/[νόμε]ṿα δεινάρια κ[β′] ὀβ[ο]λοὺς ("each paid the polis the due sum of twenty-two and a half denarii"; lines 4–5) may have referred to the payment for the children.

[55] Wilamowitz suggested amending to τὰν ἔφα ("whom he said ..."), whereas Rensch 1908,

Perhaps Aphrodisia was the spouse of Nicatour, or he had agreed to pay in return for services.[56] The use of the verb φημί in this inscription and of the verb's participle in other inscriptions may imply that the manumitted slaves had to appear before the treasurer or some other magistrate, declare that they have been manumitted—perhaps with the supporting declaration of their ex-owners, and pay the due money. The formula in the heading of *IG* IX(2) 463 from Krannon (49/8 BC), οἱ φάμενο[ι] [γ]εγονέναι ἀπελεύθεροι καὶ δεδωκότες τῇ πόλει τοὺς δεκαπέντε στατῆρας ("those declared to be freed slaves [or: to become freed slaves] and who paid the polis the fifteen staters", lines 5–8), supports the assumption that the inscription was a formal register of slaves who declared their freedom and paid the amount of money which the polis decided to exact from them.

These payments should not be confused with the money paid by the freed slaves to their ex-owners as the price of freedom (often described as λύτρον). The distinction can be gathered from the fact that the payments to the poleis were uniform, whereas the price of freedom was usually calculated on the basis of the individual slave's market value and varied according to his or her age, professional skills and origin.[57] This is also evident in view of the mention in some inscriptions of both the freedom price and the payment to the polis.[58] More corroboration is provided by inscriptions

94, suggested ἃ ἔφα, making the manumitted female slave the subject of the verb of declaring, in agreement with the regular formula in the inscription.

[56] Evidence from other places in Greece attests to spouses and parents paying the price of freedom for their partners and children, and to payment by a third person in return for services or as a loan; see Hopkins 1978, 165–169; Zelnick-Abramovitz 2005a, 217–222.

[57] For the term λύτρον (pl. λύτρα) as denoting the price of freedom see Bielman 1989, and n. 14 above. Sums of money paid to manumittors in return for freedom are frequently mentioned in the Delphic manumission inscriptions; see Hopkins 1978, 158–162. For a different interpretation of the payments in Delphi see Duncan-Jones 1984, 203–209. In Thessaly one slave paid as *lytron* 300 denarii (*IG* IX(2) 1117c; Demetrias, Roman period); another inscription from Demetrias, *IG* IX(2) 1119 (Roman period), also seems to record payments of *lytron*: 200 and 250 drachmai. In Pythion a slave paid 150 staters (*AE*, 1924, 188, 418a [= *IG* IX(2) 1282], lines 8–10; ca. 50 BC), and in Phthiotic Thebes (*SEG* 26.691, Roman imperial period), a *lytron* of σν′ (250) is paid by the manumitted slave in line 2, and the term *lytron*, without specifying the amount, is mentioned in other acts on the stone (lines 5 and 15).

[58] Two of these cases appear in an inscription from Doliche: *IG* IX(2) 1268 II, lines 6–7 (δοῦσαν λύτρα κὲ / τῇ πόλι τὰ γινόμενα δηνάρια κβ<′; "after paying the price of freedom and paying to the polis the due twenty-two and a half denarii"); V, lines 18–20 (ἐπὶ λύτρῳ ἔδωκεν / τὰ γεινόμενα τῇ πόλει ✳ κβ<′; "in addition to the price of freedom he paid the due twenty-two and a half denarii to the polis"). In both cases the word used to denote the payment for freedom is *lytron*, though the sum paid is not specified. See also *SEG* 23.462 (= *AE*, 1923, 150, no. 383), line 12; *AE* (1916), 78, no. 284, from Olosson; *AE* (1923), 126, no. 361, lines 24–30, from Azoros (20–18 BC), where the manumitted slave is said to have paid the *lytron* "because

which state that the slave was manumitted "for free" (δωρεάν), although the money due to the city was still paid.[59] Moreover, in some cases the text states that the freed slaves were thereby released from *paramone*, that is, from the binding clause attached to their manumission (which was performed on some earlier date), according to which they were obligated to stay and continue working for their manumittors, yet they still paid the twenty-two and a half denarii.[60] Legally, though not in practice, they were already free; therefore, the payment of twenty-two and a half denarii was not made in return for their freedom.

In many cases in Thessaly (and in three recorded in Dodona), the slaves were manumitted ξενικῇ, or ξενικῇ λύσει/λυτρώσει. Several explanations have been offered for this phrase, which undoubtedly refers to the mode of manumission or to a particular status it conferred. Since in Thessaly this phrase is found in inscriptions which mention the payment of twenty-two and a half denarii, this mode of manumission or status did not exempt the freed slave from this payment.[61]

---

of the manumission by them", i.e. the manumittors (δο[ῦσαν λύτρον διὰ τὴ]ν ὑπὸ τού[τ]ων [ἀπ]ελευθέρω[σιν).

59 See e.g. *IG* IX(2) 1296 (= *AE*, 1923, 126, no. 361), lines 18–21, from Azoroz, where the female slave is manumitted for free (δωρεάν), but a sum of twenty-two denarii and four obols is paid to the city; on this manumission see also below. Manumissions 'for free' are frequent in Thessaly; cf. e.g. from Azoros: *AE* (1945–1947) 110, no. 59, lines 23, 30; *IG* IX(2) 1299, line 11; from Demetrias: *SEG* 37.457, line 7; from Pythion: *SEG* 23.462, line 5; 26.679, line 5; *AE* (1924) 173, no. 407, line 9 (where the verb of paying seems to refer to the manumittor instead of the slave; this may be a slip—otherwise the generous manumittor not only forfeited his right to the *lytron* but also paid the polis on behalf of his former slave); for a similar expression from Kierion: *IG* IX(2) 259, line 21.

60 See *AE* (1916), 27, no. 276, lines 27–29 (= *IG* IX(2) 1295 face a; *SEG* 53.561), from Olosson (reign of Augustus); *SEG* 56.649, A (= Zachou-Kontoyanni 2006a, 99–102; *IG* IX(2) 1293b/c + 1294b), from Olosson (late first century BC); *AE* (1923), 126, no. 361, lines 5–9, from Azoros (reign of Augustus); *Gonnoi* II, 120 (= *IG* IX(2) 1044a; late reign of Augustus?).

61 For a summary of the interpretations of this phrase and the suggestion that *xenikei lysei* exempted the freed slave from taxes imposed on *xenoi* (including freed slaves), see Zelnick-Abramovitz 2005b. Dimopoulou-Piliouni 2008, 42–45, however, suggests that this kind of manumission conferred complete freedom on the manumitted slave, who thus became a ξένος (*xenos*)—free of any ongoing obligation to his or her former master. She rejects my suggestion on the ground that this phrase is also found in inscriptions which record payments to the city of the type discussed in the present book, and she cites such inscriptions as proof that "financial conditions were imposed upon freedmen via *xenikei*" (p. 44 n. 72). However, the payment to the city was either a manumission tax imposed on the manumittors (not the manumitted slaves) or registration fees, which I do not think can be defined as taxes imposed on *xenoi*; although manumitted slaves were *xenoi* in relation to the citizens of the polis in which they lived, the payment of fifteen staters or twenty-two and a half denarii was once-only payment, not an ongoing financial obligation. The fact that the

Finally, in some of the several manumission acts recorded in a second-century BC inscription from Skotoussa (*SEG* 15.370 [= *BCH* 79, 1955, 444–459, no. 1]), the payment was in χαλκοί, "bronze coins": τοὺς χαλκοῦς ἔδωκεν ("paid the bronze coins"), but the total amount is not specified.[62] The term *chalkoi* can refer collectively to money (without specification of the nominal value) or to bronze or copper coins—obols, or even drachmai, which may be the case here. As currency, eight *chalkoi* were usually the equivalent of one obol. But since in *SEG* 15.370 only the general fact that manumitted slaves "paid the bronze coins/money" is recorded and not the exact sum, we cannot be sure that they paid fifteen staters or their equivalent; in other inscriptions also from Skotoussa, although payment is mentioned the sum is not: *IG* IX(2) 399 (undated), for instance, uses the formula ἔδωκεν τὸ γινόμενον ἐκ τοῦ νόμου τῷ ταμίαι ("gave the [money] due according to the law to the treasurer").[63] But in the early Roman imperial period there is evidence of payment in Skotoussa of twenty-two and a half denarii (*SEG* 43.312 [= *AD* 43 B, 1988, 282] and 47.786 [= *AD* 48 B1, 1993, 257, no. 46]). The latter variation can perhaps be explained by the transition to Roman currency, although a manumission inscription from the first century AD is restored as recording payment in staters.[64]

---

term *xenikei* also appears in a dedication to Apollo (*SEG* 35.607 from Larisa, first century BC) and in grave inscriptions (*IG* IX(2) 851 and 866 from Larisa, probably Roman period) indicates that it was considered a privilege, not merely the status of a manumitted slave put on a par with a *xenos*; the latter, although free to go and live wherever he wished, was still of inferior status.

62 In two cases under the *strategos* Agasikrates, son of Hippolochos (ca. 160 BC), the payments were made in *chalkoi* (face A, lines 38, 41); likewise, some of the manumission acts performed at a later date, perhaps under the *strategos* Leon, son of Kleippos (who is mentioned last on face B; ca. 134 BC), use *chalkoi* (face C, lines 1, 10, 18, 26, 34, 56, 61). It is noteworthy that the heading of the inscription is missing, that lines 1–33 mention no payment at all, and that the ταμίας (*tamias*), the treasurer, is first mentioned only in line 33; similarly, on face B no mention of the payment is made until line 32 (the treasurer is mentioned in lines 33–34); and alongside the *chalkoi* mentioned on faces A and C, staters are also mentioned on face B, lines 33–34, 49–52. Pouilloux (*BCH* 79, 1955, 451) explains these differences in phrasing and currency as deriving from differences of time, but adds that even on face B there are three different formulae, so no safe conclusions can be made. Larsen 1968, 291, notes that after 146 BC, and under the principate, Thessaly continued to mint bronze coins which became the local currency; the profit from minting bronze coins, whose extrinsic value far exceeded their intrinsic value, accrued to the federal government. See also *I Thess.* I 17 A: a list of donors from Kierion in Thessaliotis (ca. 200–150 BC), where the donations are given in *chalkoi*.

63 *IG* IX(2) 399, A, lines 2–4; B, lines 3–4; C, lines 2–4 (where the name of the treasurer is given).

64 See *SEG* 23.413 = *REA* 66 (1964), 309 2b (AD 71–96), line 6: ἔδωκεν τῆι πόλ[ει τοὺς γινομένους

The first entry in the manumission inscription *AE* (1917) 18, no. 312, from Chyretiai in Perrhaibia (14–12 BC or shortly after), seems to imply that the payment had to be made within a limited time (lines 4–7):

> Ὠφελίων καὶ Λα[μπε]τία, οἱ ἀπηλ[ευθ]-
> ερωμένοι ὑπὸ Μ[ελε]άγρου τοῦ Σωπά-
> τρου, ξενικῇ, ἔδωκαν τῇ πόλι κατὰ τὸ ψήφι[σμα],
> [ἐ]ν τ[ῷ] κ[α]τὰ [τ]ὸν νόμον χ[ρό?]νῳ, ἕ[κ]αστος δι(νάρια) κβ′ (ἥμισυ).

> Ophelion and Lampetia, having been manumitted by Meleagros, son of Sopatros, *xenikei*, paid the polis, according to the decree, in the time prescribed by the law, twenty-two and a half denarii each.

It is not implausible that the ψήφισμα (*psephisma*) mentioned here regulated the payment of the registration fee within a specific time after manumission. A time limit is known from other places.[65] Since in Thessaly inscriptions often record numerous manumissions, performed over time, the question arises whether the payment was required by the time the stele was made or within a fixed period after manumission. The present state of evidence does not allow a conclusive answer.

The above analysis informs us on two important issues: slavery and manumission, and the payments made by manumitted slaves to the polis. First, the Thessalian manumission inscriptions are our only source of information on slavery and modes of manumission in Thessaly. As we saw above, chattel slavery appears to have been an important institution in Thessaly, at least since the third century BC. This can be inferred from the vast numbers of manumission records, which in itself indicates that chattel slavery was widespread. Why so many slave owners manumitted their slaves is not an easy question to answer, but the large number of manumissions may have been one of the factors that moved the Thessalian League to exact money from manumitted slaves.[66] The manumission inscriptions also reveal the important place of the slave in the household as part of its assets. This is revealed by the acquiescence given in several records by family members to the manumission act: freeing slaves meant giving up an asset hence reducing the size of the patrimony; therefore, to forestall future claims, the agreement of potential heirs was deemed essential. In other respects the

---

στατῆρας]. The inscription does not state how many staters were paid, but it seems safe to assume that this formula refers to the uniform federal payment of fifteen staters.

65 See Chapter 4 on Gortyn.

66 See Chapter 1 above on the reason given by Livy (7.16.7) for the Senate's ratification of the law establishing the *vicesima libertatis*. See also Chapter 5 below.

Thessalian manumissions resemble those found elsewhere in the Greek world: manumitted slaves paid for their freedom, but occasionally were manumitted for free; slave owners often appear to be the biological fathers of their manumitted slaves, whom they later manumitted; *paramone* seems to have been practised in Thessaly, though in some places less than in others.

Secondly, the above analysis also seems to show that, although the monies paid by the manumitted slaves to the various poleis were most probably a federal impost, no uniformity except for the amount itself can be perceived in the manumission inscriptions recording these payments, and even the sums paid are not always the same; in some cases the manumitted slaves paid a smaller sum. The wording of the inscriptions makes it very likely that the payments were made by manumitted slaves, not by manumittors, directly to the treasurers of the poleis or, in some cases, to *xenodokoi*. Nevertheless, we should not rule out the possibility of an intermediary office where the money was deposited before it was transferred to the state treasury. Since the manumission inscriptions record payments to officials, it is not inconceivable that a written manumission document was also deposited in a private or public archive in addition to the inscription, together with the registration of the payment, as was the practice in Ptolemaic and Roman Egypt.[67]

Here we should observe that the Thessalian manumission inscriptions differ from most of their equivalents in other places of the Greek world. While the great majority of the Thessalian inscriptions record numerous acts of manumissions, usually in chronological order,[68] most of the manumission inscriptions known to us from elsewhere in the Greek world are individual documents, recording the release of a slave by his or her owner, sometimes recording the release of more than one slave by the same manumittor. Such inscriptions, for instance, are those from Delphi, Chaironeia, Leukopetra, and many other places.[69] Moreover, whereas all the Thessalian

---

67 See e.g. *P. Hib.* I 29 (ca. 265 BC) from Hibeh, and *P. UB Trier* 135-2 (+ Quenouille, 2002; 132 BC) from Antaioupolis, on the *agoranomoi* who were in charge of the registration of manumissions and the tax paid for them. See also Chapter 4 below.

68 There are a few exceptions, e.g. *IG* IX(2) 1296 (= *AE*, 1945–1947, 110, no. 59) from Azoros (20–18 BC), and *SEG* 26.670 from Pythion (150–100 BC) discussed above.

69 Exceptions are found in four inscriptions from Calymna, which resemble the Thessalian inscriptions in recording various manumission acts, arranged in chronological order and made by different owners: *TC* 163, 164 (both contain the heading τοίδε ἐκαρύχθησαν ἐλεύθεροι ["these have been proclaimed free"], followed by names of manumitted slaves and manumittors), 192, 196; all four inscriptions are dated to the first century AD. But all the many other manumission inscriptions from Calymna are individual documents. Other catalogues

inscriptions record payments made to the polis on the occasion of manumission, or at least mention the polis' treasurer at their headings thus indicating a fiscal action, there are relatively a few cases in other places where such payments are recorded or alluded to. So the Thessalian manumission inscriptions are of a unique nature: on the one hand, being records of manumission acts they can be compared to other such inscriptions, like those from Delphi or Chaironeia; on the other hand, being also records of tax or fees paid to the polis they can be compared to accounts known to us from other places, for instance, the Athenian accounts of the *poletai* or the so-called *Rationes Centesimarum* which record land transactions and the tax paid on their occasion by Attic corporate groups.[70] This feature of the Thessalian manumission inscriptions will be further discussed in Chapter 4.

Yet not all Thessalian poleis yield evidence of such payments; furthermore, often the evidence is not consistent in the same polis—either chronologically or in the currency used.[71] Nevertheless, the picture that emerges appears to suggest that a federal impost was introduced sometime in the early years of the second century BC, probably after the declaration of freedom of the Thessalians in 196 BC, or more likely after the reorganization of the League by Flamininus in 194 BC. The nature of this impost is not easy to determine; the next chapter attempts to come closer to a conclusion.

---

of manumissions are *IG* IX(1) 2^2 419 from Oiniadai (third century BC); *IG* V(2) 274 II from Mantinea (103 BC–AD 15); and several inscriptions from Bouthrotos, e.g. *IBouthrotos* 18, 21, 30, 33 (all after 163 BC).

[70] For the accounts of the *poletai* see Rhodes 1981, 552–557; Langdon 1991. For the *Rationes Centesimarum* see Lambert 1997.

[71] See Chapter 5 below on the geographical and chronological distribution of the evidence.

CHAPTER THREE

MANUMISSION TAX OR PUBLICATION FEE?

Owing to the concise and often ambiguous formulation of the inscriptions, the information included in them might be taken as supporting both interpretations of the uniform payments: a manumission tax or a registration and publication fee. The inscriptions present some features that may imply state charges either way: uniformity of the payments, frequent allusion to the polis as the recipient of the money paid by the freed slaves,[1] registration of the payments with the names of those who paid, and the frequent mention of the treasurer in the headings of monthly or yearly manumissions.[2] It is therefore worthwhile reviewing the evidence—first the inscriptions that might be understood as attesting to the payment of manumission tax.

The wording of many inscriptions may favour a manumission tax. An inscription from Gonnoi (*Gonnoi* II 117 = *IG* IX(2) 1042 I, lines 3–8, ca. 10 BC?), for instance, has the following record:

οἱ ἀπη-
λευθερωμένοι καὶ δεδω-
κότες τῇ πόλει τὰ γεινόμ-
ενα τῆς ἀπελευθερώσεω-
ς αὐτῶν δεινάρια εἴκοσι
δύο ἥμυσυ.

Those slaves who were manumitted and paid the (money) due for their manumission (*apeleutherosis*), twenty-two and a half denarii.

So also *IG* IX(2) 542 from Larisa (reign of Augustus), where—after naming the treasurer—lines 5–9 state:

[ἀπολο]γισμὸς τῶν ἀπη-
[λευθερω]μένων ἐπ' αὐτ⟨ο⟩ῦ κα[ὶ]
[δεδωκ]ότων {οτων} τῇ πόλ[ει]
[τοὺς τῆ]ς ἀπελευθερώσ[εως ιε']
[στατῆρα]ς

---

[1] E.g. *IG* IX(2) 73 from Lamia specifies in line 2 that the payment was made to the polis (ἀπελεύθεροι δεδ⟨ω⟩κ̣[ότ]ε̣ς ἐ[ν] τὰν πόλιν τοὺς δεκαπέντε στατῆρας). Cf. *IG* IX(2) 463, line 7, from Krannon, 49/8 BC—“to the polis”.

[2] See e.g. *IG* IX(2) 18 from Hypata (undated), line 1; *IG* IX(2) 277 from Metropolis (undated), lines 3, 12.

> A record (*apologismos*) of those slaves who were manumitted during his (the treasurer's) time of office and who paid the polis the fifteen staters due for their manumission (*apeleutherosis*).[3]

In these inscriptions the payment is explicitly connected to, and stated to be for, manumission, not publication. Nevertheless, although such phrases might seem to refer to a tax on manumission, note that the word *apeleutherosis* is used elsewhere to denote the manumission document and not only the act itself.[4]

A clear case of manumission tax can perhaps be deduced from inscriptions that mention tax and tax collector in second- or third-century AD Demetrias (*SEG* 37.450 and 451).[5] But because the Magnesian League, with its chief city Demetrias, was not part of the Thessalian League, I defer the discussion of these inscriptions to Chapter 4, where the evidence from other places is analysed. Similarly, evidence of payments in manumission inscriptions in other places in the Greek world may also be adduced, if we accept the view that they were paid as manumission tax. Such evidence might indicate that manumission taxes were not unknown in Greek poleis. For instance, seven inscriptions from Chaironeia, dated to the late third or early second century BC, mention payment by slaves to the treasurer of the city immediately upon manumission. Of these inscriptions two also spell out the amount paid: twenty drachmai in *IG* VII 3303 and twenty-five staters in *IG* VII 3406.[6] Some scholars interpret these payments as representing a manumission tax, introduced in Chaironeia perhaps in imitation of the Roman *vicesima manumissionum*.[7] Note that the two inscriptions which specify the sums of money record different figures. As Rensch proposes, this difference may be understood as reflecting a calculation similar to that of the Romans: a fixed percentage reckoned on the basis of the slave's market value.[8] On the other hand, *IG* VII 3406 (with the sum of twenty-five staters) might have

3 Cf. *IG* IX(2) 541, lines 9–10 from Larisa (first century AD); *IG* IX(2) 545, line 12, from Larisa (AD 44–46); *IG* IX(2) 549, line 15 (= *SEG* 32.603) from Larisa (reign of Augustus). The word was also restored in *IG* IX(2) 1296, line 28 from Azoros (20–18 BC), but see the new readings in *AE* (1945–1947), 110, no. 59.

4 See e.g. *AE* (1924) 173, no. 408, lines 11, 19, 26–27, from mid-first-century BC Pythion (ὡς ἡ ἀπελευθέρωσις περιέχει), on which see also Chapter 2 above.

5 Ed. pr. Habicht 1987, 277–292, nos. 1–22.

6 See Darmezin 1999, nos. 18 and 87. The other inscriptions are *IG* VII 3307, 3339, 3344, 3354, 3398 (Darmezin 1999, 21, 47, 52, 61, 85 respectively).

7 See Calderini 1965, 141–142; Rensch 1908, 95.

8 Rensch 1908, 95. See, however, Darmezin 1999, 236, who suggests, without discussion, that this was a registration fee.

been inscribed much later than VII 3303 (with twenty drachmai); if so, the difference may reflect a raise in tax. These inscriptions too, as well as evidence of payments elsewhere in the Greek world, are discussed in detail in Chapter 4.

However, evidence is found for the collection of the Roman *vicesima libertatis* in Athens. A bilingual inscription, found in the theatre of Dionysus in Athens and dated to the second century AD (*SIA* VI 8 = *CIL* III 555 = 7287), reads:

> *Q. Calpurnio Eutycho*
> *Philetus publicus vicesimae libertatis vilicus fecit.*
>
> Κ. Καλπουρνίῳ Εὐτύχῳ Φίλητος,
> εἰκοστῆς ἐλευθερίας οἰκονόμος, ἐποίησεν γνησίῳ στρατιώτῃ.
>
> Philetos, the public slave, the administrator of the collection of the five-percent tax on manumission, made (this) to (the memory of) Q. Calpurnius Eutychus **the noble soldier** [the words in bold are found only in the Greek version].

According to this inscription, Philetos, who erected this column and saw to the inscription in honour of Quintus Calpurnius Eutychos, was apparently appointed, as a public slave, to the office of overseer or financial official administering the collection of the *vicesima*, and noted his rank in the inscription. If the dating of the inscription is correct, the *vicesima* was collected in second-century AD Athens, but presumably only from Roman citizens living there, since we have no evidence that Greeks too paid the tax before the *Constitutio Antoniniana* (AD 212) which made all the inhabitants of the Roman empire its citizens.[9] It may be significant that this post—the εἰκοστῆς ἐλευθερίας οἰκονόμος—resembles the office attested at second-century AD Hypata: the ἐπιμελητὴς τῶν ἀπελευθερικῶν χρημάτων ("the manager of the money pertaining to manumitted slaves"), who was in charge of receiving the money and responsible for inscribing the names of manumitted slaves who paid the money.[10] In Hypata, however, the payment

[9] On the implications of the *Constitutio Antoniniana* for the collection of the manumission tax, see also Chapter 4 below. Interestingly, according to this inscription the person in charge of collecting the *vicesima libertatis* in Athens is an imperial slave, as is the case in *P. Mich.* 7.462 from Egypt (mid-second century AD), a fact explained by Brunt (1990, 403) for Egypt as resulting from the absence of tax farmers willing to take on the collection of the *vicesima*. See also van Minnen and Worp 2009, 20. On collectors of the *vicesima libertatis* see also Chapter 4 below.

[10] See *IG* IX(2) 17 (ca. AD 131/132); *IG* IX(2) 19 (reign of Vespasian or Domitian), lines 1–3; *IG* IX(2) 21 (= *SEG* 3.457b[1]; Bouchon 2009, 400, face 1; AD 131/132), lines 1–4; *IG* IX(2) 22 (= Bouchon 2009, face 6), lines 1–6. On these inscriptions see below, and Chapter 2 above.

was explicitly not a percentage but the fixed sum of twenty-two and a half denarii. M. Vigié suggests that the slave in the Athenian inscription belonged to a society of tax collectors for the *vicesima*, on the basis of some illegible words at the end of the inscription, which he thinks indicate the name of the society.[11]

Finally, it has been argued that the sum paid in Thessaly could not have been a registration fee because it was disproportionally high compared with the costs of inscriptions elsewhere in Greece; therefore, it is unlikely to have been exacted for publication purposes only.[12] Rädle argues that whereas in Athens the costs of inscriptions varied from twenty to sixty drachmai according to the number of letters engraved, in Thessaly the fixed sum of fifteen staters (approximately equivalent to twenty-two and a half Attic drachmai) was paid for a very short text (i.e. for each manumission entry in the long lists).[13] He accordingly agrees with Calderini that the money paid in Thessaly under the label of publication fee was a tax on manumission which, however, differed from the Roman tax in that it was not calculated in proportion to the market value of the slave but was a fixed sum, regardless of age or other criteria. Yet the evidence we have on costs of official inscriptions in classical Athens implies that other criteria than the number of letters were also in play, since the Athenian Assembly sometimes apportioned more money for shorter inscriptions than for long and elaborate ones and it seems that the costs varied over time.[14] Moreover,

---

[11] Vigié (1881), 12. According to Epict. *Disc.* 4.1.33, collectors of the *vicesima* were called in Greek εἰκοστῶναι (see also Introduction above); being himself a former slave Epictetus has knowledge of this tax although he went to live in Greece after his banishment from Rome ca. AD 93. Bradley 1984b, 177, n. 17, notes that the term *vilicus* in connection with the *vicesima libertatis* appears in inscriptions which generally belong to the late Republic and early Empire, and that the term is best understood as denoting an agent for the *publicanus*. In 1984a, 150, Bradley cites the Athenian inscription, among others, as indicating collection of the *vicesima* in many areas of the Empire, but does not discuss the *vilicus*.

[12] See Calderini 1965, 140–141; Rädle 1969, 160–161; Meyer 2010, 23.

[13] Rädle bases his argument on W. Larfeld, *Griechische Epigraphik*, München 1914, 115 (cf. Larfeld 1971, vol. II, 723, and the tables on pp. 606–639), who adopts the theory of E. Drerup, "Über die Publikationskosten der attischen Volksbeschlüsse", *Neue Jahrbücher für Philologie und Paedogogik* 66 (1896), 227–257; "Zu den Publikationskosten der attischen Volksbeschlüsse: Nachtrag zu Jahrg. 1896 s. 227–57", *Neue Jahrbücher für Philologie und Paedogogik* 67 (1897), 871–873.

[14] On costs of inscriptions in Athens and the meaning of the formulaic provisions for payment see Henry 1989, especially Tables 1–3; Loomis 1998, 121–165 (who adopts most of the conclusions of B.T. Nolan, *Inscribing Costs at Athens in the Fifth Century B.C.* [Ph.D. diss., Ohio State University 1981], Ann Arbor 1981—a work I was not able to consult), esp. 159; Rhodes and Osborne 2003, xiv. See also Posner 1972, 98–99, who notes that inscribing texts on stone was costly.

given that one Thessalian stater (= two Thessalian drachmai) was equivalent to one Attic drachma and a half,[15] the fifteen staters (or twenty-two and a half denarii), paid by manumitted slaves in Thessaly between the second century BC and the second century AD, were equivalent to twenty-two and a half Attic drachmai—a figure which comes close to the prices of inscribed decrees in Athens in the fourth and third centuries BC: normally twenty to thirty drachmai.[16] Of course, we must take into consideration differences in time and monetary values, but the price paid in Thessaly also approximates sums exacted from manumitted slaves elsewhere (see below).

For all that, this price may indeed seem too high for publication purposes, given that it was imposed on each manumitted slave for a short entry in a long inscribed list. However, the same amount was paid whether the manumission record was a short[17] or a longer entry in lists of manumissions,[18] or a single and more detailed record.[19] This makes it quite plausible that the money was not paid for the number of letters on the stone; as in classical Athens, other considerations, which escape our knowledge, may well have been involved in determining the rate.[20] Furthermore, Rädle's suggestion that in Thessaly a manumission tax was collected under the name of publication fee looks implausible; there seems to be no reason why the Thessalian League or the individual cities would avoid declaring the actual purpose of this levy.

Finally, if the recorded payments were made as manumission tax, a reasonable assumption would be that *all* manumissions in Thessaly were

---

15 As noted in the Introduction, the Thessalian federal coinage had two standards, the Attic and the local; according to the latter the drachma weighed 3/4 of the Attic drachma, so two Thessalian drachmai, or one stater, were worth one Attic drachma and a half and four Thessalian drachmai were worth three Attic drachmai (or three Roman denarii). The local standard was counted in staters (didrachmai) and obols. On Thessalian currency and rates see Head 1911, 291; Larsen 1968, 291; Rädle 1969, 159.

16 See Loomis 1998, 164. In Delos, however, the price of inscriptions was much higher: 190 drachmai, as against six drachmai for publishing a text on wooden tablets; see Homolle 1887, 13 n. 7; Wilhelm 1909, 245; Posner 1972, 99. In Delphi, the treasurers paid Deinomachos the stone mason 140 drachmai (*CID* 2.76 = *FD* III 5.50, col. III, lines 23–24) in 335 BC, and 200 drachmai (*CID* 2.97 = *FD* III 5.58, lines 42–43) in 327/6 BC; cf. Pritchett 1996, 29.

17 E.g. the catalogue-like register of numerous manumission acts *IG* IX(2) 102 (Kophi, 185–180 BC), each entry comprising three to five lines.

18 Thus lines 21–24 of the inscription *IG* IX(2) 546 (Larisa, second century AD), which record a manumission made according to a will.

19 E.g. *SEG* 26.670 (Pythion, 150–100 BC)—nineteen lines recording a single manumission act; *AE* (1910), 363, no. 8, a record of one single manumission inscribed in 18 or 19 lines (Larisa, second century AD). On the latter inscription see Chapter 2, n. 32 above.

20 See below for a fuller discussion of registration or publication fees.

required to be registered and publicized—in order to keep track of those subject to tax and perhaps as a prerequisite to the legal acknowledgment of the freed slaves' new status. If this assumption is correct, the Thessalian law or laws occasionally mentioned in manumission inscriptions as requiring the payment may also have referred to this obligation.[21] However, the available evidence is partial and fragmentary, and no safe conclusion can be drawn: we have no information about the content of such laws, or any way of knowing whether the extant manumission inscriptions are chance findings out of many more obligated inscribed manumissions.

Yet we also need to consider the possibility of a Roman dictate, perhaps in the framework of Flamininus' reorganization of the League in 194 BC. As we saw in the Introduction, an inscription from Narthakion, dated to ca. 140 BC (*IG* IX(2) 89), notes that the Thessalians still used the laws given to them by Flamininus. But if Rome ordered the Thessalians to impose a manumission tax, it may seem strange that the tax was not modelled on the Roman *vicesima*, that is, a percentage of the slave's market value. Another opportunity to dictate to the Thessalians arose in 146 BC, when Thessaly was incorporated into the province of Macedonia, and later, after 27 BC, when the province of Achaia was organized and probably included Thessaly (see Introduction). But the payments made by manumitted slaves in Thessaly start earlier: in Achaia Phthiotis they are attested already in 185–180 BC in Kophi (*IG* IX(2) 102), and in 181/180 BC in Phthiotic Thebes (*IG* IX(2) 133).[22]

We now turn to the evidence possibly suggesting that these payments were levied for registration and publication. Again, although the uniformity of the payments and the involvement of the treasurers and other magistrates may point to a federal manumission tax, these features may also indicate a federal requirement to pay for the right to publish manumissions on stone. This requirement could have been compulsory—in which case we may assume that apart from seeking profit from private transactions, that is, manumissions, the states were also interested in keeping full records of their ex-slave populations (see below); or payment could have been optional—in

[21] For "laws of manumitted slaves" see e.g. *IG* IX(2) 1290 I (= *SEG* 26.689), lines 15–16, from Pythion (150–100 BC); *IG* IX(2) 1296 (= *SEG* 26.644), lines 31–32, from Azoros (15–13 BC); *SEG* 26.670 (= *SEG* 28.513), lines 14–15, from Pythion (150–100 BC); *AE* (1924) 155, no. 401 (133–129 BC) and 402 (after 125 BC) from Pythion. See also Helly 1976.

[22] On Thessalian history see the Introduction above. In *IG* IX(2) 274 from Metropolis, dated to 186/5 BC, the treasurer is mentioned but not payments; if we can consider this inscription as similar to inscriptions that do mention payments (see Chapter 2 above), this would be the earliest example we have. See also Chapter 5 below.

which case we may assume that not all manumissions were inscribed on stone, so their number must have been higher. The allusion to laws (see above) too may support the interpretation of the payments as publication fees, whether the law(s) required registration and payment by all manumitted slaves or merely established that whoever wished to inscribe his or her new status on stone must pay for it. The extant evidence allows no firm conclusion, but on the face of it the former possibility—that the law required all freed slaves to register and pay for publication—may seem the likelier, considering that the manumission inscriptions take the form of official and annually arranged state records. Moreover, since freed slaves in the Greek world did not become citizens automatically upon manumission, the polis had to guard against foreigners infringing on its citizens' prerogatives and regulate the privileges it *did* decide to grant them.[23]

Yet problems persist: if this impost was federal, why was it not exacted in each and every Thessalian city, or why in some cities later than in others? Of course, the geographical and chronological distribution of the evidence may be accidental. But if the payment was compulsory, aiming to create a register of all manumitted slaves in a given polis, what federal interest was involved? Moreover, if every manumitted slave was required to pay, why do many inscriptions contain the heading "(this is) a register of those who paid the money due to the polis"?[24] Were not the inscribed names themselves sufficient proof that they had? Do such phrases imply that not all freed slaves paid, therefore only those who did received formal publication of their status? These questions are further discussed below.

There are strong indications that at least in some cities the payment was intended for registration and inscription on stone. In Larisa, manumission inscriptions state that these are registers of the manumitted slaves who paid money to the polis. Thus lines 1–6 in *IG* IX(2) 1344 from Larisa, dated to the reign of Augustus, read:

[παρ]ὰ Ἀριστοφί⟨λ⟩ου το[ῦ δεῖνος]
[τοῦ] ταμίου τῆς πόλεος τὴν [α′]
[ἑξά]μηνον ẹ̀ν τῇ στ[ρ](ατηγίᾳ) Καλλι-
[στρά]το[υ] ἀναγραφὴ τῶν δεδω[κό]-
[τ]ω[ν] τοὺς γεινομέν[ους σ]τατῆρα[ς]
[τ]ῇ πόλει μ(ηνὸς) Ἰ⟨τ⟩ωνίου·

[23] For rights and privileges granted to manumitted slaves in private manumission acts see Zelnick-Abramovitz 2009, 309–312, where I suggest that these grants must have been based on laws which laid down the right of freed slaves to certain privileges (and presumably also the conditions set for such grants).

[24] For such phrases see Chapter 2 above and the discussion below.

> (Issued) by Aristophilos, son of [---], the treasurer of the city in the [first] six months of the *strategia* of Kallistratos, a record (*anagraphe*) of those who paid the due staters to the polis, in the month of Itonios.[25]

Another inscription from Larisa, *AE* (1910), 363, no. 8 (ca. AD 131/132), lines 5–10, on the other hand, is an ἀναγραφή (*anagraphe*) of a single(!) manumission act: after naming the treasurer and the *strategos*, the inscription reads:

> ἀνα]-
> [γ]ραφὴ ἀ[π]ελευ[θέρου ἐπ' αὐ]-
> [τ]οῦ ἀπηλ[ευθερωμέ]-
> νου καὶ [δ]ε[δ]ω[κ]ό[τος τ]-
> οὺς γειν[ομένου]ς
> [τ]ῇ πόλε[ι] στ[ατ]ῆρ[ας ιε'·
>
> A record (*anagraphe*) of the manumitted slave who was manumitted in his (i.e. the treasurer's) term of office and paid the fifteen staters due to the polis.

IG IX(2) 546, lines 1–10, of the same time and place, has a slightly different phrasing, using the verb instead of the noun:

> Πειθαγόρος Μεγαλοκλέ[ους]
> ὁ γεγονὼς ταμίας τῆς πόλε[ως]
> τὴν δευτέραν ἑξάμηνον ἐν στρ(ατηγῷ) Κοκηΐ[ῳ]
> Λύκῳ ἔτους ει Αὐτοκράτορος
> Καίσαρος Τραϊανοῦ Ἁδριανοῦ
> Σεβαστοῦ ἀνέγραψεν τοὺς φα-
> μένους ἀπηλευθερῶσθαι ἐν τῷ
> τῆς ταμείας αὐτοῦ χρόνῳ οἵτινες ἔδ[ω]-
> καν τοὺς γεινομένους τῇ πόλει στατῆρας
> μη(νὸς) Λεσχανορίου ει.
>
> Pithagoros, son of Megalokleos, being the treasurer of the polis in the second half of the year of the strategos Kokeios Lykos, in the fifteenth year of Imperator Caesar Trajan Hadrian Augustus, recorded (or: inscribed, *anegrapsen*) those declared to be manumitted during his time of office as treasurer—whoever paid to the polis the due staters, on the fifteenth of the month of Leschanorios.[26]

---

[25] Cf. *IG* IX(2) 547 (AD 131/132), lines 5–7.

[26] A similar phrasing is found outside Thessaly, in a second-century BC inscription from Thasos: after naming the eponymous archons, the text reads: οἵδε ἀνεγράφησαν κατὰ ψήφισμα δήμου ἐξελεύθεροι, ὁπόσους ὁ δῆμος ἠλευθέρωσεν καὶ οἱ ἐκ τούτων γεγονότες ("these were registered, according to a decree of the People, as free, all those whom the People manumitted, and their descendants") (Dunant and Pouilloux, 1958, no. 173). There follow four illegible lines that may have listed the names of the manumitted slaves. No payment is mentioned, but this looks like a public manumission, perhaps a grant of freedom to slaves who fought on the side of the Thasians; the setting up of a record may be explained not only as an honorific

These examples show that in Larisa, at least in the first and second centuries AD, it was customary if not obligatory to publicize a register (*anagraphe*) of manumitted slaves—whether of multiple acts or of a single one, for which the freed slaves paid.

Other terms used in Larisa which may indicate that the payments were made for registration and publication are ἀπολογισμός (*apologismos*), "account",[27] and ὀνοματισμός (*onomatismos*), "a list of names".[28] Moreover, lines 10–11 of *SEG* 31.577 (Larisa, ca. 136/5 BC) explicitly state that the names listed in the inscription are of "those among the manumitted slaves who paid to the polis what is due according to the law" (οἱ καττεθειούκοντες τοῦν ἀπελευθέρουν τᾶ πόλι / τὸ γινόμενον ἐς τοῖ νόμοι). Such wording might suggest—in contrast to the impression created by the formality of the inscriptions' phrasing and the uniform sum—that this payment was not required in all manumissions, as the manumission tax was; instead it was required only in the case of manumitted slaves who wished to publish on stone their new status, in addition to depositing the manumission document in the polis' archives—which might have been required in all cases. I shall return to this question in Chapter 5.

The term *anagraphe* is also used in Phthiotic Thebes: the heading of a long inscription (*IG* IX(2) 109a, 47/6 BC?) names the *strategos* and the treasurer of the first half year and then states, "(this is) a record (*anagrapha*) of the manumitted slaves who have paid the polis what is due" (lines 4–6: ἀναγραφὰ τῶν δεδωκότων τᾶι / πόλει ἀπελευθέρων τὸ γινόμενον τᾶι πό/λει). The inscription then lists names of manumitted slaves and their manumittors in chronological order by month; when the treasurer is replaced by another

---

token to these slaves (if indeed they were rewarded for helping the city), but also as an expression of the need of Thasos to monitor its inhabitants' status. Whereas the noun *anagraphe* usually denotes an inscription, the verb ἀναγράφειν (*anagraphein*) is used for both inscribing on stone and recording on any material, papyrus or wood; see e.g. Arist. *Pol.* 6, 1321b34–40; *IG* XII(5) 595, face B, lines 3–9, from Ceos (where the verb is used for writing on λεύκωμα (*leukoma*), a whitewashed board, and on stone); *IG* XII(7) 515, lines 131–134, from Aigiale (for writing on both *deltoi* and stone). Similarly, while πίναξ is usually translated as "wooden writing tablet", Aristotle mentions a dedication of a *pinax* by a *choregos* in Athens (*Pol.* 8, 1341a36) which seems to imply that it was inscribed on stone.

27 As in *IG* IX(2) 542 (reign of Augustus): [ἀπολο]γισμὸς τῶν ἀπη/[λευθερω]μένων ἐπ' αὐτ⟨ο⟩ῦ κα[ὶ] / [δεδωκ]ότων {οτων} τῇ πόλ[ει] / [τοὺς τῆ]ς ἀπελευθερώσ[εως ιε'] / [στατῆρα]ς ("the account [*apologismos*] of those manumitted in his [i.e. the treasurer's] time of office and who paid the polis the fifteen staters due on the occasion of manumission [*apeleutherosis*]").

28 As in *AE* (1910), 361, no. 7 and *AE* (1910), 361, no. 7a (= *IG* IX(2) 560), dated to the Roman period, lines 4–5: ὀ]νοματισ[μὸς τῶν ἐπ' αὐτοῦ ἀπηλευθερωμένων καὶ] / [δεδ]ωκότων [στατῆρας ιε' ("a list of names of those manumitted during his [i.e. the treasurer's] time of office and who paid fifteen staters ...").

(e.g. lines 43–45), or a new *strategos* is elected (beginning a new year, e.g. lines 60–63), the new name is given followed by the statement: "the manumitted slaves, according to the law" (οἱ ἀπελευθερω[θ]έντες κατὰ τὸν νόμον).

In an inscription from Hypata, *IG* IX(2) 13 (AD 47), lines 2–5, the phrasing is more explicit:

[– –]ΜΠ[.]ΘΥΟΝμάρχου Σεβα[σ]τήου ⟨τα⟩-
[μιε]ύοντος οἱ δόντες ἀπελεύθερο⟨ι τ⟩ὰ [γι]-
[νόμ]ενα τῆς στηλογραφίας κατὰ τὸν ν[όμον]
[ἀργ]υ[ρ]ίου δεινάρια εἴκοσι δύο ἥμισυ.

When [-----]marchos son of Sebasteos was the treasurer, the manumitted slaves who paid what was due for *inscribing the stele* (*stelographia*), according to the law, twenty-two and a half silver denarii.

According to this inscription, the payment was made expressly for inscribing the manumission records on the stele. Likewise, in lines 3–4 of the inscription *IG* IX(2) 14a from Hypata (AD 47/48), we read: [οἵδε ἀπελεύθερ]οι τῆς στηλογραφίας / [τὸ ἀργύριον ἔδωκαν] ("these manumitted slaves paid the money for inscribing the stele").[29] Later inscriptions from the same city refer to a special official (mentioned above), presumably entrusted with using the money paid by manumitted slaves to publish the manumissions on stone. Thus *IG* IX(2) 17 (ca. AD 131/132) reads:

παρὰ Νεικολάου τοῦ Νει-
[κ]ολάου τοῦ καὶ Λου[κίου] το[ῦ]
ἐπιμελητοῦ τῶν ἀπελε[υ]-
θερικῶν χρημάτων ἀναγρα-
φὴ τῶν δεδωκότων εἰς
τὴν πόλιν τὰ γεινόμενα αὐ-
τοῖς εἰς τὴν στήλην στρα-
τηγοῦντος Ἑλλανοκράτους.

---

[29] The term στηλογραφία (*stelographia*) and the verb στηλογράφειν (*stelographein*) are also found in dedication-manumission inscriptions from Macedonia, e.g. Petsas et al. 2000, no. 44 (second century AD); no. 78 (third century AD); *EKM* 1. *Beroia* 50 (= *SEG* 48.749), 51 and 52 (= *SEG* 49.683)—none of which mentions payments; but see *SEG* 51.833 (third century AD)—where the words ὧν]ἡ κὲ τὴν τ[ιμὴν ἔχει (lines 12–13) indicate the purpose of the *stelographia*. The dedicators bear Roman names, but this does not necessarily indicate that this was a Roman rather than a Greek practice, as argued by Meyer 2002, 139; the manumittors in Thessalian Hypata, where the same term is used, bear Greek names. The verb is also used in a first-century BC manumission inscription from the Kabeirion in Lemnos (*ASAtene* 1941/1942, 96, no. 16, line 5), where the ἱεροκῆρυξ (*hierokeryx*, the herald of sacred matters) is said to have inscribed on a stele, according to a decree of the people, the names of those who were manumitted during the festival of Horaia; and in a different context in an inscription from Pergamon (*I.Perg.* I 245, line 60, before 133 BC).

(Issued) by Nikolaos son of Nikolaos and also Lucius (or: who is also called Lucius?), the manager (or curator) of the money pertaining to manumitted slaves (*epimeletes ton apeleutherikon chrematon*), a record (*anagraphe*) of those who have paid to the polis what is due from them *for the stele*.

Likewise *IG* IX(2) 19, lines 1–3 (second century AD):

[– – – – – – – – – – –]ου ἐπιμελητοῦ τῶν ἀπελευθερικῶν
[χρημάτων – – – – – –]υτω ἀπελευθέρων τὸ τῆς στηλογρα-
[φίας – – στρατηγοῦντ]ος Εὐβιότου·

[---] the manager of the money pertaining to manumitted slaves [---] of the manumitted slaves the (money?) for inscribing the stele, in the year of the *strategos* Eubiotos.[30]

In *IG* IX(2) 22 (AD 131/132), lines 1–4, the task of this *epimeletes* is made clear:

Ζω⟨ΐ⟩λο[υ το]ῦ Παραμόνου ὁ γεγονὼς ἐπιμελητ[ὴς]
τῶν ἀπελευθερικῶν χρημάτων προσα̣ν[α]-
φέρω καὶ Ἀλέξανδρον Ἀσκληπιάδου
ἀπελεύθερον ξενικῇ δεδωκότα μοι τὰ τῆ[ς]
στηλογραφίας ✻ κβ<ʹ.

Zoïlos, son of Paramonos, being the manager of the money pertaining to manumitted slaves, I also report (or declare) Alexander, the manumitted slave of Asklepiades, he having paid *me* what (is due) *for inscribing the stele* (*stelographia*).[31]

The *epimeletes* who appears in these four manumission inscriptions has no parallel in other manumission inscriptions or in other epigraphic documents from Hypata.[32] Nor is this office attested in any other polis.[33] Since the manumission inscriptions from Hypata that mention this official are of a later date than those that do not, it may be inferred that this office was introduced into Hypata in the second century AD, if not earlier.[34] It is possible that

30 On this inscription see also Sekunda 1997, and Chapter 2 above.

31 Cf. *IG* IX(2) 21 (= *SEG* 3.457b[1]; 16.376), which is of the same year as no. 22 and in the office of the same *epimeletes*, lines 1–4: Ζω⟨ΐ⟩λο[υ το]ῦ Παραμόνου τοῦ ἐπιμελητοῦ τῶν / ἀπελευθερικῶν χρημάτων ἀναγραφὴ τῶν δεδω/[κότων –]ην τῇ πόλει τὸ τῆς στηλογραφίας ἀργύρι/[ον] ("When Zoïlos, son of Paramonos, was the manager of the money pertaining to manumitted slaves, a record [*anagraphe*] of those who paid the polis the money for inscribing the stele [*stelographia*]").

32 *IG* IX(2) 44, lines 7–8 (Hypata, reign of Augustus) mentions an ἐπιμελητὴς τοῦ κοινοῦ τῶν ἀμφικτυόνων, but not the one in charge of the money paid by manumitted slaves.

33 *IG* XII(1) 49, line 50, from Rhodes (after 188 BC) mentions ἐπιμεληταὶ τῶν ξέ[νων] ("managers/overseers of foreigners"), but nothing indicates that they handled taxes.

34 *IG* IX(2) 14a—the latest of the inscriptions which do not mention this epimeletes—is dated to AD 47/48 (though it does say [οἵδε ἀπελεύθερ]οι τῆς στηλογραφίας / [τὸ ἀργύριον

the title ἐπιμελητὴς τῶν ἀπελευθερικῶν χρημάτων is a Greek translation of a Roman office; according to Apuleius in his *Metamorphoses*, written in the second century AD, Lucius' old friend Pithias was an aedile in Hypata.[35] If so, it is tempting to compare this *epimeletes* to the collectors of the *vicesima libertatis*, perhaps even the *procuratores* in charge of this tax, who probably in the second century AD replaced the tax farmers in collecting this tax.[36] But as noted above (concerning the collection of the *vicesima* in Athens), the money paid in Hypata by manumitted slaves was not a percentage of the slave's market value but the same fixed amount as in other Thessalian poleis; moreover, the *epimeletes* in Hypata was clearly in charge of the registration and publication of manumission acts—a task not attested for the Roman *procurator*. Nevertheless, the *epimeletes* of Hypata may have been a *procurator* appointed for the particular task of receiving the registration fees and seeing to the publication of a stele bearing the names of those who paid.[37]

An attractive interpretation has been offered by Richard Bouchon (2009). He suggests that the texts inscribed on three faces of one block (*IG* IX(2) 21, 16, 56, and 22) belong together and form part of a larger inscription, whose other parts were inscribed on three faces of a joint block which is now lost.[38] Bouchon argues that the lists contained in this larger inscription were the accounts of the *epimeletes* Zoïlos (mentioned in *IG* IX(2) 21 and 22; see above), recording his income and expenses during his time of office and issued perhaps when he finished his term, which lasted for more than five years. He also suggests that since the manumission documents on the block were inscribed by different hands, the acts were perhaps engraved once a year, between AD 128/9 and 132/3.[39]

ἔδωκαν, lines 3–4). Bouchon 2009, 402, suggests that this office was created after AD 42/3, because *IG* IX(2) 13, dated to the third year of Claudius' reign, mentions the *tamias* as receiving the money from the manumitted slaves. But some of the manumission inscriptions are too fragmentary to know whether or not they mentioned the *epimeletes*, and some are undated.

35 Apul. *Met.* 1.24: *"Annonam curamus," ait "et aedilem gerimus, et si quid obsonare cupis, utique commodabimus".*

36 See Brunt 1990, 402–404; van Minnen and Worp 2009; and Chapter 4, n. 17, below.

37 If indeed this was a translation of a Roman office, we should consider the possibility that the word χρημάτων did not mean money but the general affairs concerning manumitted slaves (e.g. *procurator rerum libertorum*).

38 Bouchon 2009, 396–402. Bouchon's reconstruction is: face 1: *IG* IX(2) 21 + face 2: *IG* IX(2) 16 + faces 3, 4, and 5 (on a lost block) + face 6: *IG* IX(2) 56 + 22.

39 Ib. 399.

According to Bouchon, this *epimeletes* was in charge of receiving from the manumitted slaves the money (which Bouchon understands as a tax paid for recognition of the slaves' new status) and registering the payments in this special fund (that is, τῶν ἀπελευθερικῶν χρήματα—"the money pertaining to manumitted slaves"), from which he allocated money to various magistrates—in this case to the gymnasiarchs for the repair of the gymnasium and to the treasurers (face 6 = *IG* IX(2) 56).[40] Bouchon rightly remarks that what this inscription teaches us is that although the impost was federal, each city had its own financial system.[41]

In Lamia too there are very strong indications that the money was paid for inscribing the manumission acts in stone, as can be deduced from lines 1–3 of *IG* IX(2) 71 (after 60 BC):

> 1 στραταγέοντος Ἀγαθάνορος τοῦ ⟨Ε⟩ὐ⟨ρυ⟩δάμαντος Γομφέος, ταμιεύοντ[ος]
> [τ]ᾶς πόλιος Σωσι⟨π⟩άτρου τοῦ Δάμωνος ἀπελεύθερο⟨ι⟩ δεδ⟨ω⟩κότ⟨ε⟩ς [ἐ]ν
> ⟨τ⟩[ὰ]ν στα[λογρα]-
> [φί]αν τοὺς δεκαπέντε στατῆρες· μηνὸς Βωμίου·
>
> When Agathanor, son of Eurydamnas, of Gomphoi was the *strategos*, when Sosipatros, son of Damon, was the treasurer of the polis, the manumitted slaves who paid *for inscribing the stele* (*stelographia*) the fifteen staters: In the month of Bomios:[42]

In another inscription from Lamia (*SEG* 30.531A, lines 23–24 = *IG* IX(2) 74, lines 1–2; ca. 150–100 BC), although no mention of payment is made, the following is the heading of one of the lists of manumissions on the stone:

> 23 στραταγέοντος Λέοντος τού[σδε ὁ τα]-
> μίας Κλέων Θεύρωνος ἀνέγρα[ψε·
>
> When Leon was the *strategos*, the treasurer Cleon, son of Theuron, inscribed (or registered) the following: (here follow names of manumitted slaves).

---

40 *IG* IX(2) 56 (= Bouchon 2009, 401, face 6, lines 1–9) records the payment of 1,500 denarii to each gymnasiarch and 847.5 denarii to the *tamiai*. The total, 3,847.5, divided by twenty-two and a half (the amount paid by each manumitted slave) gives 171, whereas on the extant block the number of the paying manumitted slaves is only 54, in addition to the manumitted slave Alexandros whom Zoïlos forgot to register and added him later (*IG* IX(2) 22). Bouchon (2009, 397–398) suggests that the remaining 116 names were engraved on the missing block. In Echinos, the money paid by the manumitted slaves to the treasurer was given to the priests of the imperial cult (*SEG* 36.543= Gounaropoulos 1987, 253 A–D; *SEG* 39.493 = Zachou-Kontoyanni 1989, 213).

41 Bouchon 2009, 403.

42 Cf. *IG* IX(2) 72 from Lamia (ca. 50 BC), lines 3–4: "the manumitted slaves who had paid *for the stele* (ἐν [τὰ]ν ⟨σ⟩τάλαν) the fifteen staters".

Treasurers are often mentioned in relation to supplying the money needed for inscribing state decisions and accounts,[43] so it seems most likely that here the treasurer was responsible for ordering the inscription, covering its costs with the money paid by the manumitted slaves.

Finally, in *IG* IX(2) 280 from Metropolis (Roman period) we read:

[– – – – – – – – – – – – – – – – – – – –ἐκ] τ̣οῦ δοθέν-
[τος – – – – – – – – – – – – – – – –καὶ ἐκ] τῶν κοινῶν τῆς
[πόλεως προσόδων ἀπηλευθερωμέν]οι ὑπὸ Κλεομάχας τῆς Κλεομέ-
[νους ἔδωκαν τὸ γινόμενον τῇ π]όλι μ δ(ηνάρια) ε ταμίᾳ Λέοντι Ἀντι-
[– – – – – – – – – – – – – – –] μ(ηνὸς) Ὁμολῴου #^{7}[– – – – –]
[– – – – – – – – – – – – –]ους μ(ηνὸς) Ὁμολῴου Παρμένων Λ[– –]
[– – – – – – – – – – –ὑ]π̣ὸ Φείδωνος τοῦ Φείδωνος ἔδωκεν [– – –]
[– – – – – – – – – – – –]ιγόνῳ τῷ ταμίᾳ.

[---] from the given[44] [--- and from] the public revenues of the polis, those manumitted by Kleomacha, daughter of Kleomenes, paid what is due to the polis, forty-five denarii, to the treasurer Leon, son of Anti[---]. In the month of Homoloios [------] by Pheidon, son of Pheidon, paid [-----]igonos the treasurer.

Since the inscription lists manumitted slaves, with the names of their manumittors, who paid what was due to the treasurer, the reference to the public revenues (*koinai prosodoi*)[45] may imply that the money for inscribing and setting up the stele was taken from the public coffers, into which went the money paid by the freed slaves. The allusion to the public revenues in the context of inscriptions, although largely restored here, finds parallels in other Thessalian inscriptions: *IG* IX(2) 460, a decree of the city of Krannon (second century BC), includes a proviso to inscribe the resolution on a stone

43 E.g. *IG* IX(2) 1103, line 31 (Demetrias, 130–126 BC); *IG* IX(2) 460, lines 8–9 (Krannon, second century BC); *SEG* 33.450, lines 5–6 (Atrax, second century BC). In other places: see e.g. *IG* II^{2} 21, lines 4–5 (Athens, 390/89? BC); *IG* IV 755, lines 9–10 (Troizen, third century BC); *IG* V(1) 4, line 18 (Sparta, after 188 BC); *Milet* I(2) 10, line 38 (Miletos, 289/8 BC).

44 In other Thessalian inscriptions that specify the source of funding for the inscription of state decisions we find the phrase δοθέντος τοῦ εἰς ταῦτα ἀνηλώματος ὑπὸ τοῦ ταμίου (e.g. *SEG* 36.552 from Pythion, ca. 180–170 BC), which seems to be too long to fit in the missing parts of lines 1 and 2 of our inscription. The word ἐκ in line 1 is baffling and seems to have been restored as a parallel to the words καὶ ἐκ] τῶν κοινῶν τῆς [πόλεως προσόδων in lines 2–3, but there too the word is restored.

45 Line 3 of the inscription was restored by Hiller. See Chapter 2 above and n. 31 on the problem posed by the phrasing of the inscription: if the restoration of lines 1–3 is correct, it leaves no room for the names of the manumitted slaves in the first act recorded on the stone, as cited here.

pillar and to set it up in the sanctuary of Athena; the money for the stele and for the inscription is to be given by the treasurers from the public revenues (line 9: ἀτ τᾶν κοινᾶν ποθόδου[ν]).[46] Therefore *IG* IX(2) 280 may attest to the use in Metropolis of public revenues to inscribe documents on stone and to the procedure by which manumitted slaves paid money to the public treasurer for the right to publish their manumission on stone.

Still, the present restoration of the inscription poses serious problems, to which I have already referred. First, the mention of the public revenues in the context of manumission inscription is unique, and as the text stands now it looks as if only in the first of the two manumission acts recorded here was the money taken from the public coffers; alternatively, this source of funding was given in a heading which referred to the entire record of manumissions. But second, if lines 1–3 are correctly restored, no names of those who were manumitted by Kleomacha were inscribed—which is also unique.

Although the evidence discussed above is by no means conclusive, this survey seems to show that there is good reason to understand the payments as made for the purpose of registering the manumitted slaves and publicizing the acts of manumission on stone. Despite differences in wording and in time, the uniformity of the payments makes it plausible that manumitted slaves paid for the same purpose in second-century BC Lamia as in second-century AD Hypata. But a better evaluation may be obtained through a comparison of the Thessalian payments with similar evidence from other parts of the Greek world.

---

[46] Cf. *IG* IX(2) 461a (Krannon, before 168 BC), lines 11–13; *IG* IX(2) 517 (Larisa, 214 BC), lines 45–46; *IG* IX(2) 1231 (Phalanna, ca. 200–150 BC), lines 17–19; *IG* IX(2) 1229 (Phalanna, early second century BC), lines 39–41; *SEG* 33.450 = *ZPE* 51 (1983), p. 162 (Atrax, second century BC), lines 6–7; *Gonnoi* II, 111 (Gonnoi, 206–203 BC), lines 18–19.

CHAPTER FOUR

EVIDENCE FROM OTHER PLACES

Epigraphic and papyrological evidence shows that in several places other than Thessaly money was collected on the occasion of manumission. There too it is not always easy to determine whether the money was paid as a manumission tax or publication fee, but in most cases the latter seems more probable.

I start with Demetrias, the head city of the Magnesian League, a place geographically part of Thessaly but politically independent of the Thessalian League. The Magnesians were declared free by Titus Quinctius Flamininus in 196 BC, but eventually came under the control of Philip V after the war with Antiochos III.[1] The Magnesian League was re-founded after the Third Macedonian War (171–168 BC) and kept its independence until Diocletian's reign (AD 284–305).[2] Many manumission inscriptions have been found in the Magnesian cities of Iolkos (some undated), Pagasai, and Demetrias (dated to the "Roman period" or to the second or third century AD), but most of them contain no indication of payment.[3] *IG* IX(2) 1119 from Demetrias (Roman period) records payments of a different kind:

I.
στρ(ατηγοῦντος) Οὐήρο[υ] ⟨τ⟩ὸ β
Ζωσίμου τοῦ Παν-
θήρα ἠλευθέρω-
σεν Φίλιστον
✳ σ'.

II.
στρ(ατηγοῦντος) Ἰουλίου Ἑρμείου
Πάνταυχος καὶ Τήρης οἱ Στάχυος
ἠλευθέρωσαν Λύκον ξενικῇ ✳ ⟨σ'⟩.
Vacat

---

[1] See Liv. 39.23.11.

[2] See Larsen 1968, 295; Graninger 2011, 33.

[3] For inscriptions from Iolkos see e.g. *AE* (1930), 99, no. 1; *RPh* (1911), 298, no. 47(1); *SEG* 23.460 (where only the term *lytron*, the price of freedom, is mentioned). Pagasai: e.g. *IG* IX(2) 359b.

III.
[– – – –]δι[– – – – – –]
πελωΙΙΛC[– –] Ἀπ̣πίου
ἀπηλευθέρωσεν
Τρόφιμον μηδενὶ
προσήκοντα λύτρον
λαβοῦσα παρ̣' αὐτοῦ
✳ σν'.

I. When Verus was the strategos for the second time, Zosimos, son of Pantheras, manumitted Philistos; 200 drachmai.

II. When Iulius, son of Hermeios, was the strategos, Pantauchos and Teres, sons of Stachys, manumitted Lykos *xenikei*;[4] 200 drachmai.

III. When [-----], daughter of Appius, manumitted Trophimos, as belonging to no one, after taking from him as *lytron* 250 drachmai.

The sums of 200 (σ') drachmai or denarii, recorded in lines 5 and 8, and of 250 (σν') in line 15, undoubtedly refer to the price paid by the manumitted slaves to their ex-owners for their freedom rather than to some tax paid to the polis. This is made explicit in lines 13–15, where the payment of 250 drachmai is described as *lytron*. In another manumission inscription from Demetrias, *IG* IX(2) 1117c, the slave paid 300 denarii as lytron.[5]

But two other inscriptions from the second or third century AD mention a tax collector (*SEG* 37.450, line 18; *SEG* 37.451, line 20) and a "tax relating to manumission" (*SEG* 37.450, line 23). These inscriptions, part of a group of manumission records inscribed on reused blocks from a Hellenistic equestrian statue group, were first edited by Christian Habicht.[6] No. 13 of Habicht's edition (= *SEG* 37.450), which contains six manumission acts under four different *strategoi*, i.e. acts made in four different years (and engraved by different hands),[7] includes no payment formula in the form we see in the Thessalian inscriptions. But in the section that records the manumission of Nikeson (lines 15–18) we read:

[σ]τρ(ατηγοῦντος) Νεικίου τοῦ Πολυδώ-
[ρ]ου Μένανδρος Παρμε-
νίσκου ἠλευθέρωσεν Νεικη-
σῶν τελωνοῦντος Βίωνος.

---

[4] For the *xenikei* manumissions see Chapter 2 and n. 61 above.

[5] On the *lytron* as the ransom money see Bielman 1989, and Chapter 2 above. In *IG* IX(2) 1100b, line 12, the word *lytron* (the sum paid has not been preserved) is mentioned as paid to the polis; see below.

[6] Habicht 1987, 277–292, nos. 1–22.

[7] Lines 10–14 record the manumission of two slaves by the same female owner.

When Nikias, son of Polydoros, was the *strategos*, Menandros, son of Parmeniskos, manumitted Nikeso, when Bion served as the tax collector.

The next and last manumission on the stone, performed under another *strategos* (hence another year) is formulated differently from the previous entries (lines 19–24):

[σ]τρατηγοῦτος Κρείτωνος
τοῦ Κρείτωνος ἠλευθέρω-
σε Ἀνδρομάχα Τύχην *vv*
τὴν ἑαυτ(ῆ)ς οἰκετίδα καὶ ἔδ-
ωκε τὸ ἐλευθερικὸν τέλες
Πολυξένῳ Εὐβιότου. *vacat*

When Kriton, son of Kriton, was the *strategos*, Andromacha manumitted Tyche, her own housemaid, and paid the tax related to manumission (*eleutherikon telos*) to Polyxenos, son of Eubiotos.[8]

No. 14 of Habicht's edition (= *SEG* 37.451) records five manumission acts under four different *strategoi*. The fourth act, which records the manumission of the female slave Hermione, was done in the year of the *strategos* Nikias son of Polydoros, the same *strategos* mentioned in no. 13, lines 15–19, and by the same manumittor. Not surprisingly perhaps, this record too mentions the tax collector Bion (line 17–21):

στρ(ατηγοῦντος) Νεικίου τοῦ Πολυδώ-
ρου Μένανδρος Παρμενί[σ]-
κου ἠλευθέρωσεν Ἑρμ[ι]-
όνην τελωνοῦντος Βίω-
νος. *Vacat*

When Nikias, son of Polydoros, was the *strategos*, Menandros, son of Parmeniskos, manumitted Hermione, when Bion served as the tax collector.

Since the last manumission record in no. 14 was also made in the year of the *strategos* Nikias, Bion might have been mentioned there too, but the text breaks off here. These three manumissions then—no. 13, lines 15–19 and no. 14, lines 17–21, 22–26—were done in the same year.

In contrast to the manumission inscriptions issued in cities of the Thessalian League, where the payment (when mentioned) was made "to the polis", to the treasurer, or to the *xenodokos*, here a tax collector is alluded to

8 The grammatical construction of the sentence (two finite verbs with one subject) makes it most likely that the manumittor paid the tax, not the manumitted slave. For the dialectical form τέλες (instead of τέλος), see Habicht 1987, 286.

explicitly. The absence of any extant mention of tax collectors in the context of manumission in the cities of the Thessalian League is not, of course, proof that they were not employed there to collect the money paid by freed slaves. The treasurer or the *xenodokos* may well have been responsible for receiving from tax collectors the money due for registering and publishing the manumissions. But the specific mention of the word "tax" (τέλες) in no. 13, line 23, and the likelihood that it was the manumittor who paid the money (whereas in the inscriptions from the Thessalian League the manumitted slaves apparently paid) seem to confirm Habicht's conclusion that this was a manumission tax, established by law and farmed out by the polis to tax collectors.[9] We know from these two inscriptions that Bion was the collector of this tax in the year of the *strategos* Nikias son of Polydoros. Polyxenos son of Eubiotos, mentioned in no. 13, line 24, as the person to whom the "tax relating to manumission" (τὸ ἐλευθερικὸν τέλες) was paid, may well have been the tax collector in the year of the *strategos* Kriton son of Kriton, by whom this act of manumission is dated.

Habicht supports his interpretation that these cases refer to a statutory manumission tax by citing another inscription from Demetrias, *IG* IX(2) 1100b III, of unknown date.[10] Lines 10–13 of the inscription, very poorly preserved, allude to the laws of the Magnesian League which apparently governed the manumission procedure, and to what seems to be a payment made to the polis (lines 9–13):

> [ἐπὶ στρατηγοῦντος τοῦ δεῖνα] μη(νὸς) Δημητριῶνος
> [– – – – – – – – – – – – – –]ιαιος ἀπηλευθε-
> [ρώθη – – – – – – – – – –κατὰ τοὺς Μαγ]νήτων νόμους
> [– – – – – – – – – – – – – – – – –ὑπὲρ] αὐτοῦ λύτρον τῆ
> [πόλει? – – – – – – – – – – – – – – –] ṃηθὲν ἐπιζητησ[---].
>
> [---]iaios manumitted by [--- according to the Mag]nesian laws [--- for] him *lytron* to the [polis? ---] nor demand [---].

This makes it plausible that the Magnesian League legislated laws which regulated the manumission procedure and established a payment for it. But the payment is here described as *lytron* (line 12), a word that usually denotes payment to the manumittor in exchange for freedom, as Habicht himself recognizes; moreover, the word "polis" in line 13—supposedly the recipient of the money—is a restoration by the editor, and it seems hardly likely that

[9] Habicht 1987, 287.
[10] Ib. and n. 43.

the *lytron* was paid to the polis.[11] In any case, the *lytron* cannot explain the mention of tax and tax collector.

Habicht suggests that in inscriptions nos. 13–22 (= *SEG* 37.450–459) the manumissions were registered over a span of ca. thirty years, are all post-Trajanic, and date to the second or third century AD. However, the exact time of these thirty years is not clear. Sekoundos son of Menandros, mentioned in *SEG* 25.680, lines 8–10, might be the father of Timasitheos, son of Sekoundos, the manumittor in Habicht's no. 16, lines 19–20 (= *SEG* 37.453), or of Philemon, son of Sekoundos, the *strategos* in no. 20, lines 22–23 (= *SEG* 37.457); if so, these inscriptions would date to ca. AD 200–250. Habicht indeed suggests that they do belong to the first half of the third century AD, "from the late Severans to about the time of Philip the Arab (AD 244–249)".[12]

If Habicht's suggested dates are correct, these texts may have been inscribed after the *Constitutio Antoniniana* was issued by the Roman emperor Caracalla in AD 212. This edict made all free inhabitants of the Roman empire citizens, therefore subject to the taxes imposed on citizens.[13] As mentioned above, a five-percent tax (the *vicesima manumissionum*, or *libertatis*) was exacted in Rome in all cases of manumission from 357 BC. In fact, Caracalla re-imposed this tax and raised it to ten percent, although shortly afterwards it was lowered by Macrinus back to five percent.[14] Caracalla's edict would have made the citizens of Demetrias, like those of other poleis, Roman citizens; hence when manumitting their slaves they would have had to pay the *vicesima libertatis*. I suggest therefore that the *eleutherikon teles* and the tax collector mentioned in the inscriptions from Demetrias may well have referred to this Roman tax. Grammatical considerations may also support my suggestion: the tax collector Bion is twice referred to in the absolute genitive construction (τελωνοῦντος Βίωνος, "when Bion served as the tax collector"), as was the custom with eponymous magistrates (e.g. στρατηγοῦντος, to refer to the eponymous *strategos*, both in the Magnesian and the Thessalian Leagues, and ταμιεύοντος, to refer to the treasurer in the latter). But

---

11 Habicht 1987, 287. But see below on Gortyn, where—according to Magnelli 1998—the price of freedom too was paid to the polis, or at least was regulated by it.

12 Habicht 1987, 288–291. The quotation is from p. 291.

13 On the nature of this edict and its effects see Sherwin-White 1973, 380–394.

14 See Cassius Dio 78.9.4–5 (Xiphilinus), who explicitly connects the edict which conferred Roman citizenship on all free inhabitants of the empire to the new taxation, explaining that Caracalla wished to increase his revenues. Whether these allegations have any truth in them need not concern us here. See Vigié 1881, 3; Sherwin-White 1973, 281 (who, however, refers only to the inheritance tax); Bradley 1984a, 105; 1984b, 176.

nowhere in other Greek texts, literary or epigraphic, do we find this construction used with tax collectors.[15] This may mean that the tax collector in second- and third-century AD Demetrias had some official function; furthermore, the absence of any mention in these two inscriptions of the treasurer (*tamias*), in contrast to the Thessalian manumission inscriptions discussed above, may imply that here we indeed are dealing with a manumission tax, collected by officials who were specially appointed to this task and paid to the imperial *fiscus*, and not with a fee paid directly to the treasury of the polis for the registration of the manumission act. The use of the absolute genitive construction may also have been influenced by the Roman practice of farming out the collection of taxes in specific provinces and regions to individuals who were identified in inscriptions by the tax they collected.[16] So although we lack clear-cut proof and do not know how much was paid, the payment recorded in Demetrias in the context of manumission may well have been the Roman manumission tax.[17]

---

[15] In Thrace, ca. 425–400 BC, a dedication to Aphrodite was made by Zenokles and his [συ]ṇτελῶναι ("fellow tax collectors") (*I.Thrace.Aeg.* 401 = *SEG* 48.904), but this may simply mean that the tax collectors formed a *collegium*, not that they were named as such in formal documents. Elsewhere in epigraphic sources the title *telones* is recorded only in funerary inscriptions of the Roman era (e.g. *SEG* 7.591); it is frequently used in literary sources but never as an eponymous term.

[16] See e.g. *CIL* II^2/5, 1322 (= *SDHI* 49 (1983), 400–403; *AE* 1984, 511; *AE* 1993, 1003a–b; *AE* 1996, 881) and the funerary inscriptions *CIL* VI 38003 (*act*(*ori*) *vic*(*esimae*?)); X 3875 (*soc*(*iorum*) *vices*(*imae*) *liber*(*tatis*)), for collectors of the *vicesima*. See Bradley 1984a, 150; 1984b, 177; Brunt 1990, 373, 402–403. The contractors of the *vicesima* are sometimes also called *vicesimarii* (Petr. *Sat.* 65; *CIL* III 13798) or εἰκοστῶναι (e.g. Epict. 4.1.33). See also *IEphesos* 517 (reign of Trajan), where Crispinus' title as a *promagister* in his fourth year as the contractor of the *portoria* and in his third year as the contractor of the *vicesima libertatis* is rendered in the Greek version of the inscription as ἀρχώνης τεσ[σα]/ρακοστῆς λιμένων Ἀσίας [δ'] / καὶ εἰκοστῆς ἐλευθεριῶν γ', lines 15–17; cf. Brunt 1990, 391 and n. 125, who argues that the use of the Greek ἀρχώνης in another case, that of C. Vibius Salutaris (*ILS* 7193), refutes the view that the man was acting in an official capacity. The Greek term ἀρχώνης is used in fifth-century BC Athens by Andocides (1.133) to describe Agyrrhios as the chief contractor for the two percent customs duties levied on all goods imported and exported in the Piraeus. See also Eck 1999, 120–130, on the collection of the *vicesima libertatis* in Italy. My suggestion may still hold even though the second tax collector in our inscriptions from Demetrias is mentioned only by his name as the recipient of the tax (ἔδ/ωκε τὸ ἐλευθερικὸν τέλεˢ / Πολυξένῳ Εὐβιότου: Habicht 1987, no. 13, lines 22–24 = *SEG* 37.450); although the sentence is constructed differently, the mention of the *eleutherikon teles* makes it very likely that Polyxenos' position was identical to Bion's. For evidence of the *vicesima* and its collectors see also Vigié 1881, 9–13.

[17] See, however, van Minnen and Worp 2009, 21 and n. 18, who tend to accept Pflum's dating of the introduction of *procuratores* for the collection of the *vicesima libertatis*—mentioned also in the Latin manumission tax tablet they publish—under Septimius Severus (AD 193–211). Whether this is correct or whether *procuratores* were introduced earlier (see

Why other acts of manumission in these inscriptions do not mention the tax and the tax collector is of course open to discussion. This 'silence' may be accidental, i.e. the manumittors or the authorities responsible for inscribing the manumissions did not find it necessary to note the payment in each and every case. Or the reason may be that the manumissions inscribed do not follow a successive chronological order; the same *strategoi* appear in different inscriptions, preceded and followed by other *strategoi*. Thus the *strategos* named in no. 14, lines 9–10, Sopatros son of Sosipatros, is followed by Onesimos son of Onesimos, but in no. 16 Sopatros (lines 1–3) is followed by Simas[?] son of Agathokles (who may be the Agathokles son of Demetrios mentioned in no. 14, lines 2–3); and the last *strategos* featuring in no. 16—Aristokles son of Eumenes (lines 18–19)—is the same *strategos* mentioned in the manumissions recorded in no. 13, lines 1–3 and 6–7. The *strategos* Hegesias son of Diokles appears in two manumission acts in no. 17 (= *SEG* 37.454), c: lines 8–9 and e: 17–18,[18] interrupted by a record made in the year of another *strategos*, Aristonikos son of Aristonikos. So in the years of the *strategoi* Nikias son of Polydoros (no. 13, lines 15–18, and no. 14, lines 17–21) and Kriton son of Kriton (no. 13, lines 19–24), where the *eleutherikon teles* and the tax collector are mentioned, the tax on manumission might have been first(?) introduced in Demetrias—possibly after AD 212. We may perhaps similarly explain the absence of any mention of the *vicesima* in manumission documents postdating AD 212 from other places, such as the many acts of consecration of slaves to the Mother of Gods in Leukopetra in Macedonia. The concise inscriptions from Leukopetra record only the act of consecration, its principals, and any conditions attached to the manumission. If a tax was exacted in these cases (which is not certain, given the ambiguous nature of the act of consecration), the dedicators presumably did not find it necessary to mention its payment in the inscribed document.[19]

Bradley 1984a, 150; 1984b, 178; Brunt 1990, 404) might undermine my assumption, since the use of τελωνοῦντος in our inscriptions seems to indicate a τελώνης, tax farmer, not a *procurator*—which in Greek perhaps would have been rendered ἐπιμελητής; see Chapter 3 above. But see Brunt 1990, 404, who argues that the functions of the *procuratores*, who are also attested for the *vicesima* in first-century AD Italy, could have been only supervisory. See also Luzzato 1984, 708.

18 Habicht notes that these two documents were engraved by the same hand.

19 See Frank 1959, 456, who notes, on the basis of manumission documents from Delphi and Thessaly, that the Roman *vicesima libertatis* might *not* have extended to all parts of the empire, at least initially, and that free states and leagues were possibly permitted to retain their own systems of manumission without paying any tax to Rome. This would explain why the *vicesima libertatis* is hardly ever attested in manumission acts from Greece before AD 212

In Chaironeia, an inscription, already mentioned above (*IG* VII 3303, late third/early second century BC), records an act of manumission by way of consecration of a slave-woman to the god Sarapis:

> Καλλίκωνος ἀρχῶ, μεινὸς Δαματρίω πεντεκηδεκάτη,
> Πούριππος Προξένω ἀντίθειτι ἱαρὰν τὰν ϝιδίαν θεράπη-
> γ̣αν Ἀφροδιτίαν τῦ Σαράπι, παραμείνασαν ἀσαυτῦ κὴ τῆ γου-
> [νη]κ̣ὶ αὐτῶ {Γ} Ἀγα{Ι}θείν̣⟨η⟩ {[26]Ἀγαθείνη}[26]ἇς κα ζώωνθι, τὰν ἀνάθεσιν ποϊόμε-
> [νο]ς διὰ τῶ σουνεδρίω κὰτ τὸν νόμον, κὴ κατέβαλε τῦ ταμίη
> [τῦ] ἐπὶ τῶν ἱαρῶν τὸ γινιούμενον δραχμὰς ϝίκατι παραχρεῖμα.
>
> When Kallikon was the archon, on the fifteenth day of the month of Damatrios, Pourippos, son of Proxenos, dedicates as sacred his own maid Aphroditia to Sarapis, on the condition that she stay with him and his wife Agathina as long as they live, having made the consecration through the Council according to the law, and paid the treasurer of the sacred finances the due twenty drachmai right away.[20]

The construction of the sentence seems to imply that the manumittor paid the money.[21] Darmezin believes that the payment was made *prior* to the manumission itself and before the end of the *paramone*, to which the consecrated slave was obligated, and that this may be why the owner paid and not the slave (who would reimburse him later). Yet when the payment is made at the end of a *paramone*, as in *IG* VII 3354 (= Darmezin, 1999, no. 61), it is the slave who pays (though the price is not specified).[22] Darmezin suggests that

---

(but see Chapter 3 on Athens), but not why the *vicesima* does not appear in the consecration manumissions in Leukopetra. For an edition of the inscriptions commemorating the consecrations of slaves in Leukopetra, with a good introduction and commentaries, see Petsas et al. 2000. Meyer 2002, 139, suggests that the ruling (ἀπόφασις) of M. Ulpius Tertullianus Aquila, governor of Macedonia in AD 213, settled the status of consecrated slaves there. See, however, Ricl 2001, who argues that Tertullianus' *apophasis* simply imposed the obligation to display for 30 days the details of the consecration and the documents proving the dedicator's legal ownership of the slave. On the manumissions of Leukopetra and the ruling of Tertullianus see also Harper 2011, 369–378, who suggests that the *apophasis* concerned a dispute about *paramone* obligations; the Romanization of the place is evident from the Roman names of the manumittors and priests, but the immediate effect of Caracalla's decree is apparent from the fact that nineteen inscriptions mention Tertullianus with reference to his *apophasis*. The *vicesima libertatis*, as well as the *vicesima hereditatis*, may have been cancelled by Diocletian; see Vigié 1881, 2–4.

[20] The 'treasurer of the sacred finances' was an office well known in Boiotia, but in *IG* VII 3354 (= Darmezin 1999, no. 61, see below) the money was paid to "the treasurer of the people" (as restored by Dittenberger), for which office there is no other testimony.

[21] See Darmezin 1999, 38, no. 18; contra Calderini 1965, 141–142.

[22] Lines 8–9 of this inscription read κατέβαλεν [τὸ τῷ ταμίᾳ τοῦ δή]/μου γινόμενον ("paid to the treasurer of the people the due money").

perhaps another tax was paid at the end of the *paramone* by the manumitted slaves. But it seems more likely that the concise language of the inscriptions and an error of the stonecutter are to blame for this ambiguity.

Another inscription from Chaironeia, of mid- or late-second century BC (*IG* VII 3406), where the identity of the person who pays is again ambiguous, mentions a higher sum—twenty-five staters, and five other inscriptions have a similar formula but do not state the sum paid.[23] Darmezin would date no. 3406 at least half a century later than no. 3303; possibly the price had risen over time from twenty drachmai to twenty-five staters. Rensch, on the other hand, takes the difference in prices to mean that this was a manumission tax which, similarly to the Roman, was proportional to the slave's market value.[24] Since all the manumission inscriptions in Chaironeia which mention payment to the treasurer were inscribed roughly between the late third and early second century BC, and appear only in manumissions through consecration, authorized by the Council, such payment was presumably introduced by the polis of Chaironeia in the late third century, at least in manumissions by consecration.

Calderini, followed by Rensch, interpreted this payment as a tax on manumission, similar to the Roman *vicesima manumissionum*, whereas Darmezin considers it "une taxe d'enregistrement".[25] But it is not clear why the payment—however we understand it—is mentioned in only seven of these inscriptions. Darmezin believes, despite the scant evidence, that all manumitted slaves were subject to this levy, which may be why it was not considered necessary to mention it in most cases. She considers the inscriptions that do mention it exceptional: these were the cases, she argues, where the tax was paid by the master at the time of the manumission because the slave—bound by *paramone* obligations—was not yet free therefore not legally capable of transacting in his own person. I am not convinced that it

---

23 See Darmezin 1999, 32, no. 18 on *IG* 3303, and 63, no. 87, where she restores the last line of *IG* 3406 to match that of *IG* VII 3303, so that the price is given in drachmai and paid to the treasurer of the sacred finances (AỊ[– – – – – – ἀνατίθησι τὴν ἰδίαν δούλην, ᾗ ὄνομα] / Ἑρμαί[α, ἱερὰν τῷ Σεράπιδι· τὴν ἀνάθεσιν ποιούμενος] / διὰ τοῦ σ[υνεδρίου κατὰ τὸν νόμον καὶ κατέβαλε τὸ γινόμενον παραχρῆ]/μα, εἴκοσι πέν[τε δραχμὰς τῷ ταμίᾳ τῷ ἐπὶ τῶν ἱαρῶν]). In *IG* VII 3307, which Darmezin 1999, 33, no. 21, dates to the late third/early second century BC, the same formula is restored, but the sum has not survived (lines 5–6: κατέβαλε] / [δὲ τὸ] γενόμενο[ν τῦ ταμίη τῦ ἐπὶ τῶν ἱαρῶν]). Cf. *IG* VII 3339 (= Darmezin 1999, 46, no. 47, who suggests restoring the sum of twenty drachmai); 3344 (= Darmezin 1999, 45, no. 52); 3354 (= Darmezin 1999, 51, no. 61); 3398 (= Darmezin 1999, 62, no. 85).

24 Rensch 1908, 95.

25 Calderini 1965, 141–142; Rensch 1908, 94–95; Darmezin 1999, 236–238.

was necessary to state that the manumittor paid the fee in such cases; the numerous Delphic sale-manumissions attest that legal fictions were common. But it does seem likely that all slaves manumitted in Chaironeia by consecration and with the authorization of the Council had to pay the registration or publication fee.

Is this fee comparable to the sums paid in Thessaly? According to Roberts and Head, between 244 and 197 BC the standard of the silver drachma of Boiotia was the Aitolian (weighing about 80 grains = 5.184 grs.); between 197 and 146, owing to financial problems, they suggest, the federal Boiotian state started issuing bronze drachmai (δραχμὴ χαλκοῦ) and made them legally equal to silver drachmai.[26] The Thessalian local drachma after 196 BC weighed about 80 grains.[27] Hence the Boiotian drachma, at least in the first half of the second century BC, was of similar value to the Thessalian; therefore manumitted slaves in Thessaly paid a little higher than in Chaironeia, either as a tax on manumission or to publicize their new status.

If no firm conclusion can be drawn as to whether the payments mentioned in the inscriptions of Chaironeia were a manumission tax or a publication fee, a first-century BC inscription from Orchomenos in Arcadia, *IG* V(2) 345 (= Reinach, *BCH* 28, 1904, 5–19; *IJG* II, 309, no. 43; 76/5 BC) is unequivocal.[28] The inscription records two manumission acts performed by private owners; each is preceded by the resolution of the archons and the Council of Orchomenos to inscribe the manumission document (*apeleutherosis*) on the altar of Aphrodite, since the manumitted slave had paid the Council (in the first act, the secretary of the Council) the money due for his manumission. In the first document the sum paid is half a mina (lines 1–5):

> I. [ἐπειδὴ – – – – – – –]έος Ὀρχομενῶι κατοικῶν εἰς τὸν γραμματῆ τῶν συνέ-
> [δρων κατέβαλε ἐ]κ τᾶς ἀπελευθερώσιος ἀργυρίου ἡμίμναιον κατὰ τὸν νόμον,
> [ἔδοξε τοῖς ἄρχου]σι καὶ συνέδροις δαμιοργοὺς τοὺς τὸ ἑβδομηκο-
> [στὸν ἄρχοντας γρά]ψαι τὰν Σωσικλέος ἀπελευθέρωσιν εἰς τὸν βωμὸν
> [τᾶς Ἀφροδίτας. *vacat*]

---

[26] Roberts and Head 1974, 86.

[27] See Gardner 1963, xxi. This standard, as noted in the Introduction above, was used for internal needs, along with the Attic standard which served foreign trade purposes.

[28] Hiller's reading in *IG* V(2) 345 differs from that of Reinach, who rightly discerns two manumission acts (as against the three argued by Hiller). Reinach dated the inscription to 164/3, supposing that the "seventieth year" refers back to the date when Orchomenos entered the Achaian League (ca. 234 BC); here I follow Grandjean, *BCH* 119 (1995), 14, in dating the inscription to 76/5 BC. See also the discussion of this inscription by Rädle 1969, 114–123.

> Since [---], who resides in Orchomenos, paid the secretary of the Councillors, on account of his manumission, half a silver mina according to the law, it was decided by the archons and the Councillors that the δαμιουργοί (*damiourgoi*) of the seventieth year shall inscribe the manumission of Sosikles on the altar of Aphrodite.

In the second document the sum paid is eight staters and nine obols (lines 15–18):

> II. ἐπεὶ Ἀντίγονος κατέβαλε ἐν τῶι συνε-
> [δρίωι τᾶς ἀπελευθε]ρώσιος τὸ ἐκ τοῦ νόμου στατῆρας ὀκτὼ ἐννέ'
> [ὀβολούς, γράψαι αὐ]τοῦ τὰν ἀπελευθέρωσιν εἰς τὸν βωμὸν τᾶς
> [Ἀφροδίτας εἰς τὸ βάθρ]ον.
>
> Since Antigonos paid the Council the eight staters and nine obols, due according to the law, on the occasion of his manumission, (it was decided) to inscribe his manumission on the base of Aphrodite's altar.

In both cases the payment to the Council is explicitly distinguished from the money paid to the manumittors as the price of freedom (lines 7, 22) and is described as made "on account of manumission, according to the law". In these two cases at least, the manumitted slaves in Orchomenos seem to have paid the Council for the right to have their manumission documents inscribed in public.[29] In the first document the manumitted slave paid half a mina (= 35 drachmai, in the Aeginetan standard); in the second the sum is eight staters and nine obols. Rädle explains the different prices paid for publication by age difference: he believes that the second manumitted slave was a child, probably because he is described in the inscription as παιδίον (*paidion*), "little boy" (line 20), who thus paid only half the sum imposed on the first manumitted slave.[30] This interpretation is plausible, but two points must be considered: first, the word *paidion* is a restoration, and second, the word was frequently used for adult slaves too, as a demeaning appellation. Whether or not the second freed slave paid less because he was then a child, the sum he paid comes closer to the sums paid in Thessaly than does that registered in the first document.

There is no other explicit evidence of such payments in the extant inscriptions from Orchomenos, but in Mantinea in Arcadia an inscription dated to 102 BC–AD 16, which records the manumission of a slave-woman and her son according to the last will of the owner, mentions as one of the eponym

---

29 See Rädle 1969, 118–119; Zelnick-Abramovitz 2005a, 192, 200.

30 Rädle 1969, 160. But see above (Chapter 2) on the possible explanations for differences in the sums paid in Thessaly.

officials the δεκτήρ (*dekter*)—probably an official responsible for receiving and allocating revenues (*IG* V(2) 274 I [= *IJG* II, 305, no. 40 I]).[31] *IG* V(2) 274 II (103 BC–AD 15), which was inscribed on the same stone but seems to belong to the previous year,[32] does not mention the *dekter* but the inscription was most likely intended as a record of all manumissions proclaimed in the same year (and perhaps also in subsequent years), because although only one manumission act is recorded in this section it is preceded by the words οἱ ἀποκαρυχθέντες ἐλεύθεροι ("those proclaimed free", lines 20–21). Likewise, another fragmentary inscription from Mantinea (*IG* V(2) 342a, first to second century AD) probably recorded acts of manumission in chronological order, because in each year the names are arranged under the heading "Those proclaimed free", and it also mentions a treasurer (ταμίας, lines 6–7).[33] So although no payment is mentioned, the documents' form and phrasing suggest that in *IG* V(2) 274 II and 342a too, a fee was paid to the *dekter* or to the *tamias* for the proclamation and the publication of the manumission acts. Other manumission inscriptions from Mantinea (admittedly, very few have been discovered) may also have been inscribed only upon payment.[34]

In Ptolemaic Egypt also, as noted above, taxes were imposed on slave sales and the slave trade, and apparently also on manumissions. In the case of manumission, the evidence is not easy to interpret and several names

---

[31] See Hesychius, s.v. δεκτήρ: ἀποδοχεύς. The function of the *dekter* can perhaps be compared to that of the board of ἀποδέκται (*apodektai*) in Athens, who were responsible for receiving payments of various kinds and distributing them to the various magistracies (see *Ath. Pol.* 48.1–2). The editors of *IJG* II, 306, n. 1, do not commit themselves: "Il y avait probablement une taxe à payer pour chaque affranchissement". Rädle 1969, 113, 158, also calls it a tax, but believes it was also used for publication.

[32] The heading of *IG* V(2) 274 I names Apollonios as the eponymous priest of Poseidon who served in the forty-seventh year (lines 1–3, 5–7); in no. 274 II the priest is Gorgippos and the year is the forty-sixth (lines 16–19). This may be due to a mistake by the stonecutter, but also implies that he was copying from written documents (on tablets or papyri); see below the discussion on the Attic *phialai*-inscriptions and the act of inscribing documents in stone.

[33] Line 2 of *IG* V(2) 342a reads τ]ούτοις δὲ καὶ ἀποκεκαρ[ύκασι], "and also [to t]hose proclaim[ed]" (probably proclaimed free); lines 6–8 read [ἐπὶ ἱ]ερέος τῷ Ποσειδᾶνι Εὐτελίνου, τα/[μία] δὲ Διονυσοδώρου οἱ ἀποκαρυχθέ/[ντες ἀ]π̣ελεύθεροι, "when Eutelinos was the priest of Poseidon, and when Dionysodoros was the treasurer, those proclaimed free". Cf. Rädle 1969, 113.

[34] *IG* V(2) 275 from Mantinea is judged to be of a much later date (second to third century AD). The stone contains two manumissions, probably inscribed in successive years, in a way reminiscent of the Thessalian lists of manumissions or even the altar from Orchomenos; but no *dekter* or *tamias* is mentioned. Likewise, the manumission inscription *IG* V(2) 277 from Mantinea (after AD 130) mentions no financial magistrates, no payment, and no proclamation. In Mantinea in the fourth century BC a board, the σταλογράφοι, was in charge of inscribing steles (*SEG* 37.340, line 18).

of levies seem related to it. A ten-drachma tax, called ἀπαρχή (*aparche*), is attested in one papyrus from Antaioupolis, *P. UB Trier* 135-2 (+ Quenouille, 2002), of 132 BC. This is a manumission record of a six-year-old slave girl, consisting of a notarized manumission document and a bank receipt for payment of the *aparche*. A note attached specifies the date and venue of the public proclamation of the manumission by a herald. As Quenouille indicates, the *agoranomoi*, who are here responsible for drafting and authorizing the manumission, are already attested in *P. Hib.* I 29 (ca. 265 BC) as being in charge of the registration of slaves and the taxes paid for them, as well as drafting sale contracts. Quenouille interprets the *aparche* as a manumission tax, and because the slave's former owners paid it her interpretation may be correct.[35] If so, it is the earliest explicit evidence of manumission tax in Greek sources,[36] and a precursor to the Roman *vicesima libertatis*. Elsewhere however the term *aparche* is used to denote a tithe; but if this is the case here, the tithe may have been calculated on the basis of the price paid for the girl's freedom or of her market value, and this might support the assumption that the *aparche* in this document is a levy similar to the Roman *vicesima libertatis*. Quenouille indeed believes that here for the first time the word has a different meaning, namely a manumission tax. To sustain her interpretation she refers to *P. Tebt.* III 1, 811 (= *SB* I 4233, Crocodilopolis, 165 BC), a declaration to a contractor for the tax on sales, concerning a manumission, where she restores line 22, τεταγμένος τὰ[, to read τεταγμένος τὰ [καθήκοντα τέλη on the basis of *SB* I 463, line 22. But except for its restoration, the word *aparche* does not appear here.

As mentioned in Chapter 2, another tax, imposed *ad valorem* on all transfers of property, was the ἐγκύκλιον (*enkyklion*), which is also mentioned in manumission documents. However, evidence concerning this tax is quite limited and its rate is uncertain. There is in fact scant certain testimony—in only one papyrus from the Ptolemaic period—that *enkyklion* was the name of the tax on manumission; sometimes the general tag *telos* is given to this levy.[37] A levy on the proclamation of manumission by a herald is explicitly

35 Quenouille 2002, 87. However, the fact that the tax was paid by the manumittors may have been due to the young age of the manumitted girl.

36 Even in the earlier consecration inscriptions from Chaironeia, as we have seen, it is not at all easy to understand the payments as manumission tax.

37 On the rate of the *enkyklion* see Chapter 1 and n. 48 above. In the context of manumission, the *enkyklion* is first mentioned in *P. Tebt.* III 1, 811 (= *SB* I 4233, Tebtynis, 165 BC), line 12, and is still attested in the Roman period: *P. Turner* 19 (*BL* X, p. 278) (Oxyrhynchos, AD 101), which confirms that the *enkyklion* was paid to the tax farmers before the latter ordered the

attested as paid by the manumitted slave-woman in one papyrus—*P. Strasb.* III 135 (provenance unknown, AD 198–211), where lines 17–21 read τὸ̣ [τ]ῆς ἀνακη/ρύξεως τῆς̣ ἐλ[ευ]/θερώσ[ε]ως αὐτῆς / κηρυκ[ι]κὸν τέλος / πλήρη[ς] ("the herald-tax [paid] in full for the proclamation of her manumission"). This duty, however, may well have been levied regularly whenever manumissions were announced by a herald, for instance, in *P. UB Trier* 135-2, discussed above, where the note announcing the place of the manumission's proclamation also refers to a πράκτωρ (*praktor*), perhaps the πράκτωρ ξενικῶν (*praktor xenikon*), who may have been in charge of receiving the proclamation fees.[38] But we do not know the rate of this tax. In *P. Strasb.* III 135 an official specifically responsible for the collection of the proclamation fees is mentioned, there tagged the ἐπιτηρητὴς φόρου κηρυκίος.[39] So unlike the *aparche* and the *enkyklion*, which may have been taxes levied on the manumission act itself, the proclamation fee was clearly paid for publication of the freed slave's new status, but it does not seem to have been compulsory.

More puzzling is the fixed sum of ten drachmai attested in several manumission documents from Oxyrhynchos.[40] It is called [πρ]οπρατικόν (*pro-*

agoranomos by letter to execute the manumission; *P. Freib.* II 10 (= *SB* III 6293 = *Jur. Pap.* 7 [*BL* II 2, p. 60 and 123; VII, p. 190; VIII, p. 134]) (Ptolemaïs Euergetis, AD 196); *P. Turner* 26 (= *BL* VIII, p. 498) (Ptolemaïs Euergetis, AD 195–198). See also *P. Oxy.* XLV 3241 (Oxyrhynchos, AD 163), lines 5–6 (τὸ [τῆ]ς ἐλευθερώσεως αὐτῆς ἐνκυκλιαχ̣ὸν), where the editor suggests that the rate of this toll was ten percent (comparing the sum of 52 drachmai paid in this case [line 7] with the sums mentioned in other papyri) and was usually paid by the manumitted slave—not by the manumittor, as seems to be the case in this papyrus. If the *enkyklion* was a ten percent levy, might it be compared to the *aparche*? Another papyrus of the Ptolemaic period, *P. Hib.* I 29 (Hibeh, 265 BC), states at line 7 that the manumitted slave had to pay the τέλη, but the name and rate of this tax (or taxes) are not given. Cf. *P. Strasb.* II 122 (Arsinoïtes, AD 161–169), line 12, which refers to taxes relating to manumission (κα̣ὶ̣ τ[ῶ]ν τελῶν καὶ δα̣[πανῶν] πάντων τῆς ἐλευθερ[ώσ]ε̣ως [ὄ]ντων); again in *P. Tebt.* II 407 (Tebtynis, AD 199?), line 25: τέλη τῆς ἐλευθερώσεως. Straus 2009, 238, suggests that the τέλος τῆς ἐλευθερώσεως was the more specific name of the *enkyklion*. See *P. Strasb.* IV 238, lines 13–14 (AD 177 or 178), and *P. Oslo* III 129, line 9 (Antinoopolis, third century AD), where this tax is restored by the editors; but see Straus 1973a, 143. See also *P. Turner* 19, mentioned above, where both the term *enkyklion* (line 11) and the phrase τέλος τῆς προκειμένης ἐλευθερώσ[ε]ως (line 15) appear in the same context. On the *enkyklion* as a generic name of the tax on sales and transfers of property see Straus 2004, 72–77.

38 See Quenouille 2002, 90–91. A reference to the proclamation fee (as well as what might look like a tax on manumission, but see Straus 1973a, 143–144) is restored in *P. Stras.* IV 238, lines 13–14 (AD 177 or 178). Cf. *P. Oslo* III 129, line 9 (Antinoopolis, third century AD).

39 See Straus 1973a, 144, who adds that since in this case the manumitted slave herself pays the tax, it is possible that she decided on the proclamation.

40 See *P. Oxy.* I 48 (AD 86); 49 (AD 100); 50 (AD 99); XXXVIII 2843 (AD 86); XLV 3241 (AD 163).

pratikon) in *P. Oxy.* I 50, line 3 (AD 99), and προπ(ρατικοῦ) in XLV 3241, line 8 (AD 163), which—as noted above—also mentions the *enkyklion*. M.W. Haslam, who edited XLV 3241, suggests that this was "a charge for warranty against eviction": the state "undertook the liability for any eviction of the freedman from his freedom".[41] Yet in this papyrus the πρ]οπρατικοῦ of ten drachmai is distinct from the *enkyklion* (here set at 52 drachmai), so there seems to be no reason why the warranty against eviction (which in the context of manumission means the re-enslavement of the manumitted slave) should be paid separately; if it was now the state's duty, the tax on it (*enkyklion, telos eleutheroseos*, or any other) should have guaranteed it. Rather, the ten-drachma levy seems to have been for depositing copies of the manumission deeds in the state archives.[42]

Finally, the Roman tax of five percent, imposed on inheritances and manumissions (ἡ εἰκοστὴ τῶν κληρονομιῶν καὶ ἐλευθεριῶν = *vicesima libertatis/hereditatis*), is well attested in the Roman period, but it was imposed only on manumittors who were Roman citizens.[43]

Why were there several taxes on manumission? Von Reden argues that the large number of taxes in Ptolemaic Egypt is misleading since it includes the different names given to the same tax over the course of time or in different regions.[44] Collating the evidence, we may infer that the *tele apeleutheroseos*, mentioned in several papyri from the Roman period, was another name for the *enkyklion*—at least in Tebtynis.[45] But the evidence about levies on manumission in Egypt is mostly ambiguous, and unclear on whether these levies (apart from the Roman *vicesima*) were taxes on manumission or registration and publication fees. Since manumissions in Egypt were registered, we may safely assume that paying the levies ensured registration, hence formal acknowledgment. But the only levy that seems unquestionably linked to publication is the one imposed on proclamation.

An early second-century BC inscription from Gortyn (*IC* IV 235 = *SGDI* 5009a) records payment in the event of manumission:

---

41 Haslam 1976, 102.

42 See Zelnick-Abramovitz 2005a, 201.

43 See *P. Oxy.* XX 2265 (Oxyrhynchos, AD 119); *BGU* XIII 2244 (Alexandria, AD 186), lines 12–13; I 326 (= *Chr. Mitt.* 316 = *Sel. Pap.* I 85 = *FIRA* III 50 = *Jur. Pap.* 25; Arsinoïtes, AD 189/194). On this tax in Roman Egypt see also Eck 1977, 205–206; Brunt 1990, 403.

44 von Reden 2007, 86.

45 See *P. Tebt.* III 1, 811 (= *SB* I 4233, Tebtynis, 165 BC) and *P. Tebt.* II 407 (Tebtynis, AD 199?); and see Straus 2009, 238.

[ἐπ]ι̣ Ἀντιφάτα τῶ Κύδαντος
[.]αστῶι Σώσιος ἐλευθέρα ἀπο-
[λ]αγαθένσα κατέβαλε τᾶι πόλι
[ἀ]ργύ[ρια] τριάκοντα καὶ πέντε παρι-
[ό]ντο[ς τ]ῶ ἀπολαγάσαντος Ῥ̣ανί-
[ω] τ̣ῶ Δαμάριος α.[.].. ὁ ταμίας Ῥ̣ά-
ν̣ιος Σοάρχω φέρει τὸ ἀργύριον Καν-
ν̣ήιω τρίται δεκάται. πρόκορμος
[Β]αρυθένης Σαμαγόρα.

In the year of Antiphatas, son of Kydas, [---] of Sosis being set free paid the polis thirty-five silver drachmai in the presence of the manumittor Rhanios son of Damaris. [---] the treasurer Rhanios, son of Soarchos, receives the money on the thirteenth day of the month Kanneios. The Head-*kosmos*: Barythenes, son of Samagoras.

Lines 3–4 of the inscription mention payment of thirty-five (Aeginetan) silver drachmai by a manumitted slave to the polis. Lines 6–8 mention another money payment—twelve days after the manumission, and even a treasurer (ταμίας). This document, dated by the polis' eponymous magistrates, implies that the money paid was obligatory. The sum, thirty-five Aiginetan drachmai (i.e. half a mina), is the same as in the first manumission document in *IG* V(2) 345 from Orchomenos (see above). In another fragmentary inscription from Crete (Pyloros?), *IC* I xxv 4, of unknown date, a manumitted slave pays the polis in the presence of his manumittors (as in the previous example), but the sum has not been preserved:

[– – – – – – – – – – –]
[– – – – –]α̣θη[– – – –]
[– – –] ἐλεύθερος ἀπολα-
[γαθὲ]νς κατέβαλε τᾶι πό-
[λι παρ]ιόντων τῶν ἀπολα-
[γασάν]των Εὐρυτίδα τω.
[– – –] κὴχετίμας τᾶς γυν-
[αικός· Π]ανάρης Ἀριστοφόω ἀρ-
[γύριον φέρει – – – –]κ̣οκ...
[– – – – – – – – – – – – –]

[--------------] being set free, paid the polis in the presence of his manumittors Eurytidas, son of [---------------] and Echetima(?) his wife. Panares, son of Aristophoos, received the money [-----].

Despite the fragmentary condition of the inscription some elements similar to *IC* IV 235 are discernible: the two inscriptions are formulated in the same style and order, using the same words to denote manumission (ἀπολαγαίω + ἐλεύθερος / ἐλευθέρα); the payment is made to the polis, in the presence of the manumittor(s); the treasurer (or perhaps another official in the latter inscription) receives the money; in both cases the payment is in cash.

However, fees exacted in the event of manumission were not always paid, entirely or partly, in cash. A decree from Gortyn (*SEG* 48.1208; ed. pr. Magnelli, 1998),[46] dated to 150 BC, mentions payments in both cash and vessels. The decree seems to regulate the procedure of manumission in Gortyn and to establish the financial obligations of manumitted slaves. Although the inscription is badly mutilated and not easy to understand, it contains important information and merits broader discussion. The following is Magnelli's text:

[ἐπὶ] τῶν Αἰθαλέων κορμιόν[των τῶν] σὺν Ἀκρισίῳ τῶ Δορίω τάδ' ἔϜαδε [---------- πρὸ? τᾶς]
[Ἐλ]ευσινίας νεμονηΐας τᾶς [–ca. 6–]σας τὸ μὲν γιννόμενον τᾶι πόλι τᾶς λ[--------]
[ἐπ]ιτιθέτω δὲ ὁ ἀπολαγαθθὲς [τᾶς ἀ]πολαγάξιος καὶ τᾶς χρηματίξιος· αἰ [-----------]
[ca. 3]ς φιάλαν ἀ[ργ]υρίαν εὔκονσαν ᵛ ιε̣ ├̣ ἐ[ν ταῖ]δ δεκαδύο ἀφ' ἆς κ' ἀμέρας ἀπολαγα[θθῆι ---------]
[τᾶ]ι Ἥραι τᾶι [Κ]υδίσται ἐν τῶι Ϝοίκωι κα[τὰ τ]αὐτὰ καὶ παρι[στ]άτω ὁ ἀντιθένς τ[---------]
[ca. 3]. π̣εδ̣ὰ κ[όρ]μω γένηται ἐλεύθερος [ca. 4]ι μῆνα κ' ἀμέραν [ca. 3] τὸν ἀπολαγάσα[ντα ---------]
[ca. 3] ἀπολαγαθθῆι καὶ τὰν χρημάτιξιν [διὰ τ]ῶ χρεοφυλα[κίω]· αἰ δέ τις μὴ ἀνθ[είη --------- τὰν]
[χρ]ημάτιξιν· τὰ δ' ἄλλα ἦμεν τῶι τε ἀ[πολα]γάσαντι [καὶ] τῶι ἀπολαγαθθέ [ντι –]
[ὁ ἀπ]ολελαγασμένος ἐλεύθερος μὴ [------------]ΚΕΤ[--ca. 6--]ΟΜΕΝΟ[ca. 3] ΤΑΔ[----]
[ca. 3]ος πεδὰ τοῦτο τὸ ψάφισμα παρ[--------------]ΤΩ[------------------------------]
[---]Τ[---]

In the year of the *kosmoi* of the tribe Aithaleis, with their president Akrisios, son of Dorios, it thus pleased (the polis) [----] before the beginning of the month of Eleusinios the [----] the money due to the polis [----] let the manumitted slave pay for the manumission and for the deed(?). If [----] a silver *phiale* weighing fifteen and a half staters, within twelve days from the day he/she was manumitted, to Hera Kydista in her shrine and likewise let the dedicator[47] furnish [---] together with the *kosmos*, shall be free [----] a month and a day [---] the manumittor [---- since he/she?] was manumitted

[46] For an earlier publication of fragment b of this inscription see *IC* IV 232.

[47] This is a reasonable translation if we understand the word as a present active participle of ἀνατίθημι; but see below.

and the deed through the Archive of Public Debts. Should anyone fail to dedicate [----], the deed. The other (payments?) shall be the manumittor's and the manumitted slave's [---]. The freedman shall not [-----] according to the decree [----].

Manumitted slaves seem to be required to pay before the beginning of the month of Eleusinios (hence presumably in the first half of the year) what is due to the polis (τὸ ... γιννόμενον, line 2). The payments are made for the manumission itself and for what Magnelli believes to be its registration and publication (ἀ]πολαγάξιος καὶ [τ]ᾶς χρηματίξιος, line 3),[48] and—so Magnelli suggests—for the release from the *paramone* obligations (according to his suggested restoration of lines 2–3: τὸ μὲν γιννόμενον τᾶι πόλι τᾶς λ[ύσιος πραξξάντων]).[49] But in addition to these payments, the freed slave was also required to dedicate, within twelve days of his or her manumission, a silver φιάλη (*phiale*) to Hera Kydista (line 4), a duty which Magnelli compares to the Attic φιάλαι ἐξελευθερικαί (*phialai exeleutherikai*, see below).[50] The value of the *phiale* is read as ιε̣ ├̣, that is, fifteen and a half staters (= thirty-two Aiginetan drachmai). Magnelli argues that if we take the thirty-five drachmai mentioned in *IC* IV 235 as the regular price of freedom in Gortyn, the total cost of freedom (including the value of the *phiale*) would come close to one Aiginetan mina, or seventy drachmai.[51]

The slaves are required to make the dedication in the presence of the κόσμος (*kosmos*), which Magnelli likens to the *koinos xenodokos* who is often mentioned in the Thessalian manumission acts as present when the manumitted slaves made the payment to the polis or even as receiving the money,[52] and of another person, described as ὁ ἀντιθένς (line 5). The iden-

[48] Following Bile 1988, 229, Magnelli (1998, 101) translates the noun χρημάτιξις (*chrematixis*) as "financial transaction" and suggests that it had to do with the registration and the erection of the stele in a public place (p. 102); the noun ἀπολάγαξις, "manumission", is a *hapax*.

[49] Magnelli 1998, 101–102, suggests that λύσις corresponds to the Delphic ἀπόλυσις, release from *paramone*, and he sees this decree as a regulation of the means by which manumitted slaves could release themselves from the *paramone* by paying a fixed sum of money.

[50] Magnelli 1998, 103–105, refers to Westermann's view (1946) that the Attic *phialai*-lists were the result of fictive *apostasiou* trials, whereby freed slaves were released from all obligations to their former owners and paid the polis the fees for this release (*apolysis*) in the form of *phialai*. On the diverse interpretations of the Attic *phialai exeleutherikai* see below.

[51] Magnelli 1998, 104–105. But a second possibility, says Magnelli, is to read the number in line 4 as ρε' ├, in which case the *phiale* would weigh 105 drachmai, i.e. one mina and a half—a price which comes closer to that of the *phialai exeleutherikai* in Athens, each weighing 100 drachmai.

[52] Magnelli 1998, 107; cf. Calderini 1964, 154–156. Magnelli suggests that the *kosmos* men-

tity of the latter is difficult to determine. Magnelli notes that this participle can be derived from either of the verbs ἀνατίθημι ("to dedicate") and ἀντιτίθημι ("to put/pay in place of"), in the latter case as an aorist active participle. Associating the mention of this person in line 5 with lines 8–9 of the inscription, where it seems that the absence of this same person might have financial implications for the completion of the manumission act, Magnelli suggests understanding the participle as deriving from ἀντιτίθημι, arguing that this person is a guarantor who, should the slave fail to dedicate the *phiale*, will do so in his or her stead, or pay a fine—later to be reimbursed by the freed slave.[53] The proviso requiring the dedication of the *phiale* (lines 4–5), after which act the slave becomes free, is followed by two other provisos (lines 6–7) which presumably concern the obligations that the slave must fulfil for his manumission to be ratified, and do so within a month and a day—a time limit found in treaties between Cretan poleis in the Hellenistic period.[54] Magnelli suggests that within this period the manumitted slaves have to satisfy all the requirements for attaining full freedom: pay the manumittor the price of freedom, pay the polis the due fee, and dedicate the *phiale* (which, as noted above, had to be done within twelve days of the act of manumission).[55] This would also explain the succeeding phrase—τὰν χρημάτιξιν [διὰ τ]ῶ χρεοφυλα[κίω] (line 7), which Magnelli, on the basis of a similar proviso in a treaty between Lato and Olos (*IC* I xvi 4, lines 32–33), interprets as requiring any third party to provide guarantees for the payment by depositing securities in the Archive of Public Debts, the *chreophylakion*.[56] If such guarantees are not provided, the total expenses, suggests Magnelli, are to be partly paid by the former owner and partly divided between him and the freed slave.[57]

If Magnelli is right in his readings and interpretation, the polis of Gortyn, at least in the second century BC, was in greater control of the process of

---

tioned here is the κόσμος ξενίων (*kosmos xenion*), the official in charge of non-citizens in Crete. On the *koinos xenodokos* in the Thessalian manumission acts see Chapter 2 above.

53 Magnelli 1998, 108–109.

54 This time limit is chiefly found in connection with the institution of guarantors, the collection of fines, and the erection of steles containing the terms of the agreements. See examples in Magnelli 1998, 109 and n. 59.

55 Magnelli 1998, 109–110, also suggests that if the manumitted slave could not pay, he or she made use of a guarantor who undertook to give warranties directly to the ex-owner.

56 Magnelli 1998, 111, notes that the *chreophylakion* made possible financial transactions between citizens and non-citizens in the community, as it did between citizens of Gortyn and those of other poleis bound by treaties. On the *chreophylakion* in Cretan cities see also Chaniotis 1996, 122 and n. 746, and on *IC* I xvi 4 see pp. 321–325, no. 55.

57 Magnelli 1998, 111 and n. 66 bases this conclusion on his reading of lines 7–8.

manumission than is known in other places: it established by decree the payments for both the manumission—including, according to Magnelli, release from the *paramone*—and the registration and publication of the slave's new status, and topped this off with the dedication of a *phiale*. This is the only explicit evidence of such formal regulations pointing to the direct involvement of the state in what was a private transaction between owners and their slaves; in other places, including Thessaly, the fact that payments were made to the polis, through its officials (such as treasurers or the *xenodokoi*), is the only direct indication that these payments were regulated by the poleis—and there too, what seems to have been regulated is the payment to the polis, *not* the price of freedom paid by slaves to their manumittors. Phrases such as "according to the law(s)", "according to the laws of manumitted slaves", or "(name of manumitted slave) should not fall under the law(s) of manumitted slaves", present in inscriptions from Calymna and Thessaly, do not specify the provisions of these laws.[58] Moreover, nowhere—not even in other texts from Gortyn—is there evidence of compulsory *paramone* (such evidence could have explained why the polis demanded payment for the early termination of this obligation).[59] Furthermore, if Magnelli is right in saying that the decree also dictates payment to the manumittor of the price of freedom itself, this, as far as I know, is unprecedented.

In any event, the text as it stands makes it clear that money was to be paid to the polis; payment for the *chrematixis* seems to mean that the manumitted slave was required to pay the costs of registering and publicizing his or her new status. Also, in both Gortyn and Thessaly magistrates were involved in the payment procedure. We also have a single piece of evidence of a time limit in Thessaly (*AE*, 1917, 18, no. 312 from Chyretiai, 14–12 BC or shortly after).[60] Taken together, the three Cretan inscriptions that mention payment cannot prove that everywhere or always manumitted slaves in Crete paid the polis for registration of their manumission, but at least in second-century BC Gortyn such payment had to be made within twelve days of the deed (as both *IC* IV 235 and *SEG* 48.1208 attest), and at some

---

58 On laws pertaining to manumitted slaves see Zelnick-Abramovitz 2005a, 301–306.

59 It has been argued that the 'laws of manumitted slaves' in Calymna (Babacos 1964) and Thessaly (Babacos 1966, 79–88; Helly 1976) prescribed all the manumitted slaves' obligations to the city and to their manumittors—including the *paramone*. But there is no proof that the latter was compulsory in either of these places. It seems more reasonable that the laws merely regulated in a general way the freed slaves' protracted obligations to their ex-owners, without specifying them; see Zelnick-Abramovitz 2005a, 302–305.

60 For this inscription see Chapter 2.

time during this period an obligation to dedicate a *phiale* was added. The sum of money required in *SEG* 48.1208 has not been preserved; Magnelli, as mentioned, claims that it was the same as in *IC* IV 235, that is, thirty-five drachmai (= seventeen and a half staters). Both this sum and the value of the *phiale* (fifteen and a half staters = thirty-two drachmai) come very close to the amount paid by manumitted slaves in Thessaly (fifteen staters).

In fact, I am not convinced that the dedication of the *phiale* did not serve as the registration fee; the compulsory nature of the dedication and its uniform value are elements we find in manumission regulations in other places. In Kos a second-century BC decree (*Iscr. di Cos* ED 144 = PH 29; *LSCG* 160) regulates the sale of the priesthood of the goddesses Adrasteia and Nemesis, and lists the groups subject to obligatory sacrifices. Lines 4–9 of the inscription (according to the reading in *Iscr. di Cos* ED 144) specify the obligation of manumitted slaves to sacrifice to the goddesses:

> [ρεῖ· κατὰ ταὐτὰ δὲ] θυέτω καὶ τῶν ἐλευθε[ρουμένων ἕκαστος κατὰ]
> [τὰ γεγραμμέν]α̣, καὶ τοὶ ταμίαι ⟨τὰς⟩ {^{4}καὶ}^{4} δέλτο[υς μὴ διδόντω τοῖς ποι]-
> [ευμένοις τὰν ἀ]πελευθέρωσιν μηδὲ ποιεί[σθων τὰν ἀναγραφὰν]
> [τὰν δαμοσίαν τ]ᾶς ἀπολυτρώσιος αἴ κα μὴ ὁ ἱερ[εὺς ἐμφανίσηι τὰν]
> [τεταγμέναν θ]υσίαν ἐπιτετελέσθαι, ἢ ὀφειλό[ντω ἐπιτίμιον δραχ]-
> [μὰς – – – – – –] ἱερὰς Ἀδραστείας καὶ Νεμέσιο[ς.

> Likewise (i.e. like the other groups listed previously), let each one of the manumitted slaves sacrifice according to what has been ordered, and the treasurers may neither hand over the written tablets (*deltoi*) to those who performed the manumission nor make the public register (*anagrapha damosia*) of the payment for the manumission, unless the priest shows that the sacrifice demanded has been made; otherwise they will be liable to a fine of [...] drachmai.[61]

---

[61] PH 29 and *LSCG* 160 have slightly different readings. PH, lines 3–8: παραπλησίως δὲ θυέτω καὶ τῶν ἐλευθερουμένων ἕκαστος· ---- δὲ καὶ τοὶ ταμίαι καὶ δέλτον δόντω τοῖς ποιοῦσιν τὰν ἀπελευθέρωσιν, μηδὲ ποιεύντω τὰν ἀναγραφὰν τᾶς ἀπολυτρώσιος αἴ κα μὴ ὁ ἱερεὺς ἀπαγγείλη τὰν θυσίαν ἐπιτετελέσθαι ...; *LSCG*, lines 4–10: [κατὰ δὲ ταὐτὰ] θυέτω καὶ τῶν ἐλευθε[ρούμενων ὑπὸ κυρίων οἰκε]/[τᾶν ἕκαστος καὶ τοὶ ταμίαι καὶ δέλτους μὴ διδότω τοῖς ποιευ]/ [μένοις τὰν ἀ]πελευθέρωσιν μηδὲ ποιε[ίσθων τὰν ἀναγραφὰν τὰν] / [δαμοσίαν τᾶς ἀπολυτρώσιος, αἴ κα μὴ ὁ ἱερ[εὺς ἐμφανίσηι τὰν] / [τεταγμέναν θυσίαν ἐπιτετελέσθαι ἢ ὀφειλόντω ἐπιτιμι]/[ον δραχμὰς ἱερὰς Ἀδραστείας καὶ Νεμέσιος. So according to PH's reading, the treasurers are instructed to give the δέλτος (*deltos*), but not make the *anagrapha*—which does not make sense. I have translated τᾶς ἀπολυτρώσιος as "the payment for the manumission" because the use of *apolytrosis* in proximity to *apeleutherosis* in the same inscription seems to imply two different meanings; and since ἀπολύτρωσις (*apolytrosis*) usually means ransoming I believe that here it denotes the payment made to the manumittor for freedom, the registration of which will attest to the former slave's new status. On this inscription and the cult of Adrasteia and Nemesis see Farnell 1896, 488–500; Sherwin-White 1978, 173, 325, who suggests that these

The text makes it eminently clear that these sacrifices served as a kind of registration and publication fee: no official record of manumission—whether written on a tablet (*deltos*) or inscribed on stone (*anagrapha*)—could be issued without the manumitted slave first making the sacrifice.[62]

Another inscription from Kos, concerning the sale of the priesthood of Aphrodite Pandamos and Pontia (ed. pr. Parker and Obbink, 2000; ca. 125–100 BC), again specifies groups that must offer a sacrifice or pay money instead, in addition to an offering (or a tithe) paid to the treasurers.[63] Lines 25–27 (text and translation are those of Parker and Obbink) read:

> ἀπαρχέσθων δὲ καὶ τοὶ ἐλευθερούμενοι ἐν ὧι κα ἐνιαυτῷ ἐλευθερωθῶντι σὺν τῶι πρότερον καταβαλλομένωι δραχμὰς πέντε ποιούμενοι τὰν καταβολὰν ἐπὶ τὸς ταμίας·
>
> Those too who are being freed, in the year in which they are freed, shall make an offering, in addition to what is paid earlier, of five drachmai, making the payment to the treasurers.

Parker and Obbink liken the requirement of manumitted slaves to pay an offering as a registration fee to other imposts: religious—as in *Iscr. di Cos* ED 144 (discussed above) and in inscriptions from Macedonia (see below) and Athens; and 'civil'—as in the examples from Thessaly, Chaironeia, and other places discussed above.[64] As for these two Koan inscriptions indicating

---

goddesses presided over manumissions, perhaps because of their concern for the human fate. This notion has already been postulated by Calderini 1965, 106, who believed that the inscription refers to a form of sacral manumission; so also Sokolowski *LSCG* 281. Against this interpretation see Bömer 1960, 116–117. Parker and Obbink 2000, 442, argue that the goddesses were involved only as recipients of the fee. On the selling of priesthoods and obligatory sacrifices by certain groups in Kos see Rostovtzeff 1964, 241–242; Parker and Obbink 2000, 419–429; Wiemer 2003.

[62] *Deltoi* were used as master documents or copies of state documents and impending lawsuits, and were deposited in public archives. Laws: see e.g. *IG* XII(3) 330, lines 272–279, from Thera (ca. 210–195 BC), where an *epissophos* (a supervisor) is instructed to write down all the dictates of a law on a *deltos* and deposit it in the state archive; and *IG* XII(7) 515, lines 131–134, an honorary decree from Aigiale in Amorgos (end of second century BC), where the secretary is instructed to write the decision on *deltoi* and deposit them in the archive "where laws are written down", and the beneficiary, Kritolaos, is given permission to inscribe it on a stele and set it up where the monuments stand; it is noticeable that the same verb, *anagraphein*, is used for both writing on *deltoi* and inscribing on stone. Lawsuits: see e.g. *IG* V(2) 357, lines 32–33, from Stymphalos (second half of second century BC). On the word *deltos* and its uses see Wilhelm 1909, 244–245. On the *anagarapha* / *anagraphe* and its possible meanings see Chapter 3 n. 26 above.

[63] Cf. *SEG* 50.766. The inscription was found in 1903 by R. Herzog, who published lines 16–21 in *ARW* 10 (1907), 211, and lines 40–43 in his *Heilige Gesetze von Kos*, Berlin 1928, 50–51.

[64] Parker and Obbink 2000, 441–442. On the dedication of silver *phialai* in Athens in what until recently was universally assumed to be the context of manumission, see below. See also

different deities as recipients of the payment, the authors argue that "a registration fee retained elsewhere by the city was at Kos distributed to the benefit of a number of cults (more perhaps than the two we know)".[65]

Obligatory dedication of vessels to a deity by manumitted slaves is also attested in Beroia, in three inscriptions from the second to the first century BC. The inscriptions record the dedication by manumitted slaves to Herakles Kynagides of a silver cup (σκύφος) weighing 50 drachmai. For instance, *EKM* 1. *Beroia* 31 (second or first century BC) reads:

> Δημήτριος, Παρμονίδης, Εὐφράντα, Ζωίς, Παραμόνα,
> Ὀ̣νήσιμος, Ἐπίκτησις, Εὐφροσύνη, Ἀφροδεισία, Βεῖθυς,
> Ἀθηναΐς, ἀπελευθερωθέντες ὑπὸ Κρίτωνος τοῦ Εὐτυχίδου
> Ἡρα ⟦.c.3.⟧ κλῆ {26Ἡρακλῆ}26 Κυναγίδαι σκύφον οὗ ὁλκὴ εἰς τὸ αὐτὸ
> δραχ(μαὶ) φν′.
>
> Demetrios, Parmonides, Euphranta, Zoïs, Paramona, Onesimos, Epiktesis, Euphrosyne, Aphrodisia, Bithys, Athenaïs, being manumitted by Kriton, son of Eutychides, (dedicated) to Herakles Kynagides a cup, whose total value is 550 drachmai.[66]

Another example is *EKM* 1. *Beroia* 32 (100–50 BC):

> Ἰταλία ἀπελευθερωθεῖσα ὑπὸ Νικά-
> νορος τοῦ Λυσιμάχου σκύφον οὗ ὁκλὴ
> δραχ(μαὶ) ν′. *vacat*
>
> Italia, being manumitted by Nikanor, son of Lysimachos, (dedicates) a cup of the value of fifty drachmai.

The editors of these inscriptions, Gounaropoulos and Hatzopoulos, argue that fifty drachmai was one tenth of the average value of a slave, hence a tithe paid on account of manumission.[67] The practice of dedicating a cup to Herakles Kynagides on the occasion of manumission predates Demetrios II, who in a letter sent in 248 BC to Harpalos, the *epistates* of Beroia, says (*EKM* 1. *Beroia* 3, lines 9–13):

> Δημήτριος Ἁρπάλωι χαίρειν· ο̣ἱ̣ [ἀπε]λευ[θ]ερο[ύ]-
> μενοι πρότερον φαίνονται φιάλ[ας ἀνατίθ]ε̣σ̣[θαι]
> εἰς τὸ ἱερόν· ἐπεὶ οὖν [ἔστιν] π̣ε̣[ριο]υσία εἰς τὴ̣[ν]
> χρείαν τὴν τοῦ θεοῦ ἀνατιθέτ̣ωσαν ἀντὶ
> τ̣ῶν φιαλῶν κ̣έρατα [κ]α̣ὶ σ̣κ̣ύφους· ἔρρωσο.

Wiemer 2003, 295–296, who argues that since the manumitted slaves are obligated to sacrifice to Adrasteia and Nemesis, and also to pay a tithe of five drachmai to Aphrodite Pandamos, they had no exclusive link as a group to either of these goddesses.

65 Parker and Obbink 2000, 442.

66 That is, 11 times 50 drachmai—the number of slaves manumitted.

67 See *EKM* 1. *Beroia*, p. 135. For another example see no. 33, and cf. *SEG* 46.731, Ia.

> Demetrios to Harpalos, greetings. It seems that the manumitted slaves used formerly to dedicate *phialai* (bowls) in the sanctuary (of Herakles Kynagides). Since there are now too many for the god's use, let them dedicate instead of *phialai* drinking-horns and cups.[68]

The same practice is most likely documented in another inscription of unknown date from the city of Elimeia in Macedonia (*EAM* 30):

> 1 Θευδᾶς Νειχ̣ά̣[νο]ρ̣ο̣[ς]
> ἀπελεύθ̣ερος Ἡρα-
> κλεῖ φιαλί[σ]κ̣ον.
>
> Theudas, the manumitted slave of Nikator, to Herakles a small bowl (*phialiskon*).[69]

A similar practice may also lie behind the inscriptions found on seats of the theatre in Epidauros, dated to the third century BC. Most of these seats bear a simple formula: "(name of manumitted slave) of (name of manumittor)". Bömer interprets these inscriptions as indicating the slaves' commitment to subsidize the stone seats to mark their manumission.[70]

Many scholars who discuss the payments, sacrifices, and dedications by manumitted slaves in the above cities interpret in the same context the Attic inscriptions which record the dedications of silver bowls, known as the *phialai exeleutherikai*, that is, the "*phialai* (bowls) of manumitted slaves".[71] The inscriptions list names of prosecutors and defendants as a legal formula, which with slight variations reads "X, living in (name of deme), having escaped (i.e. escaped conviction by) Y of (name of deme), a *phiale* weighing 100 drachmai".[72] Since the late nineteenth century it has been widely

68 Cf. *SEG* 43.379. See Ricl 2001, 146, who describes these manumissions as 'secular'.

69 The editors of *EAM* compare this practice to the Attic *phialai exeleutherikai*.

70 *IG* IV 1^2, 353–379; Bömer 1960, 63. Some inscriptions contain a dedication to Asklepios, which Bömer explains by noting that the theatre stood in the sanctuary of that god. For other manumission inscriptions in theatres see *IG* IX 1^2 2, 419 (Oiniadai, third century BC); *IG* XI(2) 106, line 14 (Delos, 282 BC—a single record of manumission in a list of *choregoi*); *IG* XII(3) 336 (Thera, second century BC). On manumissions in theatres see Rädle 1971; Mactoux 2008. Cf. *SEG* 35.696, 38.522–524 (Nikaia): dedication of λίθοι.

71 The name *phialai exeleutherikai*, found in two inventory lists of the late fourth century BC (*IG* II^2 1469A, lines 5–6, 15–16; 1480A, line 9) which record the melting down of silver bowls, has been widely accepted, since the nineteenth century, as connected to the *phialai* inscriptions discussed here.

72 E.g. *IG* II^2 1570, face A, col. II, lines 36–38: Ἡρακλεόδωρος μάγειρος ἐγ Κολλ[υτῶι] /οἰκ· ἀποφυγὼν Ἐπικράτην Φιλοκλέ/ους Ἀγγελῆθ, φιάλη σταθμὸν :Η·. In another formula, the name of the ex-owner appears in the nominative case, followed by the name of the manumitted slave in the accusative case, with his deme of residence, and the record of a *phiale* worth

accepted that these inscriptions record the verdicts of trials in a procedure known as δίκη ἀποστασίου (*dike apostasiou*)—whether actual trials or fictive procedures disguising manumissions of slaves. This action, according to Harpocration (s.v. δίκη ἀποστασίου), could be brought by manumittors against their manumitted slaves if the latter abandoned them or registered another person as their *prostates* (a citizen responsible for the appropriate behaviour of a freed slave or a metic), and disregarded the laws; defendants who were convicted reverted to slavery, but if they were acquitted they became completely free.[73] Accordingly, it was generally believed that these *phialai* were dedicated by slaves who won freedom (if these were manumissions), or by already freed slaves who were acquitted and were now released from any remaining obligation to their former masters (if these were real trials).[74] As mentioned above, it has also been suggested that the *phialai*, like the vessels dedicated in Macedonia, were paid (also) as a registration fee.[75]

Recently, however, Elisabeth Meyer suggested disconnecting these dedications from the context of manumission altogether. Her two main contentions are (a) that the *phialai* were dedicated as the tenth of a fine of 1,000 drachmai, imposed on defeated prosecutors in a lawsuit known as γραφὴ ἀπροστασίου (*graphe aprostasiou*), brought against metics who failed to register a *prostates* or to pay the μετοίκιον (*metoikion*), the metic tax; and (b)

---

100 drachmai; e.g. *IG* II² 1556, lines 36–38: Πολύστρατος Πολυστράτ {ατ} Ἐπ-ικη[φ]ίσιος Σωσίαν γεωργὸν ἐν / [Ἡ]φαιστια(δῶν) οἰκõντα, φιάλ :Η.

73 The notion that these *phialai* dedications were connected to *apostasiou* trials was first suggested by H. Schenkl in 1881; Wilamowitz-Möllendorff 1887, 110, corroborated it by restoring ἀπο]στασίου in the heading of *IG* II² 1578, line 2. Klees 1998, 340–341, argues that according to a law of Lykourgos (Ps.-Plut. *Mor.* 841f–842a), freed slaves who were convicted in *apostasiou* procedures were sold into slavery by the state.

74 For the most recent re-edition and discussion of these inscriptions and a review of former interpretations see Meyer 2010, 11–28. Westermann 1946, 96–99, takes a middle way, arguing that these legal proceedings were feigned trials, used not as a guise for manumissions but as a device for releasing freed slaves from obligations to their former owners, similar to the release (*apolysis*) from *paramone* obligations known from the manumission inscriptions in Delphi. A similar view is postulated by Schmitz 2012, 82, arguing that the manumitted slaves were fictitiously sued after fulfilling their obligations to their masters and by dedicating the *phialai* and being recorded on stone they were documented as unconditionally free.

75 Westermann 1946, 97, who believes that the *phialai* were dedicated by freed slaves who were now released from *paramone* obligations, argues that the 100 drachmai covered the tax on the release from *paramone*, court charges, and publication fee; cf. Klees 1998, 308, 351–354, who argues that the *phialai* were a tax imposed on winners in *apostasiou* trials to cover publication costs and also help replenish the public coffer. Bömer 1960, 9 n. 3, 63, 117 n. 6, interprets these lists as manumissions and the dedication of *phialai* as a means by which the state controlled manumission. See also Sokolowski, *LSCG* 160, 280–281; Sherwin-White 1978, 325; Parker and Obbink 2000, 441; Zelnick-Abramovitz 2005a, 83–84, 289.

that the inscriptions as we have them are inventories of *phialai* dedicated at an earlier date and melted down as part of Lykourgos' policy of the 330s and 320s BC to melt down and re-use old metal dedications.[76] Meyer also argues that since the *prostates* is hardly mentioned in the second half of the fourth century BC, the trials in these cases were brought only on the charge of failure to pay the *metoikion*. Rejecting the view that the *phialai* were a manumission tax or fees collected on the publication of manumission acts, Meyer reviews the evidence on "manumission fees" elsewhere and concludes that such cases are either late or record prices much lower than the Attic *phialai*.[77]

This is not the place to consider Meyer's contentions in detail, but serious questions crop up. Meyer envisages a process whereby any defeated prosecutor in the *graphe aprostasiou* procedure (that is, any prosecutor who failed to receive one-fifth of the votes) was fined the fixed sum of 1,000 drachmai, of which he paid 900 in cash and ordered or paid for a silver *phiale* weighing 100 drachmai and bearing the inscribed information (which later was copied by those who made the inventories before melting down the *phialai*): "so-and-so, living in deme X, having escaped (conviction by) so-and-so of deme Y, (dedicates) a 100-drachma silver bowl"; the date may also have been added.[78] Now Meyer may be correct in arguing that as part of Athenian general policy to attract metics after 353 BC it was decided to impose heavy penalties on losing prosecutors in *aprostasiou* lawsuits.[79] In that case, such a measure should have been a serious deterrent to using the *aprostasiou* procedure.[80] But if she is right in arguing that the *phialai* lists as we have them are inventories of the original dedicated *phialai*, that is, of unsuccessful prosecutions only, we have no way of knowing how many prosecutors, having ventured to prose-

76 Meyer 2010, Part I. On Lykourgos' activity and legislation in the religious sphere see Schwenk 1985, 108–126; Klees 1998, 334–354.

77 Meyer 2010, 23 and nn. 53, 54.

78 Ib. 48, 66–67.

79 Ib. 48.

80 Meyer claims (ib. 51) that the fact that anyone could bring an *aprostasiou* suit, as well as the prospect of financial reward for both the city and the prosecutor if his case was won, "encouraged prosecutions and emphasized that revenues were important, while financial penalties for a failed prosecution would urge caution and the exercise of good judgment, and would probably discourage very many repeated attempts if the first effort failed". See Schmitz's remark (2012, 102) that Meyer's thesis presupposes that a plaintiff in a lawsuit against an entire metic family, as e.g. in *IG* II^2 1558, lines 66–76 (where five metic family members, residing in the deme of Keriadai, were sued by Menites son of Menon of the deme Kydathenaion, and were acquitted), risked having to pay a fine of up to 5,000 drachmai and dedicate five 100-drachma *phialai* for the acquitted metics.

cute despite the risk, won their cases. Moreover, the high number of failures recorded on stone implies that this measure—if such it indeed was—was not very successful.[81] This seems odd, considering that losing prosecutors had to pay a heavy fine, and were further humiliated by being compelled to make or pay for the making of *philalai* commemorating their failure. Moreover, most of the entries in the *phialai* lists (or, according to Meyer, the original inscribed *phialai*) were phrased as if the acquitted metic dedicated them.[82]

Also problematic is Meyer's argument that the dedicators of the *phialai* were not manumitted slaves but metics acquitted in a *graphe aprostasiou*. Some of the prosecutors listed in the *phialai*-inscriptions were metics themselves. Even if metics could bring *graphai* (which is not at all certain)[83] it is not clear what their motive in suing other metics was, if they all suffered hybristic harassment, as Meyer stresses, and if the general policy was to ameliorate their condition in Athens and lessen the legal dangers they were subject to.[84] Moreover, Meyer suggests that the *phialai* were called *exeleuthrikai* because they were dedicated in the first place to Zeus Eleutherios and that the acquitted metics called themselves ἐξελεύθεροι (*exeleutheroi*), "free"; hence the *phialai exeleutherikai* were, by her interpretation, "'*phialai*, those *characterized* as *out of* or *from within*' something having to do with *eleutheria* or (Zeus) *Eleutherios*, *ek* with its specifically geographical meaning

81 See Meyer's calculation (ib. 51, n. 140) of the odds as against the minimum yearly average of failed cases from 353 (when she believes these trials began) to 323, on the basis of a minimum total of 413 cases extant on stone (n. 141).

82 In the most common formula, the name of the defendant is in the nominative case ("X, having escaped Y, *phiale* weighing 100"), so the dedication part seems to describe his or her action. Another formula which appears on these stones, but much less frequently, has the name of the prosecutor in the nominative and no verb describing the legal result; here it might be inferred that the prosecutor performed the dedication. See also the objections of Vlassopoulos 2011b.

83 See the discussion by Meyer 2010, 45 and n. 126.

84 Ib. 47–52. Meyer argues (at 46) that not taking a *prostates* and not paying the *metoikion* were an insult to the polis, which "is a very good reason for allowing ὁ βουλόμενος, Athenian or metic, to prosecute". This may well have been so, given many metics' desire to assimilate into Athenian society. But that would mean attributing to metic prosecutors, about whom we know practically nothing, motives founded on no solid evidence. The same problems apply if we assume that they acted against their fellows of the same status out of spite. Meyer postulates (74–78) that many prosecutors of metic status (as well as many of citizen status) were contractors for the collection of the metic tax, the *metoikion*, and sued other metics for failing to pay the tax. She bases this postulation on the fact that the *prostates* is seldom heard of in the fourth century BC—hence the *aprostasiou* procedure involved almost exclusively failure to pay the *metoikion*, and on an analysis of the prosecutors' socio-economic standing. Attractive as this speculation may be, proofs are lacking.

(Smyth 1956, p. 377 no. 1688a)".[85] This seems to be going to too much trouble to explain an expression found in only two inscriptions[86] and whose connection to the *phialai*-inscriptions Meyer on the whole rejects. What is more, her explanation puts excessive weight on *ek*, which here is not an independent preposition but is prefixed to an adjective ending in *-kos*, that is, to an adjective describing, in this case, what belongs to freed slaves.[87]

Finally, Meyer's argument that the *phialai* inscriptions are inventories of *phialai* dedicated at earlier and apparently various dates indeed presents an attractive explanation for the multiplicity of cases. But this is not necessarily the only solution, if we consider the multiplicity of manumissions in the Thessalian inscriptions discussed in the present book, where numerous acts are recorded for a single month and even a single day.[88] Although the work

---

85 Meyer 2010, 54, quotation taken from n. 148 there (italics in the original).

86 See n. 71 above.

87 It would seem better to consult Smyth p. 378, no. 1688, 2, on ἐξ or ἐκ in composition: "*Out, from, off, away* (cp. ἐξελαύνειν drive out and away); often with an implication of fulfilment, completion, thoroughness, resolution (ἐκπέρθειν sack utterly, ἐκδιδάσκειν teach thoroughly)". Although Smyth's examples are only of verbal forms, the notion of the perfection of action is also implied in compound adjectives. So even if the *phialai* were originally dedicated to Zeus Soter/Eleutherios, perhaps in his sanctuary in the Piraeus, the *phialai exeleutherikai* would still be the *phialai* belonging or related to *exeleutheroi*—a term which is attested for freed slaves but never for metics winning cases. In this respect I cannot see the advantage of Meyer's explanation over those which she rejects (ib. 55 and n. 154). Hyperides' comment, that Zeus has acquired the name Eleutherios because the *exeleutheroi* built a stoa near him (Harpocration, s.v. Ἐλευθέριος Ζεύς), cited by Meyer (ib. 55 n. 155), may well refer to a stoa built in honour of Zeus in the Piraeus, but despite Didymus' objection that the term meant the Athenians being freed from the Persian danger (in the same lemma in Harpocration), the possibility that by *exeleutheroi* Hyperides meant freed slaves is not weakened. See also Vlassopoulos 2011b.

88 See Meyer 2010, 22. On numbers of manumissions per months and days in Thessaly see e.g. *SEG* 15.370 (= Pouilloux, *BCH* 79, 1955, 444–459, no. 1) from Skotoussa (second century BC): seven manumissions in the month of Itonios (lines 24–30); *IG* IX(2) 13 (AD 47): the remains of this inscription record at least thirteen manumissions in a single year; *IG* IX(2) 546 from Larisa (AD 131/132): seven manumissions in the month of Leschanorios. The heading of *IG* IX(2) 553 from Larisa (early first century BC) is missing, so there is no way of knowing the year or the month of the manumissions listed in lines 1–13, or whether the five extant entries were the total in that month; in the month of Homoloios, however, twelve manumissions are listed; in the month of Hippodromios two manumissions are extant, but there were seemingly at least three or four; since, according to the editor, about seventeen lines are missing and each entry covers three to four lines, the inscription as a whole would have listed roughly some 25 manumissions. *BCH* 95 (1971) 277 from Larisa (197–186 BC; cf. *ZPE* 9, 1972, 22–34; *SEG* 33.460) has at least nine manumissions in the first recorded month, whose name has not survived, five in the month of Hippodromios, and two in the month of Phyllikos. *BCH* 95 (1971) 562, from Larisa, has at least eight manumissions, apparently performed in one month. *AE* (1930) Chr., 176, A1 from Larisa, 26/5 BC (= *SEG* 28.505 + p. 154 corr.; McDevitt,

of inscribing them may have been done much later than the actual manumissions (perhaps at the end of each year), this was not the reason why numerous manumission documents were assembled under a single day or month. It is not implausible that the inscriptions record the actual number of manumissions performed on those dates, just as it is not implausible that the number of Attic *phialai* dedications on each stele represents the number of trials held on a single day.[89] Meyer also notes that names of some prosecutors on the 'Great Stele'[90] are not listed in chronological order—which, she claims, supports her conclusion that the *phialai* were first gathered and only later inventoried.[91] This too has a parallel in Thessaly: in a second-century BC inscription from Skotoussa, the entry belonging to the nineteenth day of the month of Leschanorios, in the year of the *strategos* Damothonios son of Leontomenes, precedes that of the fifteenth day of the same month and year.[92] Here too we may assume that the inscriber was given the information in random order, or that he made a mistake which he did not bother to correct. But this does not necessarily prove—as Meyer would like to believe in the case of the *phialai exeleutherikai*—that the manumissions were performed many years before being inscribed, that the information, gathered

1970, 349), has fifteen manumissions recorded for the month of Leschanorios. *RPh* (1936) 152, no. 44, from Larisa, late second century BC, has some seven manumissions in the first month recorded, and about eight in the next month. From *SEG* 27.203 (Larisa, ca. 150 BC) it appears that in the first recorded month, five or six manumissions were performed—or at least registered—on five or six different days, and three more on three different days in another month (see lines 14–19, 20–25). The extant and legible manumission records in *SEG* 31.579 (Larisa, 100–80 BC) give for five months respectively four, six, four, seven and six entries. *SEG* 31.580 has fifteen manumissions for the month of Leschanorios. *ZPE* 49 (1982), 161–167, no. 1 from Larisa (early first century BC), has four, six, four, seven and nine manumission acts in five successive months. Ib., 168–170, no. 2 (mid-first century BC), has nineteen manumission acts recorded for the month of Leschanorios. But the most striking example is *IG* IX(2) 568 from Larisa, which—if I have not miscalculated—has at least thirty-six(!) entries in a single month (Aphrodisios).

89 See Zelnick-Abramovitz 2005a, 285–288, where I discuss the possibility that at some stage the *apostasiou* cases were included among the δίκαι ἔμμηνοι (*dikai emmenoi*), the 'monthly trials'. According to Cohen 1973, 38–40, charges falling under this category could be brought only once a month, on a specific date, and were tried within a month. The possibility that the *phialai exeleutherikai* were connected to the *dikai emmenoi* was raised already by Foucart 1873, 49, but for a different reason.

90 I.e. *IG* II^2 1554–1559+*Agora* inv. I.3163+*SEG* 25.178. Face B of the stele was inscribed later than face A.

91 Meyer 2011, 63–66, with some examples.

92 Pouilloux, *BCH* 79 (1955), 444–459, no. 1 (= *SEG* 15.370), lines 8 and 10. See also Pouilloux's discussion of the calendar in Skotoussa and other places in Thessaly.

from archives, was given to inscribers much later, and that the dates on the inscriptions are those of the publication on stone, not of the manumissions.[93]

Still, Meyer is right in arguing that a price of 100 drachmai seems too high as a manumission tax or a publication fee, in comparison with other places.[94] She also notes that as a tax or a fee these 100-drachma *phialai* should have been paid to the state treasury (the *demosion*), but points out that income to the treasury was not inventoried at Athens whereas the *phialai* inscriptions are undoubtedly inventories of dedications.[95] In Athens, tithes of fines were indeed paid to Athena.[96] The goddess also received a percentage of some taxes, such as the 1/60 *aparche* taken from the tribute paid by members of the Delian League and registered in the Athenian Tribute Lists, and the *hekatoste*—a one-percent tax on land sales.[97] On the other hand, other *phialai* dedicated to Athena were of lower value. Such are the silver *phialai* dedicated by liturgists, perhaps in accordance with a law introduced by Lykourgos, which weighed only fifty drachmai, that is, half the value of the

---

93 Another example is found in a group of manumission inscriptions from Demetrias (two of which were discussed above): Habicht 1987, 277–292, nos. 13–22 (= *SEG* 37.450–459). The names of the *strategoi* in whose years of office the manumissions were made do not follow a consistent order; some appear on different stones, preceded and followed by other *strategoi* who are mentioned in other inscriptions in a different order. For instance, lines 15–18 of no. 13 (= *SEG* 37.450), lines 17–26 of no. 14 (= *SEG* 37.451), and lines 1–4 of no. 17 (= *SEG* 37. 454) record four manumissions made in the same year; but the manumission documents preceding the one in no. 13 and the manumissions preceding those in no. 14 come from sundry non-successive years. See Habicht's suggested chronology of the stones (1987, 289). It looks as if the documents were haphazardly inscribed on the stones, or perhaps some were added to another stone when the mistake was detected—which might explain the numerous errors (see Habicht 1987, 285–286).

94 Meyer 2010, 23 and n. 53.

95 Meyer 2010, 59 and n. 169; but see Davies 1994, 207, who classifies the *phialai exeleutherikai* as a "less directly" recorded income. Cf. Lambert 1997, 274, who describes the *phialai exeleutherikai* as, "in a sense", accounts of receipts like the *Rationes Centesimarum* (recording the *hekatoste* on land sales) and, like them, belonging in the same context of accountability. Parallel to the *phialai* inscriptions and the *Rationes* were also the Athenian Tribute Lists (*IG* I^3 259–290), which actually recorded not the taxes paid but the payments of tithes due to Athena. See also Lewis 1973, 191.

96 For the evidence and bibliography on tithes in Athens, see Meyer 2010, 43 n. 119, 52 and n. 143; Papazarkadas 2011, 275–276.

97 See more examples in Meyer 2010, 52 and n. 143. On the *aparche* in the Athenian Tribute Lists, see Harris 1994, 216; Samons 2000, 35–41, 313. On the *hekatoste* see Lambert 1997. Mention should also be made of the *hekatoste* in the form of gold *phialai*, made on the commission of the treasurers "from the monies brought to the Acropolis by the archon Archippos" (*IG* II^2 1471 + *SEG* 38.138; 321/0 BC), which Lambert (1997, 277) suggests might be identical to the *hekatoste* on land sales.

phialai called *exeleutherikai*: in 1968 Lewis published four fragments of a list of dedicators of silver *phialai*, weighing fifty drachmai each, which he dated to 331/0 BC Lewis suggests that this inscription refers to a law which precedes a list of citizens who performed liturgies in one year, most of them dedicating fifty drachmai; the list is recorded in *IG* II[2] 417, dated to 333 or 332 BC.[98] Lines 1–7 of the inscription published by Lewis (no. 51) read:

> [– – – φιάλας λητουργι]κὰς ἐπ' Ἀ[ριστοφάνο]υς ἄρχοντ[ος]
> *Vacat*
> κυκλίοις π̣[αίδων]
> Σωσίστρ[ατος – – – –]
> Εὐωνυμ[εύς, σταθμόν 𐅄]
> Θυμοκλῆς – – – – – –
> Πρασιεύ[ς, σταθμόν 𐅄]

> [--- liturgic *phialai* in the year of the archon Aristophanes.
> At the performance of the dithyrambic choruses of [boys]
> Sosistr[atos ----]
> Of the deme Euonym[on, weight 50 drachmai.]
> Thymokles ----
> Of the deme Prasia [weight 50 drachmai.]

Lines 1–8 of *IG* II[2] 417 read:

> σιν ἐξεῖναι γράψαι I#7#7#7O#7E – – – – – – – – – – – – – – – –
> ου καὶ : I : κατὰ τὸν ἄνδρα· εἰς δὲ – – – – – – – – – – – – –
> τῶι δήμωι δοκῆι.
> οἵδε ἐλητού[ργ]ησαν ἐπὶ [– – – –ἄρχοντος]·
> [ε]ὐταξίας·
> Ἐρεχθηΐδος·
> Κηφισόδωρος Μειδίου Ἀ[να]γυράσιος : 𐅄
> Ἀρχέβιος Ἀρχεβιάδου [Λα]μπ[τ]ρ[εὺ]ς : 𐅄

> [---] possible to write
> [---] and one drachma each man. To [-----]
> decided by the people.
> The following performed liturgies in [the year of the archon].
> In the Eutaxia:
> From the tribe Erechtheïs:
> Kephisodoros, son of Midias, of the deme Anagyrous, 50 drachmai.
> Archebios, son of Archebiades, of the deme Lamptrai, 50 drachmai.

It may be significant that the list of the dedicating liturgists, published by Lewis in 1968, was inscribed on the reverse of a stele recording *phialai exeleutherikai* (*IG* II[2] 1575); apparently these two lists were deemed to belong

---

[98] Lewis 1968, 374–380, no. 51 (= *SEG* 25.177); see *IG* II[2] 417. Cf. Lambert 2001, 52–59.

to the same sphere. If this is correct, Meyer's assumption that the *phialai exeleutherikai* were dedicated or paid for as a fine imposed on defeated prosecutors seems to stand in sharp contrast to the respectable context of dedications by liturgists. Lewis assumes that Lykourgos strove to strengthen public devotion and the state's finances by imposing a compulsory dedication on liturgists, "just as the law in *IG* II^2 1560 seems to have added the compulsory dedication of the φιάλαι to the previously existing manumission institution".[99] Alternatively, of course, these fifty-drachma *phialai* may be presented as evidence that as a 'fee' the hundred-drachma *phiale* was too high a price. Meyer takes these liturgists' *phialai* as the closest parallel to a compulsory dedication which might be interpreted as a 'fee', but elsewhere she comments that the law prescribing this dedication is phrased as a permission—ἐξεῖναι γράψαι (*IG* II^2 417, line 1).[100] However, the dedication might have been compulsory and the registration on stone optional (to which perhaps the payment of one drachma per person, mentioned there, refers).

In this context we may perhaps consider another inscription, dated to 315/14 BC and recording a decree of the deme Acharnai in honour of their treasurer Phanomachos, who, among other things (*AE*, 1992, 179–193, A, lines 3–8 = *SEG* 43.26),

> τάς τε θυσίας τέθυκεν τοῖς θεοῖς καὶ τοῖ-
> ς ἥρωσιν ὑπὲρ τῶν δημοτῶν ἁπάσας [ἐ]ν τ[ῶ]ι ἐ-
> [νι]αυτῶι καὶ τῶν Διονυσίων ἐπεμελήθη κα-
> λῶς [καὶ φιλοτίμως] μετὰ τοῦ δημάρχου Οἰν-
> ο[φ]ί[λ]ου καὶ [φ]ιάλην πεπόηται μ[ν]ᾶν ἄγουσα-
> ν ἀργυρίου [κ]ατὰ [τὸν νόμον]
>
> ... conducted the sacrifices to the gods and to the Heroes on behalf of all the demesmen in the current year, and administered the Dionysia well and zealously, together with the demarch Oinophilos, and made a *phiale*, weighing one silver mina, according to the law.

The *phiale* of one mina (= 100 drachmai), made or ordered by Phanomachos, of course immediately brings to mind the *phialai exeleutherikai*; and since Phanomachos' *phiale* seems to have been a token of his good management—including his personal expenditure on administering the Dionysia, one is also reminded of the *phialai* dedicated by liturgists, possibly as an outcome of Lykourgos' law (even though those weighed half Phanomachos'

99 Lewis 1968, 376.

100 Meyer 2010, 23 n. 53, and 58 n. 164, respectively.

phiale), discussed above. So dedicating *phialai*, either as thanksgiving or as a compulsory offering imposed by law on liturgists, was apparently quite common in the last third of the fourth century BC.[101]

If, as Meyer argues, the *phialai exeleutherikai* were paid by losing prosecutors in *aprostasiou* trials they must indeed have been compulsory, but were not necessarily so if these *phialai* lists recorded manumissions or the results of *apostasiou* trials. Since the Athenians did not inscribe in stone *all* their financial records[102] but stored many documents in various archives or published them on perishable material, records of the results in *apostasiou* trials—real or fictive—may well have been published on wood or kept in archives, and only the names of those who decided to dedicate *phialai* (as testimony to their manumission or acquittal in an *apostasiou* trial) were inscribed; the motivation could have been religious, as Samons has suggested,[103] or a wish to gain more publicity for their new status. Although evidence relating to the publication of trial verdicts is scarce and ambiguous, it is still possible that the Athenians did have such public records;[104] if future

---

101 *AE* (1992), 184–185. The editor, G. Stainhauer, suggests that the 100-drachma *phiale* was a tithe on the revenues in Phanomachos' year of office. In some cities of Asia Minor, magistrates were obligated to dedicate a *phiale* of 100 drachmai or thereabouts at the termination of their office: see Bresson 1991, 74–75, no. 48 (an inventory of a sanctuary in Amos, 220/201 BC). Evidence can perhaps be inferred from *IosPE* I² 105 from Olbia (second or third century AD). *Phialai* of 100 drachmai were quite common: e.g. Holleaux, *REA* 21, 1919, 1–19 (= *Et. épig.* II 179–198); *IMylasa* 301, lines 9–11 (= Sokolowski, *LSAM* 62; *SEG* 15.648) from Mylasa, second century BC; *MDAI*(I) 1977–1978, 261–266 (= *SEG* 27.730) from Didyma, 288/7 BC (cf. *IDidyma* 427, of 276/5 BC); *SEG* 36.1047, from Miletos, late third or early second century BC.

102 See Lambert 1997, 273.

103 Samons 2000, 316.

104 The Athenians published impending court cases and arbitrators' decisions on whitewashed wooden boards (Davies 1994, 205). Although no explicit evidence exists, court decisions may well have been published in this way too, in keeping with what Aristotle suggests (and implies to have existed in other places) in *Pol.* 6, 1321b34–40: the officials who are elsewhere called *hieromnemones* or other names are to register private contracts and the verdicts of the law courts, as well as prosecutions and the authorities that introduce them to the court. See Newman 1902, 553–554, who suggests that Aristotle meant verdicts delivered in trials involving private contracts. The only literary evidence concerning Athens is an anecdote told in Athenaeus' *Deipnosophistai* (9, 407c) on Alkibiades who entered the Metroon, where registers of indictments were stored, and erased an indictment deposited there against his friend; and Strepsiades' words in Ar. *Nub.* 769–774, which relate to waxed tablets. These examples, however, concern archival records, not inscriptions. In two publications (1994, and 1998, 91–100), Stroud suggested that the meaning of *P.Oxy.* XVII 2087, lines 16–18, which refers to the Aiakeion in Athens, is that in this shrine of Aiax lawsuits were written up (Stroud's reading: [ἐπὶ or ἐν δὲ] τῷ Αἰακίῳ δίκαι ἀναγράφονται). Stroud believes that the Aiakeion was located at the south-west corner of the *agora*, where remains of a large enclosure were found,

finds confirm this hypothesis there will be no obstacle to assuming that the *phialai* lists were records of the verdicts—whether of *apostasiou* (as I tend to believe), perhaps disguising manumission acts, or even of *aprostatsiou* trials. Definite proof, however, is still lacking.

True, the Attic *phialai* were worth about 3.33 times the price paid by manumitted slaves in Thessaly, even though the value of the Attic drachma slightly decreased after Alexander (from about 66.5 grains to 63).[105] But this price is perhaps not exceptional considering that even dedications made as a tithe could be regarded as 'income', or 'reserves' entrusted to a deity for safekeeping. In this sense the *phialai* could have been both a tithe to Athena (or even to Zeus Eleutherios, as Meyer suggests) and a registration fee—similar to the prices paid at Delphi by slaves for their freedom and for their release from *paramone* obligations. Although the sums paid by manumitted slaves at Delphi are believed to have been based on the slaves'

---

identified in earlier publications as the ἡλιαία (*heliaia*). He further suggests that the numerous fragments of white wall plaster (found by Vanderpool in 1953) bearing large letters smeared in thin red paint, came from the north wall of the same building and may have been records of *dikai*. The *dikai* mentioned in *P.Oxy*. XVII 2087, of course, may have indicated impending suits and not their results. But at least two verdicts were perhaps recorded on stone: *Agora* XXVIII no. 159 (= *IG* II² 1646), which comes from a fragmentary Delian Amphictyionic record, mentions in line 12 the Parabyston court; line 8 reads [-πλήρεις HHHHΔΔΔΔIII, which has been interpreted to mean that 443 judges acquitted the defendant (but see Stumpf 1987, who reads the number 444 and suggests that it represents the figure of the fine imposed). Lines 25–33 of *Agora* XXVIII no. 163 (= *IG* II² 1641) mention an acquitted person in a trial held at the Stoa Poikile; 399 judges voted for his acquittal against 100, which oddly gives the total number of judges as 499, less than the expected 501. This inscription too comes from a *stele* bearing records of the Delian Amphictyones. See Meyer 2010, 66–67 n. 194, who takes these inscriptions as proof that inventories were based on information gathered from the dedications themselves or some tags attached to them. But in the case of these two inscriptions, the information was obviously taken from records of verdicts. Cf. the way the Lindians gathered information about the old dedications in the sanctuary of Athena Lindia in 99 BC (*Lindos* II, 2; see now Higbie, 2003). Boegehold 1995, 7–8, notes that inscriptions were an expensive form of publication and it was not customary to record verdicts; that is why, he suggests, such records appear among the other yearly records of the relevant magistrate and not separately. If the *phialai* lists were indeed records of legal verdicts (and not an inventory of dedications), the reference to a date (of the trial), to the name of the court ('the middle of the New Courts'), and to court officials in lines 12–19 of a fragment of these lists (Lewis 1968, 369–374, no. 50 = *Agora* XXVIII no. 148 = *SEG* 25.180) acquires a clearer context ([Μαιμ]ακτηριῶνο(ς) / [---2–3]τηι ἐπὶ δέκα· δικαστή-/[ρι]ον μέσον τῶν καινῶν· / [ἐ]πὶ τὸ ὕδωρ Μενεκλῆς Εὐω-/νυμεύς· ἐπὶ τὰς ψήφους / Ἱεροφῶν Ὤαθεν [:] Π [-----4–5] / φης Ἀλωιεύς : Ἀριστολέων / Ἁλιμούσι).

[105] At 0.75 of an Attic drachma, or one Roman denarius, for every 1 Thessalian drachma, the manumitted slaves in Thessaly paid a sum roughly equivalent to twenty-two and a half Attic drachmai—less than a quarter of the value of one *phiale exeleutherike*. On Thessalian coinage and its rates see above and n. 27, and the Introduction.

real market value, to compensate the manumitting owners for the loss of property, part of the money the freed slaves paid very likely went to Apollo's priests as fees covering the costs of the manumission procedure and the publication on stone.[106] Note too that in the city of Phalanna in Perrhaibia the sum of fifteen staters was the best *xenia* granted to foreign benefactors, as an inscription dated 196–146 BC shows.[107] This may mean that as a registration fee, fifteen staters was not considered a low price in Thessaly.

A different way of extracting money from manumitted slaves for public and religious purposes is demonstrated by a trilingual inscription (in Greek, Lykian, and Aramaic; 337 BC?) which records a decree of the city of Xanthos in Lykia and its *perioikoi*, concerning the foundation of a cult for Basileus Kaunios and Arkesimas. The inscription stipulates that the maintenance of the cult be partly funded by imposing, among other things, a payment of two drachmai on all slaves upon their manumission (lines 18–20: καὶ ὅσοι ἂν ἀπελεύθεροι γένωνται ἀποτίνειν τῶι θεῶι δύο δράχμας).[108] This levy is indeed much lower than in other examples, including the Thessalian fees. But in this case, although it may be seen as taxation on manumission, the purpose of the two-drachma payment is clearly religious, and the money is not used for registration or publication.[109]

---

106 On payment to the priests at Delphi see Hopkins 1978, 138. Westermann 1946, 97–98, argues that the 100 drachmai paid at Athens as silver *phialai* by manumitted slaves were "a blanket fixed charge" that included the manumission and release taxes, a charge on court procedures, and the publication fee. Comparing costs of slaves in Athens and Delphi and the prices of release from *paramone* in the latter, Westermann also maintains that "the ratios of the prices for release from the *paramone* to the original self-redemption payments were about the same at Athens in the fourth century BC as they were at Delphi in the second century B.C.". He adds that the 100 drachmai payments in Athens "compare fairly closely with the percentages of the taxes and fees on slaves as known to us from Ptolemaic Egypt" (both quotations from p. 98).

107 *Nouvaux Choix*, 76–78, no. 12, lines 26–28, and comments on p. 79 (= *JHS* 33, 1913, 332–337, no. 16; *AE* 1916, 21–26, no. 274, esp. p. 25). Cf. *IG* IX(2) 508 (Larisa, 49/8 BC), lines 18–19, where the value of the "greatest *xenia* according to the law" is not specified.

108 Metzger, Laroche, Dupont-Sommer, and Mayrhofer 1979: the Greek text is edited and discussed by Metzger on pp. 31–48 (*SEG* 27.942); see also Metzger 1974. Cf. Debord 1982, 203; Rhodes and Osborne 2003, 384–387, no. 78; Lupu 2005, 82–83. The money levied from manumitted slaves seems to join an annual payment of three half-minai, apparently paid as salary to the priest: see Rhodes and Osborne 2003, 387.

109 Contrary to Meyer 2010, 23 n. 54, who presents this inscription as an example of low registration fees, compared with the 100-drachma *phialai* dedicated at Athens. Rhodes and Osborne 2003, 387, commenting that in funding a cult partly from taxation Xanthos was behaving "in the same way as a Greek city", compare the Xanthian levy on manumitted slaves

Some inscriptions record a formal decision by the sovereign institutions of poleis concerning the act of manumission or its inscription in public. Although no payments are mentioned, in light of the evidence discussed above we may perhaps assume that in these places too registration and publication of manumission acts were controlled and taxed by the political authorities. Thus *IG* IX(1) 193 from Tithora, dated to the early second century AD, begins with an elaborate record of the manumission by sale to Serapis of a slave-girl by a couple (lines 1–24). The manumission took place and was inscribed in stone in the year when Ariston son of Ariston was archon, in accordance with a decree (*psephisma*) which the "lawful Assembly" issued in the year when Hellanikos son of Hellanikos was archon (lines 26–28). Although no payment is mentioned, it is conceivable that the inscription of this state-authorized manumission was taxed. Another couple manumitted their slave-woman in Elatea (*FD* III 2.120, 150–130 BC). The record of the manumission act, which was found in Delphi, is preceded by a letter from the archons of Elatea to the archons and the polis of Delphi, asking them to acknowledge the "freedom" (*eleutheria*, i.e. both the act of manumission and the status of the woman) which was engraved in Asklepios' sanctuary in Elatea, the text of which was sealed and attached to the letter; they also sought permission to engrave the same manumission document (*apeleutherosis*) in the sanctuary of Apollo in Delphi (lines 1–7). The text of the manumission itself (lines 8–28), which as noted was performed in Elatea, further mentions that the act was carried out in the "lawful Assembly" (lines 8–9). After authorizing the inscription of the manumission in Elatea, this city's magistrates sent a formal request to the Delphians, and since the inscription was found in Delphi the latter apparently consented. Again, it is reasonable that the Delphians charged money for the inscription—whether from the manumittors or from the manumitted slave. In another inscription from Elatea (*IG* IX(1) 109) the Council, and then the Assembly, authorize in a decree an act of manumission by a woman and give their permission to engrave the manumission document in the temple of Athena Kranaia.[110] The use of political institutions

to the Attic *phialai exeleutherikai*. However, both the purpose of the payment and the amount paid are different.

[110] On this inscription see my discussion in Zelnick-Abramovitz 2005a, 189, 190. On the other hand, the fact that the legal status of the manumitting couple (or at least one of them) in *IG* IX(1) 36 from Stiris (200–150 BC) was that of non-citizen residents is perhaps the reason why they requested the polis' permission to engrave the act of manumission and consecration in Asklepios' sanctuary.

in acts of manumission is known from other places in Greece and may also be connected to the cities' policy of keeping registers of their freed slaves.[111]

In Calymna most of the manumission inscriptions seem to be private publications, but some are 'collective',[112] in which case—especially where proclamation of manumissions is mentioned—the publication looks official. Although no payment for this purpose is mentioned, the existence of 'laws of the manumitted slaves' (e.g. in *TC* nos. 167 and 176) may imply that such a fee was imposed. Some freed slaves are also exempted from the "legal procedures pertaining to manumitted slaves" (ἀπελευθερικαὶ δικαίαι).[113]

From the foregoing evidence we may conclude that in many places in the Greek world money or dedicated objects were exacted by the polis from manumitted slaves, in addition to the price of freedom they paid to the manumittors. And although in many cases it is not easy, sometimes even impossible, to determine whether payments made by manumitted slaves in Thessaly and elsewhere were a tax on manumission or a registration and publication fee, the latter possibility is strongly indicated in Thessaly, Orchomenos, Kos, and Nikaia. This possibility is less certain in Egypt, Tithora, and Elatea—and perhaps also in Athens (though the rate there seems too high). We cannot be sure about the evidence from Chaironeia, Macedonia, Gortyn, and Xanthos, although even in these places the money paid or the vessels dedicated by the manumitted slaves were also used as fees for registration. As I suggested above, the mention of a tax and tax collectors in Demetrias can be easily explained if the inscriptions in which they appear date to after the *Constitutio Antoniniana* and concern manumittors who were now Roman citizens and had to pay the *vicesima manumissionum/libertatis*. In any case, the practice of exacting money from slaves upon their manumission seems to have been quite widespread, and in Thessaly, and other places as well, these monies were apparently levied for registration and publication.

111 See Zelnick-Abramovitz 2005a, 188–194, arguing that such manumissions, as well as the concise lists of manumission acts attested in Thessaly and other places, indicate these states' decision to authorize publication hence establish a record of their non-citizen residents.

112 E.g. *TC* 163, 164; but in e.g. 192 and 196 the texts of the manumissions are more elaborate and each has a date. See Chapter 2, n. 69.

113 E.g. *TC* 184.

CHAPTER FIVE

THE HISTORICAL AND ECONOMIC BACKGROUND

It is now time to address other questions, no less difficult to answer: why did the Thessalian League decide to impose this levy in the second century BC? Or was it collected even earlier, with no record left in the extant sources? If this was a federal impost, as implied by the uniformity of the amount paid in many cities, was the money transferred to the federal treasury, and if so, how? Or was it used by the individual cities, while the federal interest was merely to control the non-citizen population in its member cities by ensuring that they kept public records of their manumitted slaves?

Before endeavouring to answer these questions we must bear in mind that payment of fifteen staters or twenty-two and a half denarii is not attested in *all* the Thessalian cities, or even in the same region. Moreover, some cities that do show evidence of payment seem to have introduced it later than others. Of course, new finds may change the picture, but as the evidence stands now, and although there seems to be no doubt that the payment was federal because the amount paid was identical in different cities and regions, it is difficult to discern a federal policy established at one particular moment for all Thessaly; on the contrary, from the present evidence each city seems to have decided whether or not to impose the payment. A brief review of the evidence by Thessaly's *tetrades* and its perioecic regions and *ethne* gives the following results.[1]

Pelasgiotis

The earliest allusions to payments are from the second century BC in inscriptions from Larisa (in staters), where payments are still attested in the second century AD.[2] A fragmentary inscription (*SEG* 35.593) dated to the early

[1] In ca. 150–130 BC (*SEG* 34.558, lines 31–35), the division into *tetrades*, or the four regions—Pelasgiotis, Phthiotis, Hestiaiotis and Thessaliotis—was still retained. On the division see Strabo, 9.5.3. To the four main districts of Thessaly other regions and *ethne* were joined; see Introduction.

[2] E.g. *SEG* 27.203 (= *ZPE* 27, 1977, 259–262), ca. 150 BC; *SEG* 31.577, ca. 136–135 BC; *IG* IX(2)

second century BC records the payment of fifteen staters by a female slave to the *koinos xenodokos*. But since the federal payment seems to have been introduced only after 196 BC the inscription may be dated after that date. In Skotoussa payments in staters are first documented in the second century BC, and they persist in the first century AD.[3] However, slave manumissions had taken place at Larisa already in the third century BC if not earlier: *IG* IX(2) 594, dated to the third century BC on the basis of the letter-forms, reads: Λεοντίσκος ἀπελευθερουθεὶς / ἀπὺ Στράτουνος Κοττυφείοι ὀνέθειϰ[ε] ("Leontiskos, manumitted by Straton son of Kottypheios, dedicated"). This dedication perhaps amounts to giving thanks for being manumitted, as may be inferred by comparing it to another dedication, this one by a manumitted slave-woman (*SEG* 35.616; ed. pr. A. Tziaphalias), dated to ca. 200 BC: Παρμονὶς Κλεαρχεία / ἀπελευθερουθέν/σα ἀπὸ Μνασία Που/ταλείοι ὀνέθειϰε ("Parmonis daughter of Klearcheis, manumitted by Mnasias son of Poutaleios, dedicated"). However, the text inscribed on the dedicated cylindrical stone may equally have commemorated the manumission of the slave, since—according to the editio princeps—it is one of a series of manumission texts engraved on stones belonging to a third-century BC temple and reused for the theatre where *SEG* 35.616 was found. Although no safe conclusions can be drawn from such scant evidence, before 196 BC manumissions may have been recorded in a different style and their publication was a matter of choice, paid for directly to the mason by the manumitted slave; or perhaps dedications by manumitted slaves were the norm in third-century BC Larisa.[4]

In Krannon, payments first appear in the first century BC (staters),[5] and in Atrax there are two extant references to payments in denarii from very different periods: the first century BC and the second century AD.[6] Some

---

539 (+ *SEG* 31.578), 117 BC; *SEG* 31.579 (= te Riele, 1982, 161–167, no. 1), 100–80 BC; *SEG* 53.547 (ed. pr. M-E. Zachou-Kontoyanni in *Τὸ Ἔργο τῶν Ἐφορειῶν Ἀρχαιοτήτων καὶ Νεωτέρων Μνημείων τοῦ ΥΠ.ΠΟ στὴ Θεσσαλία*, 145–149), A (24? BC) in denarii; B (after 8? BC) in staters; *SEG* 35.602 = *IG* IX(2) 545 (AD 44–46) in denarii. *SEG* 33.464, mentioning payment in denarii, is perhaps from 27 BC. An inscription from Larisa, which records manumissions in the order of the months (*SEG* 44.450 = *IG* IX(2) 1232), is dated to 100–50 BC, but in the extant text there is no mention of payments.

[3] E.g. *SEG* 15.370, second century BC; *SEG* 23.413 (= *REA* 66, 1964, 309 2b), AD 71–96 (still in staters); 43.312 (= *AD* 43 B, 1988, 282), and 47.786 (= *AD* 48 B1, 1993, 257, no. 46), Roman Imperial period (in denarii).

[4] The name of the manumittor in *SEG* 35.616, Mnasias son of Poutaleios, is also attested in *SEG* 27.202, lines 3–4, from Larisa (220–210 BC), as one of the *tagoi* of the city.

[5] See *IG* IX(2) 463 (49/8 BC).

[6] The first reference is restored in *SEG* 56.621, lines 12–13 (= M.E. Zachou-Kontoyanni,

manumission documents do not mention payments but their formulation may suggest that the freed slaves paid for the publication of their manumissions.[7] The earliest extant manumission in Atrax (*SEG* 46.622; ed. pr. A. Tziaphalias, *AD* 46 B1, 1991 [1996], 224–225) is dated—like *IG* IX(2) 594 from Larisa, mentioned above—to the third century BC. The inscription is fragmentary, but in the extant text each manumission record is followed by the formula "according to the law" (e.g. lines 10–15: Ὠφελίων Λαπί/θου ὁ ἀπελευθε/ρωθεὶς ὑπὸ Νικο/λόχου τοῦ Εὐφόρ/βου κατὰ τὸν νό/μον); however, no mention of a treasurer or payment is found on the stone. If the dating is correct, the absence of any reference to the treasurer and to payment may be explained in that the Thessalians' *koinon* as organized by the Romans after 196 BC had not yet come into being (although some of the later documents of the League are formulated similarly). But the inscription proves that some legislation concerning manumission existed in Atrax already in the third century BC, perhaps independently from the League.

In Pherai, as we saw, an inscription dated to the late first century BC records the transition in 27 BC from payments in staters to payments in denarii (*IG* IX(2) 415 + Add. + *SEG* 28.527). Other manumission inscriptions from Pherai present no information regarding payments to the polis: In *IG* IX(2) 413 (dated to the reign of Augustus) and *IG* IX(2) 414 (undated) no payment is mentioned at all. *SEG* 39.506 (+ *SEG* 42.534, dated to the second/first century BC) is too fragmentary to provide any information. In light of the importance of Pherai as a prosperous city controlling the port of Pagasai (see especially Liv. 36.8–14) and the rich information contained in *IG* IX(2) 415, the relatively scanty evidence of payments made upon manumission is remarkable.

2006b—a republication of *SEG* 32.604 = *AD* 30 B1, 1975 [1983], 197), dated to 16–6/5 BC—[κατὰ τὸ διόρθω?]/μα [Δ KB <]; although the stone was found in Larisa, Zachou-Kontoyanni argues on prosopographic grounds that it originated in Atrax. The second reference is *SEG* 34.478 (ed. pr. A. Tziaphalias, *ThessHem* 6, 1984, 204–205 no. 77), dated to AD 131/132.

[7] In Atrax, *Mélanges Daux* 4, 2, mentions a treasurer in lines 4 and 12, as does *Mélanges Daux* 6, 5, line 2—both from the reign of Augustus. But in *Mélanges Daux* 3, 1, and *Mélanges Daux* 5, 4, dated to the same period, no treasurer and no payments are recorded. However, since in all these inscriptions it is stated that the manumissions were done according to the law, it may be that the law prescribed payment. Cf. *IG* IX(2) 474 (Atrax, ca. 49/8 BC).

Hestiaiotis

The only evidence of payment in staters, although the exact sum is not preserved, comes from manumission documents from Aiginion, dated to the late first century BC/early first century AD (*SEG* 53.510(1)A–C, and 53.510(2)A–B, new readings by M.-E. Zachou-Kontoyanni of *IG* IX(2) 324a–c, and 325a–b). In *SEG* 53.512 (= *IG* IX(2) 1342), dated to the second/third century AD,[8] the first manumission document notes the payment of staters (no amount is specified) to the treasurer of the polis (δοὺς τοὺς νομίμους στατῆ/ρας τῇ πόλει ταμίᾳ Πέκλῳ / Λεοντίδῃ; lines 4–6), whereas in the second document, dated by another *strategos* (hence another year) the phrasing is "paid the staters, the twenty-two and a half denarii to the treasurer" (ἔδω/κε τοὺς νομίμους στατῆ/ρες τῇ πόλι ✳ κβ′ < / ταμίᾳ Νικασικράτῃ / Ἀνδρονείκου; lines 6–10).[9]

Some inscriptions from Gomphoi explicitly mention payment in denarii and are dated to the Roman period (or, in the case of *IG* IX(2) 289b, and c, to ca. AD 131/132).[10] Other fragmentary manumission inscriptions have the formula "by (ἀπὸ) (name of manumittor in the genitive case) (name of manumitted slave in the nominative case)", and the heading of *IG* IX(2) 288 (undated) refers to manumitted slaves who paid to the polis "what is due according to the law" (lines 1–3). In Metropolis, payment in denarii is attested in one inscription (*IG* IX(2) 280), dated to the Roman period, although there are other fragmentary manumission inscriptions which may have mentioned it, since they are likewise arranged as lists of manumission acts under various months and days. Thus the heading of *IG* IX(2) 274 (186/5 BC) reads (lines 1–4) στρατηγοῦντος Λεοντομέ/νους, ταμιεύοντος Νικάν/δρου τοῦ Ἀντιγόνου οἱ γεγο/νότες ἀπελεύθεροι ("When Leontomenes was the *strategos* and Nikandros son of Antigonos was the treasurer; those who have become freed slaves: …"). If this inscription originally recorded payments it would be one of our earliest examples of it (see below on Achaia Phthiotis).[11]

---

8 Zachou-Kontoyanni 2003.

9 As we saw in Chapter 2, in some other places payments in staters are still attested in the second and third century AD: *IG* IX(2) 92 = *SEG* 39.493 from Echinos, and *IG* IX(2) 546 and 547 from Larisa.

10 Cf. *IG* IX(2) 287a, probably from the reign of Augustus, recording payment in denarii.

11 See also *IG* IX(2) 277, line 4, and *IG* IX(2) 279, line 1 (undated).

Thessaliotis

Payments in denarii are attested in only one manumission inscription of the first century AD, from Euhydrion (*IG* IX(2) 256b; new edition: *I Thess.* I 34). There is no evidence of the payment of staters. A fragmentary inscription, found at Ekkara-Agoriani (*AD* 26 B1 (1971) 236, no. 5, undated), mentions no payment at all.

Magnesia

As noted above, Magnesia, like the other Thessalians, was declared free in 196, but constituted an independent federation. In Chapter 4, manumission inscriptions from Demetrias were discussed as evidence for what seems to be the payment of a manumission tax. That no evidence for the fifteen staters/twenty-two and a half denarii has survived in Magnesia strengthens the assumption that such payments were exacted only in the Thessalian League.

Perrhaibia

Evidence of the payment of fifteen staters begins in the second century BC in Pythion and Azoros.[12] The same cities, as well as Olosson and Gonnoi, furnish evidence of payments in denarii from the first century BC.[13] However, in *AE* (1924), 188, no. 418a (= *IG* IX(2) 1282) from Pythion, dated to ca. 50 BC, a payment of twenty-two and a half denarii to the treasurer is restored in lines 2–4, which are part of the first manumission document (A) on the stone; the other manumissions (B–F) mention no payment at all save the price of freedom (150 staters) paid for the manumission of the freedwoman

---

12 Pythion: e.g. *AE* (1924), 166, no. 405 (131/0 BC?); 173, no. 407 (after 44 BC?); *IG* IX(2) 1290 I (= *SEG* 26.689; 150–100 BC); *SEG* 26.670 = Helly 1976, 147–149 (ca. 50 BC). Azoros: e.g. *AE* (1923), 126, no. 362 (ca. 30–1 BC), where, among other manumission documents recording payments in denarii, lines 17–22 record a manumission for which publication the manumitted slave paid in staters (on this manumission act see Chapter 2 above).

13 Azoros: e.g. *IG* IX(2) 1296 (= *AE*, 1945–1947, 110, no. 59; 20–18 BC); 1298 (= *AE* (1916), 86, no. 292; 14/13 BC), which records payments in denarii in the four manumission documents extant on the stone. Olosson: e.g. *SEG* 56.649 (= Zachou-Kontoyanni 2006a; *IG* IX(2) 1293b/c + 1294b; late first century BC). Cf. *SEG* 27.211, reign of Augustus; *SEG* 35.646, first century AD. Pythion: e.g. *IG* IX(2) 1290 II–III (early first century BC); *AE* (1923), 144, no. 379 A (30 BC–AD 50); Gonnoi: e.g. *Gonnoi* II 114, dated to 27 – ca. 25 BC.

in document B by a third party (lines 8–10). The restoration of the payment in denarii seems to contradict the evidence that the change from staters to denarii was introduced by Augustus in 27 BC (see Chapter 2). Kramolisch, 1978, 103, restores the name of the *strategos* in line 4, which belongs to the second manumission document on the stone, as Κ⟨λ⟩[εά]ρχ[ου, and identifies him with Klearchos, the adoptive father of the *strategos* Eubiotos in *AE* (1917), 25, no. 313 from Chyretiai (see below). If the identification is correct, it would explain the dating of *AE* (1924), 188, no. 418a to ca. 50, but not the use of denarii.[14] However, the restored payment in denarii belongs to the first document of the stone, preceding the one dated by Kramolisch to the time of Klearchos. Perhaps the first document was added later, or Arvanitopoulos' restoration is wrong.[15] Evidence of payments in manumission documents from Olosson and Pythion, which have yielded many manumission inscriptions, continues in the second century AD (Olosson) and even the third (Pythion).[16]

In Chyretiai, payments in staters are attested in the first three manumission documents on a first-century BC inscription (*AE*, 1917, 18, no. 309, lines 1–30); the fourth document (lines 31–36) records payment in denarii so it must have been inscribed after 27 BC. Another inscription, again with four manumission records (*AE*, 1917, 18, no. 310), dated to the reign of Augustus, has payments in denarii in all four.[17] However, *AE* (1917), 25, no. 313 seems to present a problem. Although in all four manumission documents recorded on the stone payments are made in denarii, the inscription was dated by Kramolisch to shortly before 31 BC,[18] that is, before the change to denarii. The dating is based on the assumed years of office of the two eponymous federal *strategoi* mentioned in the inscription: Hegesias, son of Arnagoras, for the first manumission document (lines 3–4) and Eubiotos, son of Eukolos and by adoption son of Klearchos, son of Hegesaretos of Larisa, for the other three

---

[14] Klearchos' father, Hegesaretos, was prominent from 63 to 49 BC: Kramolisch 1978, 26, 100–102, no. F8. Cf. Sekunda 1997, 211.

[15] See also *AE* (1924), 173, no. 407 (dated to after 44 BC?), which records both staters and denarii: the first manumitted slave recorded on the stone paid in the former (and only the sum of 10 staters: line 6; see Chapter 2 above); in the second manumission document (lines 9–10) no amount is mentioned; in the third entry, lines 20–21, the two manumitted slaves pay twenty-two and a half denarii each, as do the freed slaves in the following documents on the stone. Since each manumission act belongs to a different year, the change might have happened in or shortly before the third recorded year—that of the *strategos* Lycophron, which therefore may be dated to after 27 BC.

[16] Olosson: e.g. *AE* (1916), 74, no. 282; Pythion: e.g. *AE* (1923) 144, no. 378.

[17] See Chapter 2 on this inscription and Helly's new readings of lines 16–32.

[18] Kramolisch 1978, 121.

documents (lines 12–13). Arvanitopoulos, noting that Eubiotos must be the same *strategos* as the one named in *IG* IX(2) 415 from Pherai, lines 38–39, who precedes the *strategia* of Augustus in 27 BC (lines 74–78), dated Hegesias to 29/8 and Eubiotos to 28/7 BC. As we saw in Chapter 2, the manumission documents following Augustus' *strategia* in *IG* IX(2) 415 start to record payments in denarii (lines 56–61).[19] But note that in contrast to what is recorded under Eubiotos' *strategia* in *AE* (1917), 25, no. 313, in *IG* IX(2) 415 the payments during his year of office (lines 38–65) are in staters. In fact, the lines in *IG* IX(2) 415 which record the change of currency seem to belong to Eubiotos' *strategia* in 28/7 BC. Kramolisch pointed out that because Octavian adopted the title Augustus (which is recorded in *IG* IX(2) 415, line 78: Σεβαστός) in January 27 BC, his Thessalian *strategia* cannot be dated earlier.[20] We should therefore consider the possibility that Augustus' *diorthoma*, the monetary reform following which payments in Thessalian manumissions began to be registered in denarii, was issued before Eubiotos completed his year of office, since the Thessalian year began in the month of Itonios, which corresponded to June/July or to August/September.[21] Accordingly, *AE* (1917), 25, no. 313 may be seen as reflecting the decision by the treasurer of Chyretiai to register the payments in the new currency although formally both Hegesias and Eubiotos were *strategoi* when payments were still made in staters. In other words, it seems that these manumission records were inscribed after 27 BC—after the actual manumission took place, but the treasurer decided to register the payments in the new currency. The first manumission document on the stone, dated by the *strategos* Hegesias, was engraved in a different hand from those dated by Eubiotos, but still records payment in denarii; this seems to reinforce my assumption that all the documents on this stone were inscribed after 27 BC.

Other inscriptions from Chyretiai attest to payments in denarii, and records continue in the third century AD. An example is *SEG* 47.721 B (= ed. pr. A. Tziaphalias, *AD* 49 B1, 1994, [1999] 341 no. 26), from the Roman imperial period.

---

19 See Kramolisch 1978, 121–123. Larsen, 1953, 87–88, does not accept the identification of Eubiotos in *AE* (1917) 25, no. 313, with Eubiotos in *IG* IX(2) 415; and while accepting Arvanitopoulos' dating for the latter, he argues that the former was *strategos* "about the time of the birth of Christ". Kramolisch 1978, 100–102, dates Hegesaretos, the father of Eubiotos' adoptive father, to about the mid-first century BC. Hence Sekunda 1997, 211, surmises that Eubiotos' *strategia* could not have been before the last quarter of the first century BC.

20 Kramolisch 1978, 121–123. Cf. Helly 1997; Bouchon 2008.

21 See Samuel 1972, 83–84; Graninger 2011, 95. See also Bouchon 2008, 434.

But not all manumission inscriptions in Perrhaibia mention such payments, even though they are formulated like those that do,[22] or their date is uncertain. For instance, *SEG* 37.476 from Doliche and *IG* IX(2) 339 from Chyretiai mention payments of twenty-two and a half denarii, but the date is roughly given as 'Roman period'. Perrhaibia's joining the Thessalian *koinon* only in the early 140s may have had to do with the relatively late evidence of payments in this region. Here, however, we risk a circular argument: inscriptions are often dated on the basis of their mention of payments in staters or denarii and of federal *strategoi*, or on the basis of historical assumptions. Thus Kramolisch suggests dating *AE* (1924), 155, no. 400A from Pythion, the earliest Perrhaibian inscription mentioning a Thessalian *strategos* as an eponymous magistrate (which Arvanitopoulos dated to ca. 133–129 BC), to 146, on the conjecture that Perrhaibia joined the Thessalian League following the Achaian War.[23]

Achaia Phthiotis

The single manumission inscription from Halos in which payment in staters is restored (*IG* IX(2) 110) is undated, and the one that mentions denarii is generally dated to the Roman period (*IG* IX(2) 111). In Melitaia, payments in staters are recorded in the middle of the first century BC (*IG* IX(2) 206; 49/8 BC).[24] Kophi (*IG* IX(2) 102) and Phthiotic Thebes (*IG* IX(2) 133) yield evidence of payments in staters as early as 185–180 and 181/0 BC respectively;[25] in Phthiotic Thebes payments continue (in staters and denarii) in Augustus' and Hadrian's times (*BCH* 99, 1975, 648, nos. 2 and 3).[26] In Xyniai, payments

---

22 In Pythion, manumissions were recorded on stone as early as the second century BC, in the same format as in inscriptions that do mention payments; see e.g. *AE* (1924), 155, nos. 400–406, dated by Arvanitopoulos to ca. 133–129–60 BC (on the dating of no. 400 by Kramolisch to 146 BC see below). *SEG* 26.670 from Doliche (= Helly 1976, 147–149; *SEG* 23.462), dated to the second half of the second century BC, is an elaborate manumission record of a single slave, with a *paramone* clause; there is no mention of payment to the polis, but the manumission and its stipulations are said to have been done according to the law.

23 Kramolisch 1978, 61–65; Kramolisch 1979.

24 See also *IG* IX(2) 207l (undated); 207b, c, e, and i from the Roman period, record payments in denarii.

25 Phthiotic Thebes had been under Aitolian control at least until 189 or 185 BC. It seems then that the city adopted almost immediately the federal impost. An inscription found in Tsournati Vrysi and dated to ca. 49/8 BC (*IG* IX(2) 104) has the formula ἔδωκε τᾶι πόλει τὸ ὑπὸ τοῦ νόμου τίμημα ("paid to the polis the value [required] by law").

26 See also *SEG* 26.690. Cf. *AE* (1929) 148, no. 24 (Roman period); (1932), 21, no. 6 (AD 131/2); *Chiron* 5 (1975), 337 A (AD 41/2) and B (AD 52/53).

are attested only in the second century AD (*AD* 10, 1926, 53, no. 12, face A; AD 112), but in staters. A very fragmentary inscription from Thaumakoi, dated by Kern to the third century BC (*IG* IX(2) 221 + a new reading of line 3 in *SEG* 3.471), gives a date in the month of Hermaios (line 1), seems to use the manumission formula ("X by Y"), contains the word "staters" (line 5), and its last extant line reads [– – τὸ γι]νόμενον τᾶι πό[λει – – – –] ("the money due to the polis", line 7). If the dating is correct, we have unique evidence of a manumission payment to the city even before Flamininus' reorganization of the Thessalian League.

Malis

In Lamia, payments are recorded in the first century BC,[27] although manumissions there are attested already in the second century BC[28] and the city was Thessalian by 186/5 BC, as can be gathered from the earliest Lamian inscriptions dated by federal *strategoi*.[29] Inscriptions from the Roman period mention payment of twenty-two and a half denarii.[30] In a fragmentary inscription from Echinos (*IG* IX(2) 92), dated by Kern to the reign of Augustus, something is given to the treasurer and to the priest and ἀγωνοθέτης (*agonothetes*) of the cult of the Sebastoi in Hypata, since they appear in the dative case (lines 3–5). The words "according to the manumission (*apeleutherosis*)" follow, but the text is too fragmentary to infer anything conclusive. Still, Zachou-Kontoyanni offers a new dating (AD 133/4 – ca. 150) and restores lines 1–3 to read ἔδωκεν τῆ] / [πόλει τὰ γεινόμενα τῆς ἀπελευθερώσεως ἀντὶ τῶν στατήρων] / [ἀργυρίου (δηνάρια) εἴκοσι δύο ἥμ]ισον ("paid the polis the due money on the occasion of manumission, instead of the staters, twenty-two and a half silver denarii").[31] Zachou-Kontoyanni restores a similar phrasing

---

27 *IG* IX(2) 71 (after 60 BC), 72 (ca. 50 BC) and 73 (not dated, but payment is still in staters).

28 Some inscriptions, e.g. *IG* IX(2) 74–76 (= *SEG* 30.531A–C) (all dated after 150 BC), mention no payment, but the reference to the treasurer in no. 74AS inscribing the names of the manumitted slaves (τοῦ[σδε ὁ τα]/μίας Κλέων Θεύρωνος ἀνέ⟨γ⟩ρ⟨α⟩[ψε, lines 1–2) and the arrangement of the entries in chronological order, similarly to other inscriptions discussed above, may imply it.

29 See *IG* IX(2) 64 and 67.

30 See e.g. *IG* IX(2) 78b.

31 Zachou-Kontoyanni 1989, 213 (= *SEG* 39.493). See ib. 213–214 with n. 24, where the author also discusses the reference to the priest and *agonothetes* of the imperial family cult in Hypata in a manumission document from Echinos; she suggests that Echinos was somehow dependent on Hypata, and interprets the words ἐν Ὑπάτᾳ κατὰ τὴν ἀπελευθέρω[σιν] in line 5 as indicating that one priest and one *agonothetes* were in Hypata at the time of the

in another manumission inscription from Echinos (= Reilly 1971, 669, no. 1), which she dates to ca. AD 133/4–150: ἐδέδωκεν [Τα]λασείνῳ {[27]ἔ̓δ{εδ}ωκεν (= ἔ̓δωκεν) [Γε(?)]λασείνῳ [– –] / [δεῖνος τῷ ταμίᾳ τῆς πόλεως ἀντὶ τῶν] / [στατήρων ἀργυρίου (δηνάρια) κβʹ (ἥμισυ) ("paid to Talaseinos/Gelaseinos, son of [---], the treasurer of the polis, instead of the staters—twenty-two and a half silver denarii", lines 5–7).[32] I can think of no other explanation for Echinos having to note the change from staters to denarii as late as the second century AD than the ongoing registration of payments in this city in staters (at least in the case of manumission) long after the formal change. We have no earlier inscriptions to support this assumption, but evidence shows that in other places too payments were still made in staters after 27 BC.[33]

Ainis

Many manumission inscriptions from Hypata mention payments, starting in the first century BC (but we do not know what currency was used)[34] and persisting in the second century AD, when denarii are sometimes mentioned.[35] Ainis was still an independent *koinon* in about the mid-80s BC[36] and it has been assumed that it joined the Thessalian League only in 27 BC. Accordingly, we may assume that the payments were made in denarii and that perhaps all the manumission inscriptions should be dated after that year. But if the dating of *IG* IX(2) 12 to 49/8 BC is correct it may be taken as the *terminus ante quem* for the integration of Ainis into the Thessalian League,

manumission. Cf. Reilly 1971, 674, no. 3, line 3; Reilly (pp. 672–674) refers to the payments mentioned as a "manumission tax".

32 Zachou-Kontoyanni 1989, 214 (= *SEG* 39.494). Likewise in *SEG* 36.543, 544, 545, 546 (ed. pr. Gounaropoulou 1987, 253 A–D; cf. Zachou-Kontoyanni 1989, 210, proposing an amendment to line 5 of Gounaropoulou's text C); 39.496 (= Reilly 1971, 674, no. 3 = Zachou-Kontoyanni 1989, 215, no. 3)—all dated to AD 133/134 – ca. 150.

33 See Chapter 2 above. See also *AJPh* 92 (1971) 669, no. 1 from Echinos (undated), where line 5 has the word ἐδέδωκεν ("paid"), followed by a name in the dative case; and cf. *AJPh* 92 (1971) 674, no. 3.

34 See e.g. *IG* IX(2) 12 (49/8 BC).

35 See *IG* IX(2) 13 (AD 47); Bouchon 2009, 401, face 1, lines 1–2, and face 6, lines 10–11 (= *IG* IX(2) 21 and 22 respectively) (AD 131/132). Two other inscriptions, which mention the "*epimeletes* of the money pertaining to manumitted slaves" (on which see Chapter 3 above), are dated to the second century AD, but do not state the currency used (*IG* IX(2) 17 and 19). See also *IG* IX(2) 14a (AD 47/8), where neither the currency nor the amount paid is specified.

36 For decrees of the League of the Ainians see *IG* IX(2) 4a (undated); 5a and b (ca. 130 BC); 6 (ca. 130 BC); 37 (148–146 BC); 38 (88–80 BC); *Syll.*^{3} 743. For the date of Ainis' joining the Thessalian League see Larsen 1968, 282–283.

that is, before 27 BC.[37] In that case the payments in this fragmentary inscription, which only preserves the general phrase "the manumitted slaves who paid what is due, according to the law" (οἱ ἀπελεύθεροι ἔδωκαν τὸ γινόμε]/νον κατὰ τὸν νό[μον, lines 2–3), must have been registered in staters.

Dolopia

This region, which seems to have been incorporated into the Thessalian League sometime after the Third Macedonian War, yields a single manumission inscription from the city of Angea, dated to the third century AD (*SEG* 15.368c = *IG* IX(2) 228c). The text mentions an obligatory payment, but the currency and amount were not recorded or have not been preserved (ἔ/δωκον τ/ῇ πόλε[ι] τὸ ⟨γ⟩ενό[με]/[ν]ον διὰ [τ]οῦ Καλ/λικράτ/ους, lines 11–18).[38]

No manumission inscription has been found in Oitaia. However, we have some manumission inscriptions of unknown provenance. *BCH* 99 (1975), 120, no. 1, dated to 16/15 BC, notes in lines 6–7 that the manumitted slaves paid the polis, according to the amendment (*diorthoma*), twenty-two and a half denarii. All we can assume with any confidence is that this record was inscribed shortly after 27 BC.[39]

This brief survey of the last two centuries BC and the first three centuries AD illustrates the uneven distribution of the evidence on payment throughout Thessaly of what seems to be a fixed federal impost on manumitted slaves. As stated above, these finds may well be accidental, and future discoveries might change the picture considerably. Also, many of the extant manumission inscriptions which do not mention payments are fragmentary, and to judge by the layout of their texts (eponymous magistrates in the

---

37 See Sekunda 1997, 208–214, who suggests dating Ainis' joining the Thessalian League to after the battle of Pharsalos in 48 BC, or even earlier.

38 The inscription records the manumission of two slaves (the name of the first has not survived; the second is a female) by Charilaos (lines 4–10). The text ends abruptly after the mention of Kallikrates, through whom (διὰ [τ]οῦ) the manumitted slaves paid the polis, so there is no way of knowing why this was done. Perhaps he was the treasurer.

39 The extant text of the inscription contains only the heading and the formula οἱ ἀπη-λευ]/θερωμένοι καὶ δεδωκότες [τῇ πόλει τὰ κατὰ] / τὸ διόρθωμα δηνάρια εἴκοϛ[ι δύο καὶ ἥμισυ]; then follows the name of the first recorded month (Themistios), but no names of owners and freed slaves have been preserved. On the change from staters to denarii see in Chapter 2. See also *BCH* 99 (1975) 127, no. 2c, where no payment is mentioned; pp. 133, no. 3, 134, no. 4, 141, no. 5, 142, no. 6, where the sum paid is in denarii.

heading—often including the treasurer; names of slaves and their owners, with a verb or a preposition indicating that these texts record manumissions; chronological order by years, months, and days), it is very likely that originally they did register payments. However, perhaps not everywhere in Thessaly were manumissions inscribed in stone. If, as I tend to believe, the recorded payments were levied, wholly or partly, to cover inscription costs, the possibility should be considered that some cities and some freed slaves were content to record manumissions on perishable materials (wooden tablets, papyri) which were then stored in public or private archives.

Nevertheless, judging from this survey we can be certain that the fee on manumission exacted by many Thessalian poleis was a federal charge, and that it was first introduced early in the second century BC, most likely after the declaration of liberty by Flamininus in 196 or after his reorganization of the Thessalian League in 194 BC. The fee seems to have been first applied in Pelasgiotis, perhaps in Larisa,[40] and to have spread thence to other cities and regions in tandem with the League's territorial expansion.[41] However, in view of some (admittedly meagre) evidence discussed above, it must be considered that a kind of a levy on manumission was exacted in Thessaly even before the reorganization of the League since inscriptions recording dedications from Larisa and Atrax, mentioned above (*IG* IX(2) 594, and *SEG* 46.622 respectively), and one recording staters from Thaumakoi (*IG* IX(2) 221) are dated to the third century BC.[42] In any event, such fees do not seem to have been uniform in amount or imposed as federal policy.

The entire body of evidence on payments by manumitted slaves in Greece—whether in cash or in sacrifice and as dedication—starts to build up in the second half of the third century BC (Macedonia) and, where only cash is concerned, in the second century (including the substitute for sacrifice in Kos).[43] Since this evidence comes from a wide range of places it cannot be explained only by specific local circumstances nor, I believe, by Roman influence alone. Although the Thessalians' new federal organization

---

40 If *IG* IX(2) 274 from Metropolis, dated to 186/5 BC, originally mentioned payments, then our earliest evidence comes from Hestiaiotis. See above.

41 In the perioecic regions of Achaia Phthiotis and Perrhaibia, who joined the League early, evidence of payments starts in the mid-180s; see above. Evidence from the *ethne* is uneven: only one, late, inscription comes from Dolopia and no manumission inscriptions were found in Oitaia; this, however, may be accidental since in the other *ethne*, Malis and Ainis, manumission inscriptions start to record payments when these regions joined the League.

42 The inscription from Thaumakoi mentions payment in staters to the polis.

43 See Chapter 4 above.

was given to them in 194 BC by a Roman general (Liv. 34.51.4–6), the federal administration of the Thessalian League was essentially Greek (with its *synedrion* and chosen magistrates). Even after 146 BC and its probable absorption into the province of Achaia, Thessaly continued to use local manumission practices and local currency (as the persistent reference to staters and obols indicates); and it kept on doing so into the second century AD.[44] Moreover, the fact that Augustus agreed or chose to be elected *strategos* of the Thessalian League in 27/6 BC can be seen as his acknowledgment of this federation and its functioning.[45] It seems unlikely that the Romans, who allowed the Thessalians a considerable measure of autonomy in conducting their lives, would have obligated them to exact a manumission tax in the Roman way.

The motivation for introducing the levy on manumitted slaves must be sought elsewhere, and it seems twofold: economic, and the need to keep a check on the non-citizen population. As for the economic motive, in the last two decades of the third and the first half of the second century BC Greece experienced a series of political upheavals and military conflicts which carried economic consequences. The First Macedonian War and its aftermath (214–205 BC); the Second Macedonian War (200–197 BC) and Flamininus' arrangements in Greece (194 BC); the Roman war against the Aitolians and Antiochos III (192–188 BC); the Third Macedonian War and the subsequent new political arrangements (171–168 BC); the Achaian War (146 BC) with its political consequences for Greece—all exerted their effect.

Thessaly was no exception. As on previous occasions, Thessaly was one of the major theatres in military struggles and itself played a significant role in the events. The last months of the Second Macedonian War were fought on Thessalian soil, which suffered damage: forced to retreat to Thessaly in 198, Philip V destroyed the cities and crops;[46] Flamininus followed by invading Thessaly, and so did the Aitolians and Amynander, king of Athamania, who laid the country waste[47] before the decisive battle of Kynoskephalai in 197 BC. Most of the Thessalian cities chose to side with the Romans, a decision which paid off in 196, when at the Isthmian Games Flamininus declared

---

44 See Larsen 1968, 281–293. See also Paterson 2001, 368, on 'regionalism' in the economy of the Roman Empire.

45 See Larsen 1955, 110. On Augustus as the *strategos* of the League see the above discussion of *IG* IX(2) 415 from Pherai, and Chapter 2.

46 Liv. 32.13.5–8; Plut. *Flam.* 5.2. See also Salviat and Vatin 1974, 260–262, discussing an agrarian crisis in Thessaly following the First Macedonian War.

47 Liv. 32.13.10–15; 33.14.1–4.

the Thessalians free, and likewise the Perrhaibians, the Magnesians, and the Phthiotic Achaians, after being under Macedonian rule for 150 years.[48] But things in Thessaly called for profound changes, as can be seen from Livy's report of Flamininus' moves in 194 BC (34.51.4–6):

> [4] ... *pergit ire in Thessaliam, ubi non liberandae modo civitates erant, sed ex omni colluvione et confusione in aliquam tolerabilem formam redigendae.* [5] *nec enim temporum modo vitiis ac violentia et licentia regia turbati erant, sed inquieto etiam ingenio gentis, nec comitia nec conventum nec concilium ullum non per seditionem ac tumultum iam inde a principio ad nostram usque aetatem traducentis.* [6] *a censu maxime et senatum et iudices legit potentioremque eam partem civitatium fecit, cui salva et tranquilla omnia esse magis expediebat.*

> [4] ... He continued his journey to Thessaly, where the cities had not only to be set free, but also to be brought into some reasonable condition of order after all the chaos and confusion. [5] For they had been thrown into confusion not only by the faults of the times and the king's lawless and violent behaviour, but also by the restless character of the people, which from the earliest times down to the present day has never conducted a meeting or an assembly or a council without dissension and rioting. [6] He chose the senate and magistrates mainly on the basis of property and strove to make that element in the community more influential which found it advantageous to have everything peaceful and quiet.[49]

But not long after their liberation and the reorganization of their League, the Thessalians abandoned Rome. In winter 192/191 BC most of them, mindful of the fate of Pherai, went over to Antiochos III who had invaded their country.[50] This move prompted the Romans and Philip to march into Thessaly, and after Antiochos' defeat at Thermopylai (192 BC) Thessalian cities were given to the Macedonian king.[51] Thessaly became again the chief the-

---

[48] See Polyb. 18.47.6–7; Liv. 33.34.6; Plut. *Flam.* 10.4; Larsen, 1968, 282; Gruen 1984, 449; Eckstein 2008, 288. On Thessaly in the Second Macedonian War, see also Larsen 1968, 378–406; Grainger 1999, 338–404; Scherberich 2009, 157–175; Graninger 2011, 28.

[49] The English translation is by E.T. Sage for the Loeb Classical Library (1935). On these events see Larsen 1968, 282, 397–405; Gruen 1984, 455 n. 103; Graninger 2011, 29–31. For Roman intervention in internal affairs see also Flamininus' letter to the polis Chyretiai in Thessaly, *Syll.*³ 593 (= *IG* IX(2) 338), of 196–194 BC, which declares the restoration to the city property that had been considered as belonging to the Romans; cf. Armstrong and Walsh 1986. The problems in Thessaly before Flamininus' arrival seem to have involved titles to land: Larsen, 1968, 285 n. 1. The quoted passage from Livy has led most scholars to believe that the governments of the Thessalian cities after Flamininus' arrangements were oligarchic; for a different view see Walsh 2000.

[50] See Liv. 36.9–10; Gruen 1984, 478–479; Grainger 1999, 435–498.

[51] Cf. Liv. 36.9.13–14; 36.33.

atre of operations during the Third Macedonian War (171–169 BC) and was itself caught up in it, its cities being besieged and plundered.[52] In 149 BC Thessaly was invaded again, this time by Andriskos, a pretender to the Macedonian throne.[53]

Direct evidence from Thessaly of economic difficulties caused by these wars and for other reasons is sparse, but there are some indications that Thessalian cities, like cities elsewhere in Greece, suffered shortages of funds and grain, which in the 170s resulted in heavy debts and civil strife. Diodorus Siculus (29.33) says that the Thessalians emulated the Aitolians by declaring a cancellation of debts and that civil strife and turmoil broke out in every city.[54] Livy too (42.5.7–10) refers to the state of affairs in 173 BC:

> [7] *erant autem non Aetoli modo in seditionibus propter ingentem vim aeris alieni, sed Thessali etiam. ex contagione velut tabes in Perrhaebiam quoque id pervaserat malum.* [8] *cum Thessalos in armis esse nuntiatum esset, Ap. Claudium legatum ad eas res aspiciendas conponendasque senatus misit.* [9] *qui utriusque partis principibus castigatis, cum iniusto faenore gravatum aes alienum, ipsis magna ex parte concedentibus, qui onerarant, levasset, iusti crediti solutionem in decem annorum pensiones distribuit.* [10] *per eundem Appium eodemque modo compositae in Perrhaebia res.*

> But it was not only the Aitolians who were in a state of civil war because of the enormous weight of debt, but also the Thessalians; and the evil, like a pestilence, had spread by contagion even into Perrhaibia. [8] When it was reported that the Thessalians were in arms, the senate sent Appius Claudius (Pulcher) as legate to examine and settle these affairs. And he, after reproving the leaders of both factions, removed the burden of the [9] debts which had been made heavy by unjust interest, with the consent of the majority of the creditors themselves, and distributed the payment of the just debts over ten annual instalments. [10] The difficulties in Perrhaibia were settled by the same Appius in the same way.[55]

Epigraphic evidence, though fragmentary and often ambiguous, is larger and attests to earlier years. Thus Philip V's two letters to Larisa recommending the grant of citizenship to metics, with the intention of intensifying land cultivation, indicate the agricultural condition of the city.[56] What

---

52 See Polyb. 29.19.8; Liv. 42.51–62, 64, 67; Larsen, 1968, 283; Mendels 1978, 61–63.

53 Polyb. 37.2; Liv. 48–50; Paus. 7.13.1; App. *Pun.* 20.135.

54 See Walsh 2000, who takes this passage as evidence that the governments of the Thessalian cities were not oligarchic but favourable to the debtors, not to the creditors, and that it was the latter who initiated the violence.

55 See also Larsen 1968, 283; Gruen 1984, 106.

56 *IG* IX(2) 514; *Syll.*[3] 543. See Habicht 2006, 67–73.

appears to be an extensive census of sacred land in Larisa, conducted in two stages in the late third or early second century BC, attests to the effects of the wars on agriculture and on the polis' control of its sacred land.[57] The first of these inscriptions seems to be an inventory of sacred properties, drawn up as groundwork for the restoration of the sanctuaries. According to Salviat and Vatin, the lands were those of certain sanctuaries and had been partially usurped by private individuals. The purpose of the survey seems to have been the reorganization of the sacred properties. The text speaks of steles lying flat and of enclosures being levelled to their foundation stones (line 40). If the inscription indeed dates to the end of the third century BC, the troubles of 229, the Aitolian occupation, and the Macedonian re-conquest may have been the setting of this effort to restore order. But the early years of the second century BC could also explain the need to reorganize the public property after the damage inflicted by the Second Macedonian War.

Decrees issued by Thessalian cities also reveal financial difficulties. *SEG* 33.460 (= Ch. Habicht, *Chiron* 13, 1983, 21–32; Migeotte, 1992, 90–93, no. 33), dated between 197 and 186 BC, records a decision by the polis Larisa to raise funds to renovate the gymnasium. The motive given is καὶ δι/ẹ̄χ̣ι κατεπείγει ἁ χρεία ... διὲ τὸ μεὶ ἔμμεν *vac.* [χρ]ẹίμματα ἐν τοῦ κοινοῦ ("because the shortage presses hard ... because of there not being money in the common [treasury]"; lines 9–10, 12–13). The decision is followed by a list of contributors. In the first half of the second century BC the city of Gonnoi also raised money, as indicated by a very fragmentary decree (Helly, *Gonnoi II*, no. 113 = *AE*, 1913, 48, no. 177; Migeotte 1992, 96–97, no. 35). However, the reason for that fundraising has not been preserved; all that survives is some names of contributors and the sums of money they donated. Between 179 and 142 BC the city of Krannon, being in debt, decided to raise money by decreeing that every citizen must contribute to the city as much as he could from his private property (Y. Béquignon, *BCH* 59, 1935, 37, face 2= *SEG* 15.371; Migeotte, 1992, 93–96, no. 34). The motivation clause (lines 9–13) reads as follows:

ἐπειδεὶ ἁ πόλι̣[ς]
ἐν δανείοις πλειόνεσσι ὑπάρχει δι-
ὲ τὸς πεστάντας αὐτᾶ πολέμος κα̣[ὶ]
χρόνος εἴδε πλείονας ἕλκονθαι̣ τὰ
δάνεια.

---

[57] Salviat and Vatin 1971, 9, no. 1; Salviat and Vatin 1974, 251. Cf. *IG* IX(2) 1014; *SEG* 26.674. See also Helly 1974, who thinks that the first of these texts deals not only with sacred land but with sanctuaries and dedications which existed on the land when the inspection took place.

> Since the polis has incurred many debts due to the wars which surround it and because these debts have dragged on for a long time.[58]

Motivation clauses in honorary decrees issued for individuals may also reveal financial difficulties.[59] In ca. 186 BC the city of Larisa decided to praise Q. Titus Flamininus, and grant privileges to him and his descendants, because of his help and good will towards the polis in the hardships of the long war (*AE*, 1910, 344, no. 3, lines 1–6):

> [..... τῆς πόλε]ως κ[αὶ]
> [τῶν ἀγρῶ]ν ἀρουμένων ἥ[κισ]-
> [τα διὰ τὸν πο]λυετῆ πόλεμον· καὶ κιν-
> [δυνευ]ούσης τῆς πόλεως, κατ[α]-
> [λειφθείσης] ὑπὸ τῶν τηβεννοφορο[ύ]-
> [ντων, αὐτὸ]ς οὐκ ἐνκατέλιπεν ...

> [.....] the polis and the fields being hardly tilled because of the long war; and when the city was in danger, being abandoned by the toga-wearers (the Romans), he himself did not leave it ...[60]

In ca. 180–170 BC Pythion granted *proxenia* to two persons because of the help they rendered the polis in its financial difficulties (*SEG* 36.552, lines 3–6, 19–21 = *AD* 35 A, 1980, 232–240):

> ἐπειδὴ ἐν οἷς
> χρεί[α]ν εἶχεν ἡ πόλις ἡ Πυθοιαστῶν εὐ[ερ]-
> γετήθη ὑπὸ Ξενοκλέου τοῦ Δικ[α]ιοκρά-
> του Ἀσκυριέως ...
> ...
> ἐπειδὴ ἐν [ο]ἷς χρείαν εἶχ[εν ἡ]
> πόλις ἡ Πυθοιαστῶν εὐεργετήθ[η]
> [ὑπὸ – –]ΑΡΝΑΙΟΥ καὶ ΤΟ[– –]ΘΥΕ

> Since in its time of need the polis of Pythion was benefited by Xenokles, son of Dikaiokrates, the Askyrian ...
>
> Since in its time of need the polis of Pythion was benefited by [...]

---

[58] Cf. Engelmann 1999, 137–139, no. 1, on a list of contributors in second-century BC Metropolis. In this case too, the decree itself, with the reason for the fund-raising, has not been preserved.

[59] Many honorific decrees contain motivation clauses which indicate economic difficulties, but I limit my discussion to examples which also refer to the difficulties of the community as a whole.

[60] On the expression τηβεννοφοροῦντες as indicating the existence of an Italian community in Larisa, see Bouchon 2007 and his new readings. For lines 3–6 he restores: καὶ κιν/[δυνευ]ούσης τῆς πόλεως, κατα/[λειφθεῖναι?] ὑπὸ τῶν τηβεννοφόρω[ν], / [αὐτός γ]ε οὐκ ἐνκατέλιπεν ... Based on dialectical and palaeographical considerations, Bouchon re-dates the inscription to the early years of the first century BC and interprets the war mentioned there as the Mithradatic Wars (pp. 260–261).

For similar reasons the polis Krannon decided in 168 BC to praise and honour Lion, son of Pausanias, of Metropolis for helping the city as a whole and the citizens personally in times of need (χρεία) (*IG* IX(2) 461b, lines 21–26). For the same period we find a grant of *proxenia* by Gonnoi to Nikias, son of Thersimenes, of Phalanna (*Gonnoi* II 41; 180–160 BC) who, among other things (lines 15–17),

> καὶ ἐν τῶι παρεληλυθότι δὲ ἔτει
> [οὔ]σης σπανοσιτίας, εἴοι εὐχρηστή-
> [σα]ς τῇ πόλει σῖτον ἐπ' ἀναβολῇ·
>
> … in the previous year, when there was a shortage of grain, helped the polis with grain (consenting to) deferred payment.[61]

Even more explicit about the existence of financial difficulties, leading to quarrels over debt, is *IG* IX(2) 1230, a decree issued by Phalanna in honour of Glaukon, son of Apollonios, of Gyrton(?) in the second century BC, granting him citizenship and other privileges. Lines 1–17 state the reasons for this grant: Glaukon, who seems to have been invited by Phalanna to settle "the disputes and turbulence present among the citizens" (τὴν ἐ[ν]σ[τᾶσ]αν δ[ιαφ]ορὰν καὶ ταραχὴν ἐν τοῖ[ς] π̣ολίταις [δι]α̣λῦσαι), acted to resolve problems arising from contracts which those who lacked money were unable to uphold, put an end to civil strife, and restored concord to the city (κ̣[αὶ σ]τάσιν ἀνελὼν εἰς ὁμόνοια[ν κα]τή[γαγ]εν).

In the same region of Greece a decree of the Magnesian League dated to 120–115 BC (*SEG* 32.613) justifies the honours bestowed on Polemaios, son of Harpagion, of Kalydon by saying that he helped both the *koinon* (the League as a whole) and private citizens in times of need (χρεία) (lines 16–18).[62] As we saw above (Chapter 4), manumission inscriptions from Magnesia do not provide evidence of payments similar to those recorded in the cities of the Thessalian League, and the reference to what seems to be a manumission tax is of much later date.[63] But this does not rule out the possibility that in

---

61 Cf. *ISE* II, 103, lines 12–16, from Larisa (196–146 BC); *IG* IX(2) 519 face I, lines 2–8, from Larisa (late second century BC); *IG* IX(2) 259, lines 22–23 (= *I Thess.* I 16) from Kierion (ca. 125 BC). Garnsey, Gallant and Rathbone 1984, discuss an inscription dated to the mid-second century BC, which shows that Thessaly provided grain for the Roman populace in response to a request from a Roman magistrate; but the authors stress that from time to time Thessaly suffered from failure of crops caused by climatic hazards or wars.

62 Cf. *IG* IX(2) 1103, lines 14–15 (130–126 BC). Likewise, in the first century BC the Magnesian League honoured its former *strategos*, Sopatros son of Euboulos, because of his help at a time of grain shortage (*IG* IX(2) 1104).

63 Several manumission inscriptions from Magnesia, all from the Roman period, mention the *lytron* (from Demetrias: *IG* IX(2) 1100b III, line 12; 1116b, line 3; 1117c, line 2; 1119, line 13,

Magnesia too economic troubles stimulated the federal government to exact fees for the registration and publication of manumission acts—for which, however, no evidence survives. As Walsh argues, the economic crisis in the 170s was regional, affecting Aitolia, Thessaly, Perrhaibia and Boiotia.[64] But the evidence discussed above indicates that these difficulties started earlier, in the first quarter of the second century BC.

The faltering economy, then, could have been behind the decision to introduce the charge on the registration and publication of manumissions. The federal government decided or advised its members to impose this fee as a means to increase revenues—for the cities themselves and for federal needs, such as the maintenance of the federal army which had been in action almost throughout the second century BC. Part of the money was perhaps kept in the cities themselves and helped to cover publication and other costs, while the rest was probably sent to the federal treasury. This, of course, is only hypothetical, and we have only a few texts that refer to the poleis' use of the proceeds of the tax. In Hypata, as we have seen, the ἐπιμελητὴς τῶν ἀπελευθερικῶν χρημάτων administered a fund from which proceeds were allocated to magistrates.[65] In Echinos, the beneficiaries were the priests of the imperial cult.[66] In Rome, the proceeds of the five-percent *vicesima libertatis* until Caracalla were used in emergencies;[67] as noted in Chapter 4, Caracalla raised the tax to ten percent in order to increase his revenues.[68] Similar needs may have motivated the League's decision to exact money for the registration and publication of manumission acts. In fact, the creation of the office of the "*epimeletes* of the monies pertaining to manumitted slaves" in Hypata may be seen as instigated by two motives, perhaps shared by other Thessalian poleis. This office may imply that the number of manumissions in second-century AD Hypata was so high as to justify the establishment of a special fund to provide for public activities and at the same time to warrant a means to control the numbers of non-citizens.

---

but certainly intended also, without explicit use of the term, in lines 5 and 8; from Iolkos: *SEG* 23.460, line 2), but this term most probably denotes the price of freedom paid to the manumittor (although in the first case mentioned above the restored word πόλει in line 13 makes it a payment to the polis; see Chapter 4 above).

64 See Walsh 2000.

65 *IG* IX(2) 56 = Bouchon 2009, face 6, lines 1–9.

66 *SEG* 36.543= Gounaropoulos 1987, 253 A–D; *SEG* 39.493 = Zachou-Kontoyanni 1989, 213. See Bouchon 2009, 402–403.

67 See Liv. 27.10.11; Caes. *BC* 1.14.1; Cic. *Att.* 7.21.2; App. *BC* 2.41; cf. Bradley 1984a, 149–150; 1984b, 175.

68 Cassius Dio 78.9.4–5.

Indeed, as noted above, the second motive for levying payments upon manumission may have been the need to monitor the non-citizen population. Whether my interpretation of this payment is correct or whether it was a manumission tax, the freed slaves who paid it were registered on stone—and very likely also in the cities' archives. By registering manumitted slaves the cities not only increased their revenues, they were also able to ensure that non-citizens would not encroach on citizens' rights or evade fulfilling their duties as non-citizen residents. This was one of the main concerns of Greek poleis, which guarded their citizenship, and granted it to foreigners only by a special decision of the Assembly even in the Hellenistic and Roman periods. Thessalian cities occasionally granted citizenship to foreigners;[69] and in 217 BC Philip V encouraged Larisa to grant citizenship to metics in order to overcome difficulties caused by war.[70] Approximately in the same period Pharsalos granted citizenship and land to (presumably) Penestai (*IG* IX(2) 234 = *ZPE* 81, 1990, 163–184),[71] and Phalanna issued a decree granting citizenship to other Thessalians (*IG* IX(2) 1228). But such grants did not abolish the need to clearly demarcate citizens from non-citizens. The reaction of Larisa to Philip's first letter—granting citizenship to metics but then removing them again from the citizens' lists (as transpires from the second letter[72])—may indicate the deep-rooted aversion to liberally sharing the exclusivity of citizenship with foreigners. True, honorific decrees issued by Thessalian poleis, such as those mentioned above, show that the Thessalians did not entirely eschew granting citizenship and privileges to foreigners, but these decrees also prove that the boundaries between citizens and non-citizens were still protected zealously.

But if the need to register manumitted slaves can be explained on the local level, it is less easy to understand the federal interest in this act. Yet the same dual position on foreigners, revealed in individual poleis' honorific decrees, can be inferred from decrees issued in the name of the entire Thessalian League. Thus *IG* IX(2) 505 (= *SEG* 47.744, of ca. 130 BC), is a decree issued by the League (τὸ κοινὸν τῶν Θεσσαλῶν) in honour of judges from Mylasa, praising them and granting them and their descendants citizenship

---

[69] E.g. *IG* IX(2) 11 (Hypata); *IG* IX(2) 61 (Lamia); *IG* IX(2) 458 (Krannon); *SEG* 33.448 (Atrax); Habicht, 1970, 139 (Metropolis).

[70] *IG* IX(2) 517 = *Syll.*[3] 543; see Habicht, 2006, 67–73. Philip's letters, as noted above, also imply economic difficulties in Larisa.

[71] See Ducat 1994, 107–113, and the Introduction.

[72] *IG* IX(2) 517, lines 16–27: πυνθάνομαι τοὺς πολιτογραφηθέντας κατὰ τὴν παρ' ἐμοῦ ἐπιστολὴν καὶ τὸ ψήφισμα τὸ ὑμέτερον καὶ ἀναγραφέντας εἰς τὰς στήλας ἐκκεκολάφθαι.

and *proxenia*.[73] But *SEG* 29.531 (= te Riele 1982, 170–174, no. 3), a list of manumissions from Larisa, dated to the first century AD, includes an entry which reads "Philemon (manumitted) by the *koinon* of the Thessalians" (Φιλήμων ἀπὸ τοῦ κοινοῦ τῶν Θεσσαλῶν; lines 22–23). This ex-slave probably served in the League's administration and his status was similar to that of public slaves (*demosioi*) in Greek poleis.[74] Although the extant text of the inscription does not mention payments, the fact that the federal authorities saw fit to include the case of Philemon in a public manumission record may indicate that the League was interested in publicly registering freed slaves in the way suggested by the manumission records of individual poleis.

The fragmentary condition of most of the Thessalian manumission inscriptions makes it plausible to think that the actual number of manumissions in the centuries following the reorganization of the League was larger than the number of the extant records, which amounts to some 1760 manumissions; as noted in Chapter 2, the corpus of the Thessalian manumission inscriptions seems to equal or even outnumber the Delphic corpus.[75] It is not easy to assess why so many slaves were manumitted. Most likely, the economic difficulties described above motivated slave owners to minimize expenses by reducing the number of mouths to feed in the household, while making some profit from the money paid by their freed slaves in return for freedom. This, of course, was not the only reason; as we saw in Chapter 2, some of the manumitted slaves were probably spouses and children of the manumittors, and other motives undoubtedly came into play.[76] But it is also conceivable that it was this large number of manumissions that moved the federal government to impose the registration fee—both because it realised

---

73 Line 28 of the inscription states that these privileges, including citizenship, were granted to the foreign judges and their secretary, and to their descendants, "in all the poleis in Thessaly". This means that if the honorands decided to implement their citizenship, any polis to their liking had to comply with the League's decree and consider them its citizens. In any case, the grant of both citizenship and *proxenia* suggests that the citizenship was meant to be merely nominal. Cf. *SEG* 47.745 (second century BC) for a similar decree, although the part conferring the honours has not been preserved; *SEG* 34.558, lines 1–16 (ca. 150–130 BC).

74 See te Riele 1982, 174, who remarks that as far as is known this is the first case attested of a manumission by the Thessalian League. In Atrax a slave named Herakleides was manumitted by the polis, "according to the law" (*Mélanges Daux* 6, 5, lines 1–2; reign of Augustus). The inscription, which records ten manumissions in at least two years, does not mention payments at all.

75 As noted in Chapter 2, it is not easy to estimate the number of manumissions recorded in these inscriptions.

76 For the motivation for manumission see Hopkins 1978, 118–129, 134; Zelnick-Abramovitz 2005a, 147–153, 162–169.

its financial advantage for the members and for the League and because it feared infiltration of the poleis' citizen bodies by non-citizens. So it seems that where the whole League was concerned the motivation behind the federal impost was both economic and socio-political.

As noted above, the uneven distribution of the evidence on the payment of this levy in the various cities may be due to the chance survival and condition of inscriptions. Our earliest explicit evidence emanates from Larisa, the chief city of the League, and from Achaia Phthiotis, which by ca. 185 BC belonged to the Thessalian League; but the extant evidence does not necessarily follow the dates of the Thessalian League's expansion. Moreover, although it is certain that this levy represented some federal policy, we do not know if it was compulsory. If it was, the absence of evidence of payments in some cities should be considered accidental. But although the levy was federal and compulsory, engraving the acts of manumission in stone perhaps was not. As indicated earlier, it is very probable that manumission acts were registered on perishable material and deposited in local archives, solely, or in addition to the inscribed copies. If this theory is correct, we should assume that in such places the money was paid for inscribing the slaves' new status in stone. On the other hand, inscriptions comprising lists of manumissions without mentioning payments, yet dated by the *strategoi* of the League and the local treasurers, arranged chronologically, and originating from poleis yielding other inscriptions that *do* mention the payments, were almost certainly just formulated differently.[77]

But there are still some puzzling questions: if these payments were a federal impost, as their uniformity implies, where does the federation come in? Did local authorities transfer the money to the central treasury, and if so, by what means? Was the federal government satisfied with merely receiving the remittances, or was there also a central registration of the sums received? And if there was a federal registration as well, was it arranged by cities? Did such records also contain the names of the paying manumitted slaves (and perhaps also of the manumittors) and were they arranged chronologically as in the local inscribed records? It must be significant that no such record has been discovered to date; and although future finds may change the picture, we cannot ignore this 'silence', which appears to imply

[77] And since many inscriptions were found with their headings broken off, these may have included a statement such as "those manumitted slaves who paid ...", as e.g. in *IG* IX(2) 288 from Gomphoi (οἱ ἐξε/[λευθερω]θέν[τ]ες καὶ δεδωκότες τὸ γινόμενον / [εἰς τ]ὴν [π]όλιν κατὰ τὸν νόμον; lines 1–3), and many others.

that although this levy was imposed as a federal policy the payments were handled locally. If this is correct, it might add further support to my assumption that these payments were not a manumission tax levied centrally.

Moreover, as we saw in Chapter 1, evidence of federal collection of taxes is absent in the Thessalian League, as it is in other federations. This may indicate that all imposts, including the fees imposed on publication of manumissions, were collected locally. Alternatively, the Thessalians may have had an arrangement similar to the one attested in *IG* IX 1^2 2, 583 (216 BC) from Anaktorion, whereby revenues from the taxes collected during the festival to Apollo in Aktion (including a tax on slaves sales) were shared between the polis of Anaktorion and the Akarnanian League.[78]

There are other considerations that may imply that taxes were not collected centrally. Despite their federal organization, the members of the Thessalian League were considerably independent in their inter-state relations.[79] For instance, even when in 183 BC the Thessalians sent delegates to the Roman Senate to complain against Philip, "there were ambassadors from the whole nation (*koinon*), and also from each city separately" (Polyb. 23.1.10). Likewise, a number of Thessalian cities invited non-Thessalian poleis and even the Romans to arbitrate their border disputes.[80] The organization of the League was not that of a *sympoliteia*: citizens of Thessalian poleis did not possess rights in other cities of the League, as indicated by the numerous grants of *proxenia, enktesis* (ἔγκτησις), and citizenship by the assemblies of various poleis to citizens of others. So although the federal government "laid down rules applying to all the cities of the Confederacy, such as those applying to the manumission of slaves",[81] it apparently left the operation of the money collection and registration to its individual members.

Also, the grants of *ateleia* and *isoteleia* (exemption from and equality of imposts) by Thessalian poleis to foreigners, discussed in Chapter 1,[82] indicate that the individual members of the League had their separate machinery for collecting local taxes, probably tax collectors of the kind we find

---

78 See Chapter 1 above.

79 For a discussion of the Thessalian federal constitution and administration see Larsen 1968, 284–294.

80 One of the most famous cases is the dispute between Melitaia and Narthakion, settled in ca. 140 BC by the Roman Senate, according to the laws of the Thessalians, "laws given by the consul Titus Quinctius (Flamininus)" (*IG* IX(2) 89, lines 15–17).

81 Larsen 1968, 293.

82 *Ateleia*: e.g. *SEG* 23.437 (= *REA* 66, 1964, 312–315) from Krannon; *SEG* 16.373 (= *AE*, 1955, 81–84) from Lamia; *IG* IX(2) 513 from Larisa. *Isoteleia*: e.g. *IG* IX(2) 61 from Lamia; *SEG* 33.448 from Atrax.

elsewhere in Greek poleis.[83] The registration fee imposed on manumission may have been collected in the same way. However, since the manumission inscriptions often mention the local treasurers, the *xenodokoi* and, in second-century AD Hypata, the *epimeletai*, as involved in receiving the money from and the registration of the manumitted slaves,[84] payments were more likely made directly to the office of the treasurer or of the *epimeletes* who kept records of the sums and the names of those who paid them, later to be inscribed in stone. Nevertheless, besides the registrations deposited in public archives and the inscribed steles set up by local authorities, the central government may very well have also recorded the remittances on wooden tablets and stored them in some central archive so as to keep track of this source of revenue.

---

[83] On the tax collectors mentioned in inscriptions from Demetrias see discussion in Chapter 4.

[84] On these officials see Chapters 2 and 3 above.

CONCLUSIONS

In 196 BC, after 150 years under Macedonian control, the Thessalians—together with the Magnesians, the Perrhaibians and the Phthiotic Achaians—were declared free by Titus Quinctius Flamininus, the Roman consul who won the Second Macedonian War. A few years later, in 194 BC, a Roman commission headed by Flamininus made arrangements for the reorganization of the Thessalian League. The Romans apparently exerted some influence on the shape of the newly organized League. However, the latter retained considerable independence, from Rome and in inter-city relations, as indicated by the many honorary decrees issued by the various poleis to citizens of other poleis. During the second and first centuries BC the League also incorporated increasingly more regions and cities.[1]

Long years of war and invasions left their mark on the Thessalian lands. The dire economic situation, reflected in the literary and epigraphic sources, is one reason, perhaps the most important, for the introduction of a federal charge early in the second century BC. It was exacted on the occasion of manumission from slavery, as recorded in numerous inscriptions found in Thessalian cities spanning a long period, from the second century BC to the third century AD. Raising the polis' revenues (*prosodoi*) was often an acute problem and to solve it many Greek cities had recourse to taxes and a variety of other imposts. Evidence shows that from early times slaveholding and slave sales were also subject to taxation; taxing slave manumission or its registration seems therefore a reasonable means to an end, all the more so if, as was the case in Thessaly, manumission was practised extensively.[2] The Thessalian federal government, in need of money to maintain the federal army and magistracies, probably imposed the registration fee on its members as a means to increase its revenues and help the cities themselves.[3]

Another reason for the payments exacted upon manumission seems to have been the need of the poleis to control their non-citizen residents and prevent them from encroaching on citizen rights or evading the fulfilment of their duties as non-citizen residents. Despite being part of the Roman

[1] See Introduction.
[2] See Chapter 1.
[3] See Chapter 5.

Empire, and until the *constitutio Antoniniana* in AD 212 made all the Empire's inhabitants Roman citizens, citizenship in the Thessalian as well as other poleis was still regarded as exclusive, and the line demarcating citizens from non-citizens, though more blurred than in earlier times, was still kept. There are some indications that the League as a whole was interested as well in publicly registering manumitted slaves just as the individual poleis did, but its motivation for this is less clear; generally speaking, it seems that the federal interest was more economic.[4]

The Thessalian manumission inscriptions, whose nature and purpose this book examined, accordingly provide important evidence on the economic and social life of the Thessalian poleis where they were found and on steps taken by the Thessalian League to increase its revenues. They also present unique evidence of federal taxation in Thessaly besides the partial evidence we have on customs duties collected by or for the federal treasury in earlier times.

The discussion of the manumission inscriptions in Chapter 2 showed that although it is difficult to estimate the number of slaves in Thessaly, chattel slavery was an important institution there, side by side with the Penestai (at least since the third century BC) or constituting the servile labour force in their stead. The manumission inscriptions also disclose the slave's vital place in the household as part of its property, as can be inferred from several inscriptions recording the acquiescence given by family members to the manumission act. The inscriptions also seem to indicate that women could act independently as manumittors and as guardians of their children; even the consent given by family members to women manumitting slaves seems to suggest that their legal standing was not inferior to that of men.

The extant manumission inscriptions show that manumission too was widespread in Thessaly. Although exact numbers are difficult to calculate, my count of the extant and more evident cases gives the total of 1,760 slaves manumitted from the early second century BC to the middle of the second century AD and, in Demetrias, some manumission acts are dated to the third century AD.[5] Why so many slave owners manumitted their slaves is not an easy question to answer; but the enormous number reveals the important social and economic place of slaves and freed slaves in the cities of the

---

[4] See Chapter 5.

[5] New readings might affect this calculation; still, the corpus of the Thessalian manumission inscriptions equals and even exceeds that of the manumissions in Delphi.

Thessalian League. Regrettably, we have hardly any evidence about the lives and occupations of manumitted slaves in Thessaly.[6]

Manumission in Thessally seems to have been performed by a simple declaration, by proclamation or by will, followed by registration in the local archive; the recorded payments to the polis indicate that registration or a declaration of some kind was also needed in the treasurer's or other magistrate's office. Manumitted slaves paid their manumittors for their freedom (the λύτρον), but some were manumitted free of charge (δωρεάν); the reason is probably that slave owners in these cases were the biological fathers or spouses of these manumitted slaves. The deferred manumission, the *paramone*, seems to have been practised in Thessaly, though in some poleis more than in others.[7]

The manumission inscriptions are typically long lists of names of manumittors and manumitted slaves, arranged in chronological order, although some of them record single acts of manumission formulated more elaborately. The inscriptions are usually dated by local eponymous magistrates and by the annually elected federal *strategos*. These inscriptions show that the sum paid by manumitted slaves was uniform: fifteen staters per person. In 27 BC, as part of Augustus' reforms, the formal currency was changed to denarii (one stater being equal to one denarius and a half) and inscriptions start to record payments of twenty-two and a half denarii (though the Thessalians continued to use staters). The amount paid was uniform regardless of age and number of slaves manumitted by the same manumittor at the same time; that is, each manumitted slave paid fifteen staters or twenty-two and a half denarii. But there were some exceptions which cannot be explained satisfactorily from the evidence presently available, although in all the relevant cases which show payments of reduced sums the manumitted slaves seem to be females. They might have been the spouses or biological daughters of the manumittors, who helped them with the payment. The inscriptions explicitly state that the money was paid to the polis. In many cases the treasurer, and sometimes the *xenodokos*—and in second-century AD Hypata the ἐπιμελητὴς τῶν ἀπελευθερικῶν χρημάτων—is expressly noted as the official to whom the freed slaves paid the money.[8]

---

[6] Some of the manumittors in Thessalian inscriptions are described as freed slaves themselves, which at least indicates that their economic condition was reasonable: e.g. *IG* IX(2) 21, lines 6–8 (AD Hypata, 131/132); *IG* IX(2) 1344, lines 7, 12, 14, 17 (Larisa, reign of Augustus).

[7] See Chapter 2.

[8] See Chapter 2.

Throughout the chapters of this book we have seen that the evidence provided by the manumission inscriptions might in some cases indicate that the fifteen staters or twenty-two and a half denarii paid to the polis were a tax levied on manumissions, similar to the Roman manumission tax, the *vicesima libertatis*, as some scholars have suggested. This interpretation may seem reasonable considering that the Romans' entry into the Greek world had an impact on some practices, and we actually do not know whether, in addition to reorganizing the Thessalian League, they also imposed taxes and legal procedures. But in many other cases the evidence explicitly shows that the payments recorded in the manumission inscriptions were a fee exacted for registration and publication of the manumission acts on stone. Certain phrases are clear proof that the uniform payment was not a manumission tax, for example, "a record (ἀναγραφά) of the manumitted slaves who had paid the polis what is due" (*IG* IX(2) 109a from Phthiotic Thebes, 47/6 BC); "Pithagoros, son of Megalokleos, being the treasurer ... recorded (ἀνέγραψεν) those declared to be manumitted during his time of office as treasurer—whoever paid to the polis the due staters" (*IG* IX(2) 546 from Larisa, ca. AD 131/132); "the account (ἀπολογισμός) of those manumitted in his (i.e. the treasurer's) time of office and who paid the polis the fifteen staters due on occasion of manumission (ἀπελευθέρωσις)" (*IG* IX(2) 542 from Larisa, reign of Augustus); "the manumitted slaves who paid what is due for *inscribing the stele* (στηλογραφία), according to the law, twenty-two and a half silver denarii" (*IG* IX(2) 13 from Hypata, AD 47).[9]

This conclusion is corroborated by a comparison of the Thessalian inscriptions with similar evidence elsewhere in the Greek world. In many places poleis exacted money from manumitted slaves, in addition to the price of freedom paid to the manumittors. The evidence strongly suggests that payments recorded in Thessaly, Orchomenos, Kos, and Nikaia in connection with manumission were for registration and publication. This same conclusion is less safe, but still plausible, for Egypt, Tithora, and Elatea—and perhaps also Athens. We cannot be sure about Chaironeia, Macedonia, Gortyn, and Xanthos, although in these places too the money paid or vessels dedicated by the manumitted slaves also served as fees for registration. The only unequivocal reference to a tax and tax collectors in the context of manumission, and not of registration fees, comes from Demetrias. This evidence can be easily explained if the inscriptions in which the tax and tax collectors are mentioned date to after the *constitutio Antoniniana* and concern manu-

---

[9] See Chapter 3.

mittors who now, under this regulation, were Roman citizens hence had to pay the *vicesima manumissionum/libertatis*.[10] There is one piece of evidence which mentions a collector (perhaps a member in a *societas*) of the *vicesima libertatis* in second-century AD Athens, but it is likely that this tax was paid only by Roman citizens.[11] A Roman impact might also be suspected in the inscriptions from second-century AD Hypata which refer to the ἐπιμελητὴς τῶν ἀπελευθερικῶν χρημάτων, perhaps a *procurator* entrusted with the collection of the money from manumitted slaves; but this official clearly collected registration fees, not the manumission tax.[12] In any event, the practice of exacting money from slaves upon their manumission was apparently quite widespread, and in Thessaly, as well as in other places, these monies were levied for registration and publication.[13]

Despite the uniformity of the amount paid, inscriptions show a variety of formulae. Moreover, not all Thessalian poleis yield evidence of such payments; often the evidence is not of an even character within the same polis—chronologically or in the currency used. As noted, the members of the Thessalian League were considerably independent in their inter-state relations, so the operation of money collection and registration seems to have been left to each individual city to handle as it saw fit. Yet the procedures for collecting the fees and the federal government's role in this process are still far from clear. It seems likely that, being a federal impost, part of the money collected was transferred to the federal treasury in Larisa; manumission may have been registered in the federal as well as the local archive; local or federal tax collectors may have served as an intermediate stage between the paying manumitted slaves and the treasurers. But the present state of the evidence does not allow us to come to safe conclusions.[14]

Other questions regarding the payments recorded in the manumission inscriptions remain unanswered. For instance, we do not know whether slaves manumitted by Thessalians outside Thessaly had to pay the same fee and register in their manumittors' poleis or whether they were exempt because the manumission was not performed in a Thessalian polis. Some of the Thessalians who manumitted their slaves in other places took advantage of their visiting a Pan-Hellenic centre such as Apollo's sanctuary at Delphi in order, perhaps, to obtain more publicity, to fulfil a vow, or to grant their

10 See in Chapter 4 above.

11 *SIA* VI 8 = *CIL* III 555 = 7287, and see Chpater 3 above.

12 See *IG* IX(2) 17, 19, 21 22, and Bouchon 2009; see also in Chapter 3 above.

13 See Chapter 4.

14 See Chapter 5.

slaves' wishes. Thus *FD* III 2.213 (ca. 124 BC) records a manumission through sale to Apollo in Delphi of two slaves by Pyrrias son of Zopyros from Thaumakoi (in Achaia Phthiotis). Two of the three guarantors to the transaction are Thessalians (one from Melitaia, the other from Hypata) and so are two of the witnesses: Leon son of Kleippos from Atrax, and Pollichos son of Phrynos from Gomphoi. These witnesses, and one of the guarantors—Lamprochos son of Politas from Melitaia—are mentioned as *hieromnemones* sent by Thessalian cities to Delphi in ca. 130 BC (*CID* 4.414 and 416; *FD* III 2.68).[15] The other Thessalian guarantor, Pyladas son of Sosamenos from Hypata was granted *proxenia* and other honours by the polis of Delphi in 137/6 BC (*FD* III 1.261). It seems likely that these men, already connected to Delphi, went there in 124 BC, together with Pyrrias son of Zopyros, all as Thessalian *hieromenmomes*, and helped Pyrrias as guarantors and witnesses to the manumission of his slaves.[16]

Yet none of these names, or those mentioned in other Delphic inscriptions, appear in the Thessalian manumission inscriptions.[17] This absence of course may be accidental and cannot rule out the possibility that slaves manumitted outside Thessaly registered afterwards in the local archives of the Thessalian poleis, or even paid the fee and had their names entered in the inscribed lists. It may also be that some of the manumissions recorded in Thessaly were actually performed outside it, but the extant inscriptions do not inform us where the manumissions took place. *FD* III 2.213, discussed above, and *SGDI* 2138, a manumission done by a Melitaian in Delphi, are dated both by Thessalian and Delphic eponyms, so we may presume that

---

15 According to *SEG* 47.744, Pollichos son of Phrynos also served as the federal *strategos* sometime between 150 and 130 BC.

16 See Daux 1936, 349. In nineteenth-century Barbados, slave owners who wished to avoid paying the manumission tax (introduced in 1739 at the rate of £50 and raised temporarily between 1801 and 1816 to £300 for females and £200 for males) sold their slaves to captains or passengers on ships bound for England with the intention of freeing them there. The newly freed slaves would then return to Barbados, writing the details of their certificate of freedom in the local manumission registers; see Handler 1974, 39–47. It seems that no such motive can be attributed to Thessalian freed slaves because the fee seems to have been too small to make the journey worthwhile.

17 Cf. the following manumissions performed by Thessalians in Delphi: *SGDI* 2073 (198/7 BC)—by Axiochos of Hypata, who used three of his compatriots as guarantors and a witness; *SGDI* 2234 (186 BC)—by Phalakrion son of Sosikrates of Lamia; *SGDI* 2009 (182 BC)—by Archepolis son of Timokles of Larisa, who used at least one Thessalian (from Echinos) as a guarantor; and *SGDI* 2138 (150–140 BC)—by Dasymenes son of Sostratides of Melitaia, using three compatriots as witnesses (one of them, Kleitarchos son of Eubiotos, also served as the guarantor; another, Polysaon son of Politas, appears as a *xenodokos* in an arbitration decree between Halos and Phthiotic Thebes: *FD* III 4.355, line 23).

the manumittors intended the acts to be legally recognized in their poleis as well—perhaps by registering them there; but whether their freed slaves paid the registration fee, or even whether they ever returned to their manumittors' poleis, cannot be known.[18]

Nevertheless, I hope I have succeeded in dispersing some of the mists that still obscures our understanding of the economic and social life in the Thessalian League. The picture that emerges appears to suggest that a federal impost on the registration and publication of manumissions was introduced sometime in the early years of the second century BC, probably after the Thessalians were declared free by Flamininus in 196 BC, or more likely after the latter's reorganization of the league in 194 B.C, and it is reasonable to assume that besides the manumission records deposited in public archives and the inscribed steles set up by local authorities, the central government recorded the receipts of money or part thereof on wooden tablets and stored them in some central archive.

[18] Especially if the manumission agreement granted them full freedom to go and live where they wanted to, which seems to have been the case in some of the manumissions done in Delphi (see previous note): *SGDI* 2073 (line 4: ποιέουσαν ὅ κα θέληι); *SGDI* 2234 (line 7: same phrase); *FD* III 2.213 (lines 11–12: ποιέοντες ὅ κα θέλωντι καὶ ἀπο/τρέχοντες οἷς κα θέλωντι).

BIBLIOGRAPHY

Amemiya, T. 2007. *Economy and Economics of Ancient Greece*, London and New York: Routledge.

Andreades, A.M. 1979. *A History of Greek Public Finance*, Vol. I, translated from the Greek edition of 1933 by C.N. Brown, New York: Arno Press.

Aperghis, M. 2001. "Population—Production—Taxation—Coinage", in Z.H. Archibald, J.K. Davies, V. Gabrielsen and G.J. Oliver (eds.), *Helenistic Economies*, London and New-York: Routledge, 69–102.

Armstrong D. and J.J. Walsh. 1986. "*SIG*^{3} 593: The Letter of Flamininus to Chyretiae", *CPh* 81.1, 32–46.

Austin M.M. and P. Vidal-Naquet. 1977. *Economic and Social History of Ancient Greece: An Introduction*, Translated into English by M.M. Austin, University of California Press, Berkeley and Los Angeles.

Babacos, A.M. 1962. "La mention du prostate dans les affranchissements thessaliens", *BCH* 86, 494–503.

——— 1963. "Vormundschaft im alt-thessalischen Recht", *ZRG* 80, 311–322.

——— 1964. "Familienrechtliche Verhältnisse auf der Insel Kalymnos im 1. Jahrhundert n. Chr.", *ZRG* 81, 31–51(translated into German from his *Σχέσεις οἰκογενειακοῦ δικαίου εἰς τὴν νῆσον Καλύμνον τὸν α' μ.Χ. αἰῶνα*, Athens, 1961).

——— 1966. *Actes d'alienation en commun et autres phénomènes apparentés d'après le droit de la Thessalie antique: Contribution a l'étude de la copropriété familiale chez les anciens hellènes*, Thessaloniki: Université de Thessaloniki.

Baker, P. 2001. "Quelques remarques sur des institutions militaires dans les cités de Thessalie à l'époque hellénistique", *The Ancient World* 32, 191–206.

Beauchet, L. (1897) 1969. *Histoire du droit privé de la république athénienne*, Vol. II: *Le droit de famille*, Amsterdam.

Beck, H. 1997. *Polis und Koinon. Untersuchungen zur Geschichte und Struktur der griechischen Bundesstaaten im 4. Jahrhundert v. Chr.*, Historia Einzelschrift 114. Stuttgart: Franz Steiner Verlag.

Bielman, A. 1989. "Λύτρα, prisonniers et affranchis", *MH* 46, pp. 25–41.

Bile, M. 1988. *Le dialecte crétois ancien. Étude de la langue des inscriptions: recueil des inscriptions postérieures aux IC*, Paris: Librairie Orientaliste Paul Geuthner.

Boegehold, A.L. 1995. *The Athenian Agora* XXVIII: *The Lawcourts at Athens: Sites, Buildings, Equipment, Procedure, and Testimomia*, Princeton, NJ: The American School of Classical Studies at Athens.

Bömer, F. 1960. *Untersuchungen über die Religion der Sklaven in Griechenland und Rom*, Vol. II: *Die sogenannte sakrale Freilassung in Griechenland und die δοῦλοι ἱεροί*, Wiesbaden: Verlag der Akademie der Wissenschaften und der Literatur in Mainz in Kommission bei Franz Steiner Verlag.

Bouchon, R. 2007. "Les 'Porteurs de Toge' de Larissa", *Topoi* 12, 251–284.

——— 2008. "L'ère auguste: ébauche d'une histoire politique de la Thessalie sous Auguste", BCH 132, 427–471.

——— 2009. "La taxe des affranchis et le financement de la vie publique dans les cités thessaliennes: nouvelle lecture de documents du II^{2} s. apr. J.-C.", Αρχαιολογικό Έργο Θεσσαλίας και Στερεάς Ελλάδας 2 2006, Βόλος 16.3–19.3.2006 (Proceedings of the 2 Archaeological Meeting of Thessaly and Central Greece [AETHSE]), 395–407.

Bowersock, G.W. 1965. "Zur Geschichte des romischen Thessaliens", *RhM* 108, 277–289.

Bradley, K. 1984a. *Slaves and Masters in the Roman Empire. A Study in Social Control*, Collection Latomus Vol. 185, Bruxelles.

——— 1984b. "The *vicesima libertatis*: Its History and Significance", *Klio* 66, 175–182.

Bresson, A. 1991. *Recueil des inscriptions de la Pérée rhodienne (Pérée Intégrée)*, Annales Littéraires de l'Université de Besançon, 445, Paris: Les Belles Lettres.

Brunt, P.A. 1990. *Roman Imperial Themes*, Oxford: Clarendon Press.

Burford, A. 1993. *Land and Labor in the Greek World*, Baltimore and London: The Johns Hopkins University Press.

Burke, E.M. 1992. "The Economy of Athens in the Classical Era: Some Adjustments to the Primitivist Model", *TAPA* 122, 199–226.

Busolt, G. 1920. *Griechische Staatskunde*, Vol. I, München: O. Beck.

Cabanes, P. 1998. "Public et privé dans le cadre de l'*ethnos* en Grèce ancienne", *Ktèma* 23, 441–449.

Calderini, A. 1908, repr. 1965. *La manomissione e la condizione dei liberti in Grecia*, Rome.

Chaniotis, A. 1996. *Die Verträge zwischen kretischen Poleis in der hellenistischen Zeit*, Stuttgart: Franz Steiner Verlag.

Christ, M.R. 2006. *The Bad Citizen in Classical Athens*, Cambridge: Cambridge University Press.

Cohen, E.E. 1973. *Ancient Athenian Maritime Courts*, Princeton, NJ: Princeton University Press.

——— 1992. *Athenian Economy and Society*, Princeton University Press, Princeton New Jersey.

Cottier, M., Crawford, M.H., Crowther, C.V., Ferrary, J.-L., Levick, B.M., Salomies, O., and Wörrle, M. 2008. *The Customs Law of Asia* Oxford: Oxford University Press.

Darmezin, L. 1999. *Les affranchissements par consécration en Béotie et dans le monde grec hellénistique*, Paris: Diffusion De Boccard.

Darmezin, L. and Tziaphalias A. 2007. "The Twelve Tribes of Atrax: A Lexical Study", in E. Matthews (ed.), *Old and New Worlds in Greek Onomastics*, Proceedings of the British Academy 148, Oxford: Oxford University Press, 21–28.

Daux, G. 1936. *Delphes au IIe et au Ier siècle: depuis l'abaissement de l'Étolie jusqu'à la paix romaine, 191–31 av. J. C*, Paris: E. de Boccard.

Davies, J.K. 1994. "Accounts and Accountability in Classical Athens", in *Ritual, Finance, Politics: Athenian Democratic Accounts Presented to David Lewis*, ed. By R. Osborne and S. Hornblower, Oxford: Oxford University Press, 201–212.

——— 2001. "Hellenistic Economies in the Post-Finley Era", in Z.H. Archibald, J.K. Davies, V. Gabrielsen and G.J. Oliver (eds.), *Helenistic Economies*, London and New-York: Routledge, 11–62.

Debord, P. 1982. *Aspects sociaux et économiques de la vie religieuse dans l'Anatolie gréco-romaine*, Leiden: Brill.

Decourt, J.C. 1990. "Decret de Pharsale pour une politographie", *ZPE* 81, 163–184.
Dimopoulou-Piliouni, A. 2008. "Apeleutheroi: Metics or Foreigners?", *Dike* 11, 27–50.
Ducat, J. 1994. *Les Pénestes de Thessalie* (Centre de recherches d'histoire ancienne, 128 = Annales litteraires de l'Universite de Besançon, 512), Paris: Universite de Besançon, Les Belles Lettres.
Duncan-Jones, R.P. 1984. "Problems of the Delphic Manumission Payments, 200–1 B.C.", *ZPE* 57, pp. 203–209.
Dunant Chr. and Pouilloux, J. 1958. *Recherches sur l'histoire et les cultes de Thasos, II: De 196 avant J.C. jusqu'à la fin de l'Antiquité*, Études Thasiennes 5, E. de Boccard: Paris.
Eck, W. 1977. "Zur Erhebung der Erbschafts- und Freilassungssteuer in Ägypten im 2. Jahrh. n. Chr.", *ZPE* 27, 201–209.
——— 1999. *L'Italia nell'impero romano. Stato e amministrazione in epoca imperiale* (an updated translation of *Die staatliche Organisation Italiens in der hohe kaiserzeit*, München 1979), Bari: Edipuglia.
Eckstein, A.M. 2008. *Rome Enters the Greek East. From Anarchy to Hierarchy in the Hellenistic Mediterranean, 230–170 BC*, Malden, MA and Oxford: Blackwell.
Einhorn, R.L. 2006. *American Taxation. American Slavery*, Chicago: The University of Chicago Press.
Engelmann, H. 1999. "Inschriften aus Metropolis", *ZPE* 125, 137–146.
Engen, D. Tai. 2010. *Honor and Profit: Athenian Trade Policy and the Economy and Society of Greece, 415–307 B.C.E.*, Ann Arbor: The University of Michigan Press.
Étienne, R. and Knoepfler, D. 1976. *Hyettos de Béotie et la chronologie des archontes fédéraux entre 250 et 171 avant J.-C.*, *BCH* suppl. 3. Paris.
Farnell, L.R. 1896. *Cults of the Greek States*, Vol. II, Oxford: Clarendon Press.
Finley, M.I. 1973. *The Ancient Economy*, University of California Press, Berkeley and Los Angeles.
Foucart, P. 1873. *Des associations religieuses chez les Grecs*, Paris: Klincksieck.
Frank, T. 1959. *An Economic Survey of Ancient Rome*, Vol. IV, Paterson, N.J.: Pageant Books.
Gabrielsen, V. 1994. *Financing the Athenian Fleet: Public Taxation and Social Relations*, Baltimore: Johns Hopkins University Press.
——— 2008. "The Public Banks of Hellenistic Cities", in K. Verboven, K. Vandorpe and V. Chankowski (eds.), *Pistoi Dia Tèn Technèn: Bankers, Loans and Archives. Studies in Honour of Raymond Bogaert*, Leuven: Peeters, 115–130.
Gardner P. 1963. *A Catalogue of Greek Coins in the British Museum: Thessaly to Aetolia*, ed. by R.S. Pool (reprint of the 1883 edition, London), Bologna: Arnalso Forni.
Garnsey, P., Gallant, T. and Rathbone D. 1984. "Thessaly and the Grain Supply of Rome during the Second Century B.C.", *JRS* 74, 30–44.
Gounaropoulos, L. 1987. "Τέσσερις καινούριες απελευθερωτικές επιγραφές από τον Αχινό Λαμίας", in *Ἀμητός, Τιμητικός τόμος για τον καθηγητή Μ. Ανδρόνικο*, Thessalonike: Panepistemio Thessalonikes.
Grainger, J.D. 1999. *The League of the Aitolians*, Mnemosyne Supplementum 200, Leiden: Brill.
Graninger, D. 2011. *Cult and Koinon in Hellenistic Thessaly*, Leiden and Boston: Brill.
Gruen, E. 1984. *The Hellenistic World and the Coming of Rome*, Berkeley, Los Angeles and London: The University of California Press.

Habicht, Chr. 1957. "Eine Urkunde des Akarnanischen Bundes", *Hermes* 85, 86–122.

——— 1970. "Eine Bürgerrechtsverleihung von Metropolis", *Klio* 52, 139–147.

——— 1983. "Makedonen in Larisa?" *Chiron* 13, 21–32.

——— 1987. "Neue Inschriften aus Demetrias", *Demetrias V*, Die deutschen archäologischen Forschungen in Thessalien, Bonn, 269–306.

——— 2006. *The Hellenistic Monarchies: Selected Papers*, translated by P. Stevenson, Ann Arbor, Mich.: The University of Michigan Press.

Handler, J.S. 1974. *The Unappropriated People: Freedmen in the slave society of Barbados*, Baltimore: Johns Hopkins University Press.

Handler, J.S. and Pohlmann J.T. 1984. "Slave Manumissions and Freedmen in Seventeenth Century Barbados", *The William and Mary Quarterly*, 3rd ser., 41.3, 390–408.

Harper, K. 2011. *Slavery in the Late Roman Mediterranean, AD 275–425*, Cambridge: Cambridge University Press.

Harris, D. 1994. "Freedom of Information and Accountability: The Inventory Lists of the Parthenon", in *Ritual, Finance, Politics: Athenian Democratic Accounts Presented to David Lewis*, ed. By R. Osborne and S. Hornblower, Oxford: Oxford University Press, 213–225.

Haslam, M.W. 1976. "Notes on Deeds of Manumission", *ZPE* 20, 58–60.

Hatzopoulos, M. 2003. "Polis, Ethnos and Kingship in Northern Greece", in *The Idea of European Community in History* II, ed. by K. Buraselis and K. Zoumboulakis, Athens: National and Capodistrian University of Athens, Greek Ministry of Education and Religious Affairs, 51–64.

Head, B.V. 1911. *Historia Numorum. A Manual of Greek Numismatics*, revised by G.F. Hill, G. MacDonald and W. Wroth, Oxford: Oxford University Press.

Helly, B. 1970. "A Larisa. Bouleversements et remise en ordre de sanctuaires", *Mnemosyne* 23, 250–296.

——— 1976. "Lois sur les affranchissements dans les inscriptions thessaliennes", *Phoenix* 30, pp. 143–158.

——— (ed.). 1979. *La Thessalie: actes de la Table-ronde, 21–24 juillet 1975, Lyon*, Lyon: Maison de l'Orient—Paris: diffusion de Boccard.

——— 1987. "Les émissions monétaires de la Confédération Thessalienne (IIer–Ier s. av. J.C.)", in T. Hackens, G. Depeyrot and G. Moucharte (eds.), *Rythmes de la production monétaire de l'Antiquité à nos jours*, Louvain-la-Neuve: Seminaire de numismatique Marcel Hoc, 39–53.

——— 1995. *L'État thessalien: Aleuas le Roux, les tétrades et les tagoi*, Lyon: Maison de l'Orient Méditerranéen.

——— 1997. "Le diorthôma d'Auguste fixant la conversion des statèrs thessaliens en deniers. Un situation de passage à la monnaie unique", *Topoi Orient-Occident* 7.1, 63–91.

Henry, A.S. 1989. "Provisions for the Payment of Athenian Decrees: A Study in Formulaic Language", *ZPE* 78, 247–295.

Homolle, Th. 1887. *Les archives de l'intendance sacrée à Délos*, Paris: Ernest Thorin.

Hopkins, K. 1978. *Conquerors and Slaves*, Cambridge: Cambridge University Press.

Invernizzi, A. 2003. "They Did Not Write on Clay: Non-Cuneiform Documents and Archives in Seleucid Mesopotamia", in M. Brosius (ed.), *Ancient Archives and*

Archival Traditions: Concepts of Record-Keeping in the Ancient World, Oxford: Oxford University Press, 302–322.

Klees, H. 1998. *Sklavenleben im klassischen Griechenland*, Stuttgart: Franz Steiner Verlag.

Kramolisch, H. 1978. *Die Srategen des thessalischen Bundes vom Jahr 196 v. Chr. bis zum Ausgang der römischen Republik*, Bonn: Rudolf Habelt Verlag.

——— 1979, "Das ende des perrhäbischen Bundes", in B. Helly (ed.), *La Thessalie. Actes de le Table-Ronde 21–24 Juillet 1975, Lyon*, Collection de la Maison de l'Orient méditerranéen no. 6, Série archéologique no. 5, Lyon: Maison de l'Orient, 201–219.

Kyrtatas, D.J. 2002. "Domination and Exploitation", in P. Cartledge, E.E. Cohen and L. Foxhall (eds.), *Money, Labour and Land. Approaches to the Economies of Ancient Greece*, London: Routledge, 140–155.

Lambert, S.D. 1997. Rationes Centesimarum: *Sales of Public Land in Lykourgan Athens* (Archaia Hellas 3), Amsterdam: Gieben.

——— 2012. "Ten Notes on Attic Inscriptions", in id., *Inscribed Athenian Laws and Decrees, 352/1–322/1 B.C.*, Leiden: Brill, 221–239 (first published in *ZPE* 135, 2001, 51–62).

Langdon, M.K. 1991. "Poletai Records", in *The Athenian Agora* Vol. XIX, Princeton NJ: The American School of Classical Studies at Athens, 53–143.

Larfeld, W. 1902, repr. 1971. *Handbuch der griechischen Epigraphik*, Vol. II, Hildesheim and New York: G. Olms Verlag.

Larsen, J.A.O. 1953. "A Thessalian Family under the Principate", *CPh* 48.2, 86–95.

——— 1955. *Representative Government in Greek and Roman History*, Berkeley and Los Angeles: University of California Press.

——— 1958. "The Policy of Augustus in Greece", *Acta Classica* 1, pp. 126–127.

——— 1968. *Greek Federal States, Their Institutions and History*, Oxford: Clarendon Press.

Lewis, D.M. 1968. "Dedications of Phialai at Athens", *Hesperia* 37.4, 368–380.

——— 1973. "The Athenian Rationes Centesimarum", in M.I. Finley (ed.), Problèmes de la terre en Grèce ancienne, Paris: Mouton, 187–212.

Lindström, G. 2003. *Uruk: Siegelabdrücke auf hellenistischen Tonbullen und Tontafeln*, Ausgrabungen in Uruk-Warka. Endberichte 20, Mainz am Rhein: Verlag Philipp von Zabern.

Littman, R.J. 1988. "Greek Taxation", in M. Grant and R. Kitzinger (eds.), *Civilization of the Ancient Mediterranean*, Vol. II, New York: Charles Scribner's Sons, 795–808.

Llewelyn, S.R. 1992. *A Review of the Greek Inscriptions and Papyri Published in 1980–1981*, North Ryde, N.S.W.: Macquarie University, Ancient History Documentary research Centre.

Loomis, W.T. 1998. *Wages, Welfare Costs and Inflation in Classical Athens*, Ann Arbor: The University of Michigan Press.

Lotze, D. (1959), *Metaxu Eleutherōn Kai Doulōn: Studien zur Rechtsstellung unfreier Landbevoelkerungen in Griechenland bis zum 4. Jahrhundert v. Chr.*, Berlin: Akademie-Verlag.

Lupu, E. 2005. *Greek Sacral Law: A Collection of New Documents (NGSL)*, Leiden—Boston: Brill.

Luzzato, G.I. 1984, "Vicesima hereditatum et manumissionum", in R. Bonini (ed.), *Scritti minori epigrafici e papyrologici*, Sala Bolognese: A. Forni, 707–708 (first published in *Noviss. Dig. Ital.* 20, Utet, Torino, 1975, 809–810).

Lyttkens, C.H. 1994. "A Predatory Democracy? An Essay on Taxation in Classical Athens", *Explorations in Economic History* 31, 62–90.

Mactoux, M.-M. 2008. "Regards sur la proclamation de l'affranchissement au théâtre à Athènes", in A. Gonzales (ed.), *La fin du statut serville? (Affranchissement, libération, abolition)*, 30e colloque du GIREA, Besançon—15–17 décembre 2005, Besançon: Presses universitaires de Franche-Comté, 437–451.

Magnelli A. 1998. "Una nuova epigrafe Gortinia in materia di manomissione", *Dike* 1, 95–113.

Manning, J.G. 2007. "Hellenistic Egypt", in W. Scheidel, I. Morris, and R. Saller (eds.), *The Cambridge Economic History of the Greco-Roman World*, Cambridge: Cambridge University Press, 434–459.

Mattingly D. and Salmon J. 2001. "The Productive Past: Economies beyond Agriculture", in id. (eds.), *Economics beyond Agriculture in the Classical World*, London: Routledge, 3–14.

McDevitt, A.S. 1970. *Inscriptions from Thessaly. An Analytical Handlist and Bibliography*, Hildesheim: G. Olms.

McDowell, R.H. 1935. *Stamped and Inscribed Objects from Seleucia on the Tigris*, Ann Arbor: The University of Michigan Press.

Mendels, D. 1978. "Perseus and the Socio-Economic Question in Greece (179–172/1 BC). A Study in Roman Propaganda", *Anc.Soc.* 9, 55–73.

Messina, V. 2005. "Da Uruk a Seleucia pratiche amministrative e archivi della Babilonia seleucide", *Mesopotamia* 40, 125–144.

Metzger, M.H. 1974. "La stèle trilingue récemment découverte au Létoon de Xanthos: Le texte grec", *CRAI*, 82–149.

Metzger, H., Laroche, E., Dupont-Sommer, A., and Mayrhofer M. 1979. *La stèle trilingue du Létôon*, Fouilles de Xanthos VI, Paris.

Meyer, E. 2002. Review of M.B. Hatzopoulos, L. Gounaropoulos and P. Paschidis (eds.), *Inscriptions du sanctuaire de la Mère des Dieux autochtone de Leukopétra (Macédoine)*, Meletema 28, Athens: Kentron Ellenikes kai romaikes archaiotetos ethnikon idryma erevnon, 200. *AJP* 123, 136–140.

——— 2010. *Metics and the Athenian Phialai-Inscriptions: A Study in Athenian Epigraphy and Law*, Historia Einzelschriften 208, Stuttgart: Franz Steiner Verlag.

Migeotte, L. 1984. *L'Emprunt public dans les cités grecques: Recueil des documents et analyse critique*, Québec: Les Éditions du Sphinx, Paris: Les Belles Lettres.

——— 1992. *Les souscriptions publiques dans les cités grecques*, Genève et Québec.

——— 2003. "Taxation directe en Grèce ancienne", in G. Thür and F.J. Fernández Nieto (eds.), *Symposion 1999: Vorträge zur griechischen und hellenistischen Rechtsgeschichte* (Pazo de Mariñán, La Coruña, 6.-9. September 1999), Köln—Weimar—Wien: Böhlau Verlag, 297–313.

——— 2009. *The Economy of the Greek Cities: From the Archaic Period to the Early Roman Empire*, translated by J. Lloyd, Berkeley-Los Angeles-London: University of California Press.

Möller, A. 2007. "Classical Greece: Distribution", in W. Scheidel, I. Morris, and R. Saller (eds.), *The Cambridge Economic History of the Greco-Roman World*, Cambridge: Cambridge University Press, 362–384.

Morgan, C. 2003. *Early Greek States Beyond the Polis*, London: Routledge.

Muhs, B.P. 2005. *Tax Receipts, Taxpayers, and Taxes in Early Ptolemaic Thebes*, Oriental Institute Publications—Volume 126, Chicago, Illinois: The Oriental Institute of the University of Chicago.

Mulliez, D. 1992. "Les actes d'affranchissement delphiques", Cahiers du Centre G. Glotz, 3, 31–44.

Newman W.L. (ed.) 1902. *The Politics of Aristotle*, Oxford: Clarendon Press.

Newton K. and Confalonieri M.A. 1995. "Politics, Economics, Class, and Taxation", in O. Borre and E. Scarbrough (eds.), *The Scope of the Government*, Oxford: Oxford University Press, 149–164.

Papazarkadas, N. 2011. *Sacred and Public Land in Ancient Athens*, Oxford: Oxford University Press.

Parker, R. and D. Obbink. 2000. "Sales of Priesthoods on Cos I", *Chiron* 31, 415–449.

Paterson, J. 2001. "Hellenistic Economies: The Case of Rome", in Z.H. Archibald, J.K. Davies, V. Gabrielsen and G.J. Oliver (eds.), *Hellenistic Economies*, London and New-York: Routledge, 367–378.

Petsas, P.M. et al. (eds.). 2000. *Inscriptions du sanctuaire de la Mère des Dieux Autochtone de Leukopetra (Macédoine)*. Meletemata 28: Centre de recherches de l'antiquité grecque et romaine. Fondation nationale de la recherche scientifique Paris: Diffusion De Boccard.

Posner, E. 1972. *Archives in the Ancient World*, Cambridge, Ma.: Harvard University Press.

Pouilloux, J. 1979. "Avant-propos", in B. Helly (ed.), *La Thessalie. Actes de la Table-Ronde 21–24 Juillet 1975 Lyon*, Collection de la Maison de l'Orient méditerranéen no. 6, Série archéologique no. 5, Lyon: Maison de l'Orient, vii–viii.

Pritchett, W.K. 1996. *Greek Archives, Cults, and Topography*, Amsterdam: Gieben.

Quenouille, N. 2002. "Eine Sklavenfreilassung aus der Ptolemäerzeit (P.UB Trier S 135-2 und 135-12)", *Archive für Papyrusforschung* 48.1, 67–97.

Rädle, H. 1969. *Untersuchungen zum griechischen Freilassungswesen* (diss. München, 1968), München: Dissertationsdruck W. Blasaditsch.

——— 1971. "Freilassung von Sklaven im Theater (Inschriftliche Zeugnisse)", *RIDA* 18, 361–364.

Rathbone, D.W. 2007. "Roman Egypt", in W. Scheidel, I. Morris, and R. Saller (eds.), *The Cambridge Economic History of the Greco-Roman World*, Cambridge: Cambridge University Press, 698–719.

Reden, S. von. 2007. *Money in Pteolemaic Egypt. From the Macedonian Conquest to the End of the Third century B.C.*, Cambridge: Cambridge University Press.

Reger, G. 2007. "Hellenistic Greece and Western Asia Minor", in W. Scheidel, I. Morris, and R. Saller (eds.), *The Cambridge Economic History of the Greco-Roman World*, Cambridge: Cambridge University Press, 460–485.

Reilly, L. Collins. 1971. "New Inscriptions from Echinos", *AJPh* 92.4, 667–675.

Rensch, W. 1908. *De manumissionum titulis apud Thessalos*, diss. Phil. Halenses.

Rhodes, P.J. 1981. *A Commentary on the Aristotelian Athenaion Politeia*, Oxford: Clarendon Press.

Rhodes, P.J. and R. Osborne. 2003. *Greek Historical Inscriptions*, Oxford: Oxford University Press.
Ricl, M. 2002. "The Phrase ΚΑΤΑΧΘΕΙΣΗΣ ΤΡΙΑΚΟΘΗΜΕΡΟΥ in an Inscription from Macedonian Lefkopetra", *ΤΕΚΜΗΡΙΑ* 5, 155–160.
——— 2001. "Donations of Slaves and Freeborn Children to Deities", *Tyche* 16, 127–160.
Riele, G.J.M.J. te 1982. "Nouveaux affranchissements à Larissa", *ZPE* 49, 161–176.
Roberts, W.R. and B.V. Head. 1974. *The Ancient Boeotians and the Coinage of Boeotia*, Chicago: Ares Publishers Inc.
Rostovtzeff, M.I. 1932. *Seleucid Babylonia: Bullae and Seals of Clay with Greek Inscriptions*, New Haven: Yale University Press (reprinted from *YCS* 3, 1932, 1–114).
——— 1964 (1941). *The Social and Economic History of the Hellenistic World*, Oxford: Oxford University Press.
Salviat, F. and Vatin C. 1971. *Inscriptions de Grèce central*, Paris: Éditions de Boccard.
——— 1974. "Le cadastre de Larissa", *BCH* 98, 247–262.
Samons II, L.J. 2000. *Empire of the Owl. Athenian Imperial Finance*, Stuttgart: Franz Steiner Verlag.
Samuel, A.E. 1965. "The Role of the Paramone Clauses in Ancient Documents", *JJP* 15, 221–311.
——— 1972. *Greek and Roman Chronology: Calendars and Years in Classical Antiquity*, München: Verlag C.H. Beck.
Scherberich, K. 2009. *Koinè symmachía. Untersuchungen zum Hellenenbund Antigonos' III. Doson und Philipps V. (224–197 v. Chr.)*, Historia Einzelshcriften 184, Stuttgart: F. Steiner Verlag.
Schmitz, W. 2012. "'Sklavenfamilien' im archaischen und klassischen Griechenland", in H. Heinen (ed.), *Kindersklaven—Sklavenkinder: Schicksale zwischen Zuneigung und Ausbeutung in der Antike und im interkulturellen Vergleich*, Forschungen zur antiken Sklaverei 39, Stuttgart: F. Steiner Verlag, 63–102.
Scholten, J.B. 2000. *The Politics of Plunder. Aitolians and Their Koinon in the Early Hellenistic Era, 279–217 B.C.*, Berkeley: University of California Press.
Schwenk, C.J. 1985. *Athens in the Age of Alexander: The Dated laws and Decrees of 'The Lykourgan Era', 338–322 B.C.*, Chicago: Ares Publishers.
Segré, M. 1952. *Tituli Calymni*, Annuarion della scuola archeologica d'Atene, 22–23 (1944–1945).
——— 1993. *Iscrizioni di Cos* (= *Iscr. Di Cos*), Roma: "L'Erma" di Bretschneider.
Sekunda, N.V. 1997. "The Kylloi and Eubiotoi of Hypata during the Imperial Period", *ZPE* 118, 207–226.
Sherwin-White, A.N. 1973. *The Roman Citizenship*, 2nd ed., Oxford and New York: Oxford University Press.
Sherwin-White, S.M. 1978. *Ancient Cos. An Historical Study from the Dorian Settlement to the Imperial Period*, Hypomnemata, Heft 51, Göttingen: Vandenhoeck & Ruprecht.
Sordi, M. 1958. *La lega Tessala fino ad Alessandro Magno*, Rome: Istituto italiano per la storia antica.
Stählin, F. 1924. *Das hellenische Thessalien: landeskundliche und geschichtliche Beschreibung Thessaliens in der hellenischen und romischen Zeit*, Stuttgart: J. Engelhorns nachf.

——— 1934. *Pagasai und Demetrias: Beschreibung der Reste und Stadtgeschichte*, Berlin: W. de Gruyter.

Stewart, R. 2012. *Plautus and Roman Slavery*, Malden, MA: Wiley-Blackwell.

Straus, J.A. 1973a. "Deux notes sur l'affranchissement dans les papyrus de l'Égypte romaine", *ZPE* 11, 143–145.

——— 1973b. "Le statut fiscal des esclaves dans l'Égypte romaine", *Chronique d'Égypte* 48 (no. 96), 364–369.

——— 2004. *L'Achat et la vente des esclaves dans l'Égypte romaine. Contribution papyrologique à l'étude de l'esclavage dans une province orientale de l'empire romain*, München-Leipzig: K.G. Saur.

——— 2009. "L'Affranchissement dans l'Égypte gréco-romaine à propos d'une ouvrage récent sur l'affranchissement et le statut des affranchis dans le monde grec antique", *L'Antiquité Classique* 78, 233–239.

Stroud, R.S. 1998. *The Athenian Grain-Tax Law of 374/3 B.C.*, Princeton, NJ: *Hesperia* Supplement 29.

Stumpf, G. 1987. "Zwei Gerichtsurteile aus Athen: *IG* II^2 1641 und 1646a", *Tyche* 2, 211–215.

Thomsen, R. 1964. *Eisphora: A Study of Direct Taxation in Ancient Athens*, Copenhagen: Gyldendalske Boghandel.

Treggiari, S. 1969. *Roman Freedmen during the Late Republic*, Oxford: The Clarendon Press.

Van Antwerp Fine, J. 1932. "The Problem of Macedonian Holdings in Epirus and Thessaly in 221 B.C.", *TAPA* 63, 123–155.

Van Minnen, P. and K.A. Worp, 2009. "A Latin Manumission Tax Tablet in Los Angeles", *BASP* 46, 15–22.

Vanderspoel, J. 2010. "Provincia Macedonia", in J. Roisman and I. Worthington (eds.), *A companion to ancient Macedonia*, Malden, MA: Wiley-Blackwell, 251–275.

Vigié, M. 1881. *Études sur les impôts indirects romains. Vicesima libertatis. Vicesima hereditatis*, Paris: Ernest Thorin.

Vlassopoulos, K. 2011a. "Greek Slavery: From Domination to Property and Back Again", *JHS* 131, 115–130.

——— 2011b. Review of Elizabeth A. Meyer, *Metics and the Athenian Phialai-Inscriptions: A Study in Athenian Epigraphy and Law. Historia Einzelschriften Bd 208.* Wiesbaden: Franz Steiner Verlag, 2009: Bryn Mawr Classical Review 2011.02.48 (http://bmcr.brynmawr.edu/2011/2011-02-48.html).

Waldstein, W. 2001. "Zum Menschsein von Sklaven", in H. Bellen and H. Einen (eds.), *Fünfzig Jahre Forschungen zur antiken Sklaverei an der Mainzer Akademie, 1950–2000*, Forschungen zur antiken Sklaverei 35, Stuttgart: F. Steiner Verlag, 31–49.

Walsh, J.J. 2000. "The Disorders of the 170s BC and Roman Intervention in the Class Struggle in Greece", *CQ* 50.1, 300–303.

Westermann, W.L. 1946. "Two Studies in Athenian Manumissions", *Journal of Near Eastern Studies* 5, 92–104.

——— 1955. *The Slave Systems of Greek and Roman Antiquity*, Philadelphia: The American Philosophical Society.

Westlake, H.D. 1935. *Thessaly in the Fourth Century B.C.*, London: Methuen & co.

Wiemer, H.-U. 2003a. "Die koische Opfergebotsliste Syll.³ 1000—*diagrapha* oder *nomos*?", *ZPE* 145 (2003), 117–122.

——— 2003b. "Käufliche Priestertümer im hellenistischen Kos", *Chiron* 33, 263–310.

Wilamowitz-Möllendorff, U. von. 1887. "Demotika der attischen Metoeken I", *Hermes* 22, 107–128.

Wilhelm, A. 1909. *Beiträge zur griechischen Inschriftenkunde*, Wien: Alfred Hölder.

Wilson, P. 2000. *The Athenian Institution of the Khoregia: The Chorus, The City and the Stage*, Cambridge: Cambridge University Press.

Zachou-Kontoyanni, M.-E. 1989. "Παρατηρήσεις σε απελευθερωτικές επιγραφές του Εχίνου", *Egnatia* 1, 209–216.

——— 2003. "Ἀπελευθερωτικὲς ἐπιγραφὲς Αἰγινίου (Καλαμπάκας)", *Egnatia* 7, 29–49.

——— 2006a. "Ἐπιγραφὲς Ὀλοσσονίων ἐντοιχισμένες στῇ Μονὴ τῆς Παναγίας τῆς Ὀλυμπιώτισσας στὴν Ἐλασσόνα", in G.A. Pikoulas (ed.), *Inscriptions and History of Thessaly: New Evidence*, Proceedings of the International Symposium in Honor of Professor Christian Habicht, Volos: Πανεπιστήμιο Θησσαλίας Τμήμα ΙΑΚΑ: Υπουργείο Αρχαιολογικό Ινστιτούτο Θησσαλικών Σπουδών: Ελληνική Επιγραφική Εταιρεία, 91–102.

——— 2006b. "Manumissions from Atrax", in G.A. Pikoulas (ed.), *Inscriptions and History of Thessaly. New Evidence*, Proceedings of an International Symposium in honor of Professor Christian Habicht, Volos: Πανεπιστήμιο Θησσαλίας Τμήμα ΙΑΚΑ: Υπουργείο Αρχαιολογικό Ινστιτούτο Θησσαλικών Σπουδών: Ελληνική Επιγραφική Εταιρεία, 103–111.

Zelnick-Abramovitz, R. 2000. "The *Xenodokoi* of Thessaly", *ZPE* 130, 109–120.

——— 2005a. *Not Wholly Free. The Concept of Manumission and the Status of Manumitted Slaves in the Ancient Greek World*, Mnemosyne Supplements 266, Leiden: Brill.

——— 2005b. "The Phrase ξενικῇ λύσει in Manumission Inscriptions", *Zeitschrift für Papyrologie und Epigraphik* 153, 108–112.

——— 2009. "Freed Slaves, Their Status and State Control in Ancient Greece", *European Review of History: Revue européenne d'histoire* 16.3, 303–318.

——— 2012. "Slaves and Role Reversal in Ancient Greek Cults", in S. Hodkinson and D. Geary (eds.), *Slaves and Religions in Graeco-Roman Antiquity and Modern Brazil*, Newcastle upon Tyne: Cambridge Scholars Publishing, 96–132.

Zimmern, A. 1961. *The Greek Commonwealth*, 5th ed. rev., New York: Oxford University Press.

APPENDIX

THE THESSALIAN MANUMISSION INSCRIPTIONS

The following list includes the published manumission inscriptions of Thessaly,[1] arranged alphabetically according to regions, cities, and corpora of inscriptions. Inscriptions marked with an asterisk are discussed in this book (often presenting different readings and dates) and are listed in the Index Locorum. Note that the grand majority of these inscriptions register numerous manumission acts.

Achaia Phthiotis

Halos

IG IX(2) *110 (undated); *111 (Roman period).

Kophi

IG IX(2) *102 (185–180 BC).

Melitaia

IG IX(2) *206 (49/8 BC); 207a (undated); *207b (Roman period); *207c (Roman period); 207d (undated); *207e (Roman period); 207f (reign of Augustus); 207g (undated); 207h (undated); *207i (Roman period); 207k (undated); *207l (undated); 207m (undated).

Phthiotic Thebes

AE (1929) 148, no. 23 (Roman period); *148, no. 24 (Roman period); (1932), *21, no. 6 (AD 131/2).
BCH 99 (1975), *648, no. 2 (reign of Augustus); *648, no. 3 (reign of Hadrian).
Chiron 5 (1975), *337 A (AD 41/2); *337 B (AD 52/53).
IG IX(2) *133 (181/0 BC).

---

[1] Richard Bouchon (Lyon) is planning to publish new editions of the Thessalian manumission inscriptions with the *Collection Bibliothèque des Ecoles françaises d'Athènes et de Rome*, including material not yet unpublished. This much wanted corpus will undoubtedly be an invaluable contribution to the study of Thessaly in the Hellenistic in Roman times.

Thaumakoi

IG IX(2) 221 + *SEG* 3.471 (third century BC).

Tsournati Vrysi

IG IX(2) *104 (ca. 49/8 BC).

Xyniai

AD *10 (1926), 53, no. 12 (AD 112).

Ainis

Hypata

IG IX(2) *12 (49/8 BC); *13 (AD 47); *14a + *SEG* 3.456 (AD 47/48); 14b + *SEG* 3.456 (undated); 14c + *SEG* 3.456 (undated); 14d + *SEG* 3.456 (undated); 14e + *SEG* 3.456 (undated); 15 (AD 42/43); *16 + *SEG* 3.457a (AD 131/132); *17 (AD 132/133); *18 (undated); *19 + *SEG* 3.458 (second century AD); 20c (reign of Hadrian); *21 + *SEG* 3.457b, 16.376 (AD 131/132); *22 + *SEG* 3.457c (AD 131/132); 23 (undated); 24 (undated); 25a (undated); 25b (undated); 25c (undated); 26 (undated); 27 (undated); 28 (undated); 29 (undated); 30 (undated).

Dolopia

Angea

SEG 15.368b (third century AD); *15.368c = *IG* IX(2) 228c (third century AD).

Hestiaiotis

Aiginion

SEG *53.510(1)A–C = *IG* IX(2) 324a–c (late first century BC/early first century AD); *53.510(2)A–B = *IG* IX(2) 325a–b (late first century BC/early first century AD); 53.511A–B (late first century BC); *53.512 = *IG* IX(2) 1342 (second/third century AD).

Gomphoi

IG IX(2) *287a, b + *SEG* 57.504 (27 BC–AD 14); 287c (undated); *288 (undated); *289 (Roman period); 289a (Roman period); *289b (AD 131/132); *289c (AD 132/133?); 290a (reign of Augustus).

Metropolis

IG IX(2) *274 (186/5 BC); 275 (undated); 276 (undated); *277 (undated); 278 (Roman period); *279 (undated); *280 (Roman period).

Magnesia

Demetrias

IG IX(2) *1100b (undated); 1100c (undated); 1107a (reign of Claudius?); 1115 (reign of Claudius?); *1116b (Roman period); 1117b (undated); *1117c (Roman period); 1117d (Roman imp. period); 1118a (Roman period); 1118b (undated); *1119 (Roman period); 1120 (Roman imp. period); 1121 (undated).
SEG *37.450 (second-third century BC); *37.451 (second-third century AD); 37.452 (second-third century BC); *37.453 (second-third century BC); *37.454 (second-third century BC); 37.455 (second-third century BC); 37.456 (second-third century BC); *37.457 (second-third century BC); 37.458 (second-third century BC); 37.459 (second-third century BC).

Iolkos

AE (1930), *99, no. 1 (Roman period).
RPh (1911), *298, no. 47(1) (undated); 298, no. 47a (undated).
SEG *23.460 = AE (1930), 100–101, no. 2 (Roman imp. period).

Pagasai

IG IX(2) *359b (Roman period); 359c (Roman period).

Malis

Lamia

IG IX(2) *71 + *SEG* 28.505 (after 60 BC); *72 (ca. 50 BC); *73 (undated); *74 + 76 = *SEG* 30.531A (second half of the second century BC); *75 = *SEG* 30.531B (second half of the second century BC); 77 + *SEG* *28.505 (undated); 78a (undated); *78b (Roman period).
SEG *30.531C (second half of the second century BC).

Echinos

AJPh 92 (1971) *669, no. 1 (undated); 673, no. 2 (AD 131/132); *674, no. 3 (mid-second century AD?).
IG IX(2) *92 + *SEG* 39.493 (AD 133/4 – ca. 150).
SEG *36.543 (AD 133/134 – ca. 150); *36.544 (AD 133/134 – ca. 150); *36.545 (AD 133/134 – ca. 150); *36.546 (AD 133/134 – ca. 150); *39.494 (AD 133/134 – ca. 150); 39.495 = *AJPh* 92 (1971), 673, no. 2 (ca. AD 131/132); 39.496 (AD 133/134 – ca. 150).

Pelasgiotis

Atrax

IG IX(2) *474 (ca. 49/8 BC).
Mélanges Daux *3, 1 (reign of Augustus); *4, 2 (reign of Augustus); 4, 3 (reign of Augustus?); *5, 4 (reign of Augustus); *6, 5 (reign of Augustus).
SEG *34.478 (AD 131/132); *46.622 = *AD* 46 B1 (1991) [1996], 224–225 (ca. third century BC); *56.621 = 32.604 = *AD* 30 B1, 1975 [1983], 197 (16–6/5 BC);

Krannon

IG IX(2) *463 (ca. 49/8 BC).

Larisa

AAA 13 (1980), 260–261, no. 6 (mid-first century BC).
AD 11 (1927–1928), *58, no. 5 (mid-first century BC); 61, no. 6B (second century BC?).
AE (1910) *361, no. 7 (Roman period); *363, no. 8 (AD 131/132); (1930) Chr., *176, A1 + *SEG* 28.505 (ca. 26/5 BC); (1932) Chr., 22, no. 7 (second/first century BC).
BCH 95 (1971) *277 (197–186 BC); *562 (undated).
IG IX(2) *539 + *SEG* 31.578 (117 BC); *540 (48/9 BC); *541 (first century AD); *542 (reign of Augustus); *543 (reign of Augustus); *544 (AD 41/42); *546 (AD 131/132); *547 (AD 131/132); 548 (AD 131/132); *549 + *SEG* 32.603 (reign of Augustus); 550 (late first century BC/early first century AD); 551 (first century BC); *553 (early first century BC); *554 (undated); 555 (first century BC); 556 (undated); 557 (undated); *558 (undated); 559 (undated); *560 = *AE* (1910), 361, no. 7 and 7a (Roman period); *561 (Roman period); 562 (Roman period); 563 (Roman period); 564 (first century BC); 565 (Roman period); 566 (Roman period); 567 (reign of Claudius?); *568 + *SEG* 31.581 (undated); *594 (third century BC); 596 (undated); *1293 + *SEG* 28.505, 53.548 (first century AD); *1344 (reign of Augustus).
SEG *27.203 = *ZPE* 27 (1977), 259–262 (ca. 150 BC); 27.204 = *AD* 28 B (1973), 327 (Roman period); *29.532 (undated); *31.577 (ca. 136/5 BC); *31.579 = *ZPE* 49 (1982) 161–167 no. 1 (100–80 BC); 31.580 = *ZPE* 49 (1982) 168–170 no. 2 (mid-first century BC); *33.464 (27 BC?); *35.593 (early second century BC); 35.599 + 38.446 (100–50 BC); 35.600 (50–1 BC); *35.602 = *IG* IX(2) 545 (A: AD 44, B: AD 54); *44.450 = 28.505 = *IG* IX(2) 1232 (100–50 BC); *53.547 A (24 BC?); *547 B (after 8? BC).

Pherai

IG IX(2) *413 (reign of Augustus); *414 (undated); *415 + Add. + *SEG* 28.527 (late first century BC).
SEG *39.506 + 42.534 (undated).

Skotoussa

SEG *15.370 = *BCH* 79 (1955), 444–459, no. 1 (second century BC); *23.413 = *REA* 66 (1964), 309 2b (AD 71–96); *43.312 = *AD* 43 B (1988) 282 (early Roman imp. period); *47.786 = *AD* 48 B1 (1993) 257, no. 46 (early Roman imp. period).

Perrhaibia

Azoros

AE (1923), 126, no. 362 (ca. 30–1 BC).
IG IX(2) *1296 = *AE* (1923), 361 = *AE* (1945–1947), 110, no. 59 + *SEG* 26.644 (20–18 BC); *1297 (reign of Augustus); *1298 = *AE* (1916), 86, no. 292 (14/13 BC); *1299 (reign of Augustus); 1300 = *AE* (1916), 81, no. 286 (reign of Augustus); 1301a = *AE* (1923) 132, no. 363 (AD 150–200?); 1301b = *AE* (1923) 132, no. 364 + *SEG* 28.505 (Roman period); 1302 (AD 131/132); 1303 (undated); 1304 = *AE* (1916), 87, no. 293 (Roman period).

Chyretiai

AE (1917), *18, no. 309 (first century BC); *18, no. 310 + *SEG* 32.599 (reign of Augustus); *18, no. 311 (late first century BC); 18, 311C (mid-second century BC); *18, no. 312 (14–12 BC); 18, no. 312C (AD 40/41); *25, no. 313 (before 31 BC).
IG IX(2) *339 (Roman period).
SEG *47.721 B = *AD* 49 B1, 1994, [1999] 341 no. 26 (Roman imp. period).

Doliche

AE (1923) 140, no. 372 (late first century AD); 140, no. 373 (first century AD); 141, no. 375 (Flavian period); 141, no. 376 (mid-second century AD); 144, no. 378 (second/third century AD); *144, 379 (30 BC–AD 50); 148, no. 380 (reign of Augustus); 148, no. 381 (18–15 BC).
IG IX(2) *1268 = *AE* (1923) 153, no. 384 + *SEG* 30.530 (AD 131/132); 1269 = *AE* (1923) 141, no. 374 (AD 131/132); 1270 = *AE* (1923) 144, no. 377 (AD 131/132).
SEG *37:476 (Roman period).

Olosson

AE (1916) 73, no. 279 (first century AD); 73, no. 280 (first century AD); 74, no. 281 (reign of Hadrian); *74, no. 282 (second century AD); 74, no. 283 (reign of Augustus); *78, no. 284 (reign of Augustus); 78, no. 285 (reign of Augustus); 81, no. 287 (early first century AD); 83, no. 288 (early first century AD); 84, no. 289 (AD 1–50); 85, no. 290 (second century AD); 86, n. 291 (undated).
IG IX(2) *1294b + *SEG* 56.649 (late first century AD); *1295 = *AE* (1916), 27, no. 276 + *SEG* 53.561 (reign of Augustus).
SEG *27.211 (reign of Augustus); 27.212 (Flavian period); 27.213 (Flavian period); *56.649 = *IG* IX(2) 1293b/c + 1294b (reign of Tiberius).

Gonnoi

Gonnoi II *114 (27 – ca. 25 BC); 115 (ca. 25 BC); 116 (12/11 BC); *117 = *IG* IX(2) 1042 I (ca. 10 BC?); 118 = *IG* IX(2) 1042 I (before AD 14); 119 (after 12 BC); *120 = *IG* IX(2) 1044a (late reign of Augustus?); 121 (early first century AD); 122 (early first century BC); *123 = *IG* IX(2) 1040b (first century BC/AD); 124 (AD 1–50); 125 (AD 42/43);

126 (AD 45/46); 127 = *IG* IX(2) 1040d + *SEG* 28.505g (AD 45/46); 128 = *IG* IX(2) 1042 III ll. 51a–74 (after AD 45/46); 129 (first century AD); 130 (AD 54–100); 131 (AD 54–100); 132 (AD 54–100); 133 = *IG* IX(2) 1042 III ll. 75–89 (first century AD); 134 (AD 50–100?); 135 (first century AD); 136 (ca. AD 50–100); 137 = *IG* IX(2) 1042 III, lines 91–110 (first century AD); 138 = *IG* IX(2) 1042 III, ll. 110–115 (first century AD); 139 = *IG* IX(2) 1042 II, ll. 44–49a (first century AD); 140 = *IG* IX(2) 1042 II, ll. 50–51 (AD 50–100); 141 = *IG* IX(2) 1041b (first century AD); 142 = *IG* IX(2) 1041c (first century AD); 143 = *AE* (1915) 17, no. 257d (second century AD?); 144 = *AE* (1915) 21, no. 260 (second century AD).

Pythion

AE (1923) *144, no. 378 (second/third century AD); *144, 379 (30 BC–AD 50); 148, no. 380 (reign of Augustus?); 148, no. 381 (18–15 BC?); 150, no. 382 (reign of Augustus); (1924), *150, no. 383 (first century BC/AD); *155, no. 400 (late first century BC); *155, no. 401 + SEG 28.505 (133–129 BC); *155, no. 402 + *SEG* 28.505 (after 125 BC); 155, no. 403 + *SEG* 50.531 (after 125 BC); *166, no. 404 (ca. 131–129 BC); *166, no. 405 (131/0 BC?); *166, no. 406 + *SEG* 28.505 (ca. 60 BC); *173, no. 407 (after 44 BC?); *173, no. 408 (mid-first century AD); 182, no. 410 (third century AD); 183, no. 413 (reign of Augustus); 183, no. 414 (third century AD); 183, no. 415 (second century AD); 183, no. 416 (second/third century AD); 186, no. 417 (AD 131/132); 186, no. 418 (reign of Augustus).

IG IX(2) 1270 = *AE* (1923) 144, no. 377 (first/second century AD?); *1282 = *AE* (1924), 188, no. 418a + *SEG* 28.505 (ca. 50 BC); 1283 = *AE* (1924), 182, no. 411 (third century AD); 1284 = *AE* (1924), 183, no. 412 (third century AD); *1290 = *AE* (1924) 173, no. 409 = *SEG* 26.689 (150–100 BC).

SEG *23.462 = 26.670 + 28.513 (150–100 BC); *35.646 (first century AD).

Thessaliotis

Ekkara-Agoriani

AD 26 B1 (1971) *236, no. 5 (undated).

Euhydrion

I Thess. I 34 = *IG* IX(2) 256b (first century AD).

Proerna

SEG 49.629 (early second century BC).

Unknown Provenance

BCH 99 (1975), *120, no. 1 (16/15 BC); *127, no. 2c + *SEG* 26.692 (reign of Hadrian); *133, no. 3 (second century AD); *134, no. 4 (late second/third century AD); *141, no. 5 (third century AD); *142, no. 6 (ca. AD 250–300).

INDEX LOCORUM

1. Literary Texts

2. Inscriptions

3. Papyri

GENERAL INDEX

INDEX OF GREEK TERMS

www.ingramcontent.com/pod-product-compliance
Ingram Content Group UK Ltd.
Pitfield, Milton Keynes, MK11 3LW, UK
UKHW020846290926
15470UKWH00004B/1587

9 789004 253896